IMAGES
of America

Dodge Ridge Mountain Resort

Dodge Ridge Mountain Resort operates in the Stanislaus National Forest under a special use permit from the US Forest Service. We do not discriminate based on race, color, creed, sex, age, or nationality. (Courtesy of Dodge Ridge Mountain Resort Archives.)

ON THE COVER: Several age groups lined up for ski instruction class. Fashion and equipment styles have changed over time, and classes cater to children or adults separately. Family-focused fun is always the goal at Dodge Ridge Mountain Resort. (Courtesy of Dodge Ridge Mountain Resort Archives.)

IMAGES
of America

DODGE RIDGE MOUNTAIN RESORT

Tricia O'Brien

ARCADIA PUBLISHING

ISBN 978-1-4671-6278-4
Hardback ISBN 978-1-5402-9965-9

Published by Arcadia Publishing
Charleston, South Carolina

Printed in the United States of America

Library of Congress Control Number: 2025937192

For all general information, please contact Arcadia Publishing:
Telephone 843-853-2070
Fax 843-853-0044
E-mail sales@arcadiapublishing.com

Visit us on the Internet at www.arcadiapublishing.com

Contents

Acknowledgments

While researching the origin and history of Dodge Ridge, it was clear that the passion, memories, and abundant love from owners, staff, and guests are endless and truly treasured. Dodge Ridge is such a gem, and this book barely scratches the surface to show the depth and devotion that owners and employees have dedicated to this small but mighty mountain resort. It was a privilege to work on this project and get to know the people behind Dodge Ridge. This book would not have been possible without the love and support of all the owners and employees past and present. You are what brought the resort to life and made it the treasure that people hold dear in their hearts. Thank you for your time and patience as I peppered you with endless questions.

Thank you to Ralph Purdy and the entire Purdy family, Frank and Sally Helm, and Karl and Audrey Kapuscinski for allowing me to share your lives with the world. To Chucker and Debi Twining, Paul Mundy, Jeff and Rebecca Hauff, Jon Mahanna, and Andre Armand, thank you for all the extra time and going above and beyond, plus your hospitality, which was much appreciated.

Thank you to the past and present staff and family members who answered my endless questions with enthusiasm and true passion for Dodge Ridge, especially Dave Alley, Ted Beeler, Justin Calbert, Christy Cashman, Reuben Chirnside, Carol Cochran, Hanna Craig, Mike Davis, Katie Fromm, Brett Fulkerson, Don and Sally Harms, Bob Hohne, Bill and Valerie Huffman, Joe Jackson, Michael Ladinig, Mike Loy, Bobby Mackey, Dee Martin, Stacey Martin, Tom McCollum, Norman Morrison, Bob Patton, Bruce Pedretti, Jennifer Rapp, Jason Reed, Ethan Sandberg, Sam Sells, Jenni Smith, Calin and Nicole Smith, Ken Sorrick, Brian Townsend, and Sean Waterman.

I would also like to thank Erin Vosgien, Amy Jarvis, and Mike Litchfield of Arcadia Publishing for all your help, encouragement, and support. Thank you to my brilliant, loving husband, Doug Johnson, for always supporting me and to the snuggle crew, Ronald, Shyla, Charlotte, and Eberflus, also known as "Wapperflus." Unless otherwise noted, all images appear courtesy of the Dodge Ridge Mountain Resort Archives.

INTRODUCTION

The 2025–2026 ski season marks the 75th anniversary of Dodge Ridge Mountain Resort.

There's a good vibe on this mountain. People come for the camaraderie, skiing, and snowboarding and know that there's always something fun going on. It has a family-friendly focus, great terrain for beginners and beyond, plus its top-notch ski school and affordable ticket options add to its appeal. The base elevation is 6,600 feet, the summit is 8,200 feet with a vertical drop of 1,600 feet, and there are 67 trails accessing terrain for all levels.

In 75 years, Dodge Ridge has had three owners, starting with the Purdy family, who founded Dodge in 1950, followed by the Helms, who purchased the resort in 1976. In 2021, Karl Kapuscinski facilitated a purchase from the Helms with his investment partner Invision Capital.

Prior to founding Dodge Ridge, Earl Purdy had been running a general merchandise store in the San Joaquin Valley, which also housed his family above the store. His in-laws owned a cabin in Long Barn in Tuolumne County, where his wife, Mary, and the two boys, Ralph and George, spent the summer, and Earl joined them on weekends. It became clear that George's struggle with severe asthma was active in the valley but not in the mountains, so a permanent move was required.

He spontaneously submitted his application and fee after receiving a random tip about the US Forest Service soliciting bids to develop Dodge Ridge as a ski area. Earl was happy running the store and really had no interest in the ski resort. He believed that such a venture was only for someone extremely wealthy or someone with no brains. Shock hit when US Forest Service (USFS) supervisor Allen Miller called to tell Earl that his bid would be accepted if he were truly serious about accepting the offer. Earl requested a few days to consider the offer. This spurred a trek across multiple ski resorts between Colorado and California to learn as much as possible about the business. He returned convinced that he should move forward with Dodge Ridge.

Earl and his young boys, Ralph and George, stood at Dodge Ridge as Earl pulled out a matchbook and drew his plan on the inside cover. He noted where the single chairlift, several rope tows, and lodge would be located.

The project was not a simple task to accomplish. The land was raw; only a dirt logging road led to the area, and numerous trees covered the slopes. The Forest Service expected a large investment to make the resort, and it had strict rules, so Earl had to secure two special use permits from the Forest Service: one permit for the chairlift and parking lot and another for the acreage covering the slopes.

In the summer of 1949, work started on the original Chair Three (which was manufactured by Heron Engineering), two double-rope tows, and the original lodge. For the first five years, there was no electricity, and everything ran on gas-powered generators.

Jasper Meuli, who later became the assistant manager in 1952, led the construction crew. He was a hard worker who got things done. Purdy family members also jumped in to make the dream a reality. Dodge Ridge opened for skiing in January 1951 as the snow arrived a little late that winter. During the first season, Ralph and George remember their grandmother Frances Gardner cooking in the kitchen while the two of them helped other skiers sidestep up the rope tow to pack the snow. Proper snow grooming equipment came in the following year. But their efforts paid off, because even though the first season was only three months, attendance drew 19,000 skiers. It was a great place to learn how to ski. Ken Floto was the first head of the ski school for beginners and intermediate skiers. He especially enjoyed teaching local students who were allowed to leave school early one afternoon a week to ski. Eric Johnson took over as director of the ski school from 1952 to 1954. Ray Patton took over from 1954 to 1977. Patton began teaching in 1949 at Badger Pass in Yosemite Valley under Luggi Foeger, a National Ski Hall of Famer. Nic Fiore became the Badger Pass Ski School director when Patton moved over to Dodge Ridge. Patton ran the ski school as a concessionaire until 1976.

Numerous enhancements were made over the years. In 1962, Chair Five was built. In 1964, Chairs Two and Four were built, as was a ski shop that then burned that winter and was rebuilt in 1965. In 1968, construction began on the new lodge as well as on Chair One. In 1970, Chair Six replaced a Poma lift. By the mid-1970s, Purdy had expanded to six chairlifts, two new lodges, and a more spacious parking area.

When Earl Purdy was thinking about retiring, Frank Helm was looking for work. He admired what Earl had done with Dodge Ridge, so he spent a year working in various departments, learning the business and delving deeper into the reality of what it takes to run a ski resort. Eventually, Frank felt that he would really love to grow and improve upon Earl's vision. In the 1976–1977 season, Frank Helm and his wife, Judy Huddelston, purchased Dodge Ridge. Judy's father, Paul Huddelston, a rancher in Oakdale, and Frank Helm Sr., of Modesto Helm Chevrolet, helped finance the purchase. Several of the original investors carried over as part of the purchase agreement but were eventually bought out by the Helms.

Judy Helm was active in running the shop and being an ambassador for guests. She was a beloved member of the Dodge Ridge family, and her death from breast cancer in 1990 was keenly felt by the community. To honor Judy, a short but very sweet run was named after her: Judy's Run.

George Purdy continued his work at the ski area after the sale. He was a tremendous help in the office and kept meticulous notes and ledgers. He retired in 1997 but continued part-time for many more years. His knowledge of the ski area was rich, and he told many colorful stories about the Purdy years.

Frank's entrepreneurial spirit drove him to develop the ski area to its highest potential. His first major improvement in 1983 was to replace the original Chair Three with a new triple chair up to date with the latest lift technology. He had multiple environmental plans developed to map out the growth of the ski area, including one that incorporated Chair Nine, east of Chair Eight. With USFS approval, Chair Seven was installed in 1985, just in time for an incredible snow season. Chair Seven doubled the size of the skiable acreage, offering more advanced terrain, longer groomed runs, and access to the backcountry—the terrain that would eventually be serviced by Chair Eight. The Mid Mountain Lodge, also known as the Waystation, was also built that summer in a sunny location just at the base of the new chair. The roof was finished in a snowstorm.

As the ski area grew, Frank realized he had to develop a summer business to retain key employees like legends Jon Mahanna (ski school director) and Paul Mundy (children's ski school director) year-round. In 1983, the USFS offered an opportunity to bid on operating Pinecrest Campground as a concessionaire. Frank immediately submitted a proposal. Dodge Ridge became the operator of Pinecrest Campground, making the company a year-round recreation business in the Stanislaus National Forest. Not only did it allow for year-round employment, it also added a desired summer revenue stream. Dodge Ridge continues to operate Pinecrest Campground to this day.

In 1992, Frank married Sally Fromm on February 7. They share the same birthday and decided to marry on that day but only after enduring several big January snowstorms. Frank gained a family when he married Sally with her two children, Christopher and Katie.

Frank wanted Sally to learn ski area operations, but she was busy operating her own successful landscaping business. Nevertheless, Sally responded to Frank's calls to come up to help. She worked wherever a hand was needed; no job was beneath her, so she learned the business firsthand. Her participation grew, and Frank shared his knowledge about operating the resort. It became clear to Sally that her true life calling was to partner with Frank and together grow the ski area. In 1996, Sally closed her landscaping business and came on full-time as an owner. She later served as president and chief executive officer for 19 years.

Frank and Sally put their whole hearts and souls into Dodge Ridge. They were passionate about growing and developing the ski area as well as growing and developing their team. A family-friendly culture was essential to their purpose. The slogan "The Closest Snow to Home" evolved into "Family Owned and Family Loved." They took seriously their responsibilities to their employees, their guests, and the industry to operate the ski area to the highest industry standards.

From 1993 to 1995, Frank and his team were weighing the pros and cons of the next major expansion. It was not an easy choice. The current environmental assessment developed in partnership with the USFS allowed for the installation of snowmaking or the ski area expansion into the roadless area of Chair Eight. Many discussions led to the final decision to move ahead with the Chair Eight expansion.

Frank and Sally accepted that they would have to weather the lack of snow without snowmaking, and they did.

In the summer of 1997, the major logging project on Chair Eight terrain was completed; the runs were cleared and ready for the public to enjoy, and enjoy them they did. Cat skiing was offered for the first season before the lift was installed. The following summer, Chair Eight was installed, and the Main Lodge, renamed the Creekside Lodge, was significantly expanded and remodeled to enhance the guest experience.

Chair Eight opened in December 1998 for one of the best ski seasons ever. The direct north-facing slopes offered incredible snow conditions for the groomed runs, the Granite Bowl, and the other adventuresome off-piste areas. The Chair Eight expansion forever sealed the long-term success of the ski area. Frank had realized his dream; he had tripled the size of the skiing terrain and greatly enhanced the base area facilities and services.

The 2004–2005 season was another memorable one for both good and bad reasons. It began with an astonishing early opening on October 30. California was blessed with abundant cold snowstorms in October that delivered enough snow for Dodge Ridge to open. Opening this early was a credit to the outstanding mountain management team. It's important to note that not all ski areas in California were able to open that early for their guests to enjoy some of the best snow of the season. Then, sadly, on the morning of January 6, 2005, the historic Motherlode Lodge burned to the ground due to an electrical fire. Over a hundred employee lockers were lost. It burned in a matter of hours, yet the Dodge Ridge team continued to serve the guests that day despite their grief. Sally worked tirelessly with the USFS to gain approval to erect a sprung structure to restore the employee locker rooms. Just 40 days later, the structure was up and functioning.

The USFS requested a new master plan as Sally and Frank looked to the future to rebuild the base area. In partnership with the USFS, the Family Lodge was built in 2007 as part of a $6-million expansion. It opened in the nick of time to begin the 2007–2008 season on December 21.

This master plan set in place future developments, including mountain biking. In 2016, the USFS approved a mountain bike lift servicing a trail system. Thankfully, Kapuscinski and his team made that a reality in the summer of 2022.

Frank and Sally understood that it was the employees who made the guest experience welcoming, caring, and family-focused. The Dodge Ridge team was the Dodge Ridge family. In 2010, Sally and Frank were pleased to welcome their daughter, Katie, into the business. Katie's career has thrived, and she continues to work for Karl Kapuscinski in a senior management role.

Sally and Frank were both active in serving on the board of the California Ski Industry as well as on the board of the National Ski Areas Association (NSAA). Sally was one of the first women to be asked to serve on the NSAA Board and later served on the NSAA Executive Board. Sally and Frank were both honored as individuals to receive the Bob Roberts Award by Ski California. This award is given to individuals in recognition of their contribution to the

California Ski Industry.

In 2016, Sally and Frank were fortunate to hire Jenni Smith as general manager. Smith had spent her career at Park City for 33 years, rising to the role of general manager under the ski industry legend Nick Badami, owner of the resort. Jenni loved working for family-run ski areas, and Dodge Ridge fit the bill for her next career move. She continues to work for Kapuscinski, leading the team today.

Frank and Sally were dedicated owners and were widely recognized for their contribution to the ski industry. Michael Berry, NSAA president for 30 years, reflected:

> Sally and Frank Helm did something very special over the past 30 years, they nurtured and grew a truly special place. As we see fewer of these valuable family-owned resorts we need to be reminded how incredibly important they are to the future of skiing and snowboarding. Sally and Frank throughout their ownership created an experience that was treasured by their incredibly loyal customer base. The future of Dodge Ridge is secure due to the over three-decade effort by Sally and Frank to create something quite wonderful.

After Frank's 80th birthday, Frank and Sally Helm made the decision to retire. A longtime friend of 25 years and a well-respected member of the ski industry, Karl Kapuscinski had indicated he would be interested. Kapuscinski was skilled at putting together ski area purchases and facilitated a purchase with his current investment partner, Invision Capital Investment Group, in August 2021.

Sally and Frank will always have a heart full of gratitude for the Dodge Ridge family and all who contributed to making Dodge Ridge the successful mountain it is today.

Karl Kapuscinski grew up at Mount Ascutney ski resort in Vermont, owned by the parents of his best friend. His first paid job was making snow for them, which led to a variety of jobs, including teaching freestyle skiing, lift operations, and other positions in just about every department. He also wanted to play major league baseball, but he wasn't good enough to play professionally. However, while playing baseball in college, he was exposed to the California mountains.

After college, he became the assistant manager of Mount Ascutney. A year and a half later, he went on to run Hunt Hollow in upstate New York. At the time, he was one of the youngest general managers. Five years later, he was recruited to Mountain High Resort in Southern California. Kapuscinski knew that he wanted to run his own resort, so he later accepted the position of executive director at Spirit Mountain in Minnesota and ran it for two and a half years.

In 1996, Kapuscinski was recruited back to Mountain High by a group that was looking to purchase the resort. He spent that year working with the current owner, Terry Tognazzini, and he eventually put together a group to purchase Mountain High. The purchase was finalized in 1997.

There are four resorts that Karl and Invision Capital own in California, and they offer a Cali Pass, which allows skiers to ski any of the four resorts.

Karl Kapuscinski and his wife, Audrey, are very keen on continuing the "Guest First" culture by being very hands-on. While Karl is the leader of the group, he pulls from his baseball days, where he knows that he is not above anyone and appreciates the effort everyone brings because this is a team effort. It is not uncommon for Karl and Audrey to be seen serving food on busy days, helping in the parking lot, or assisting guests.

One

Creating and Expanding a Ski Resort

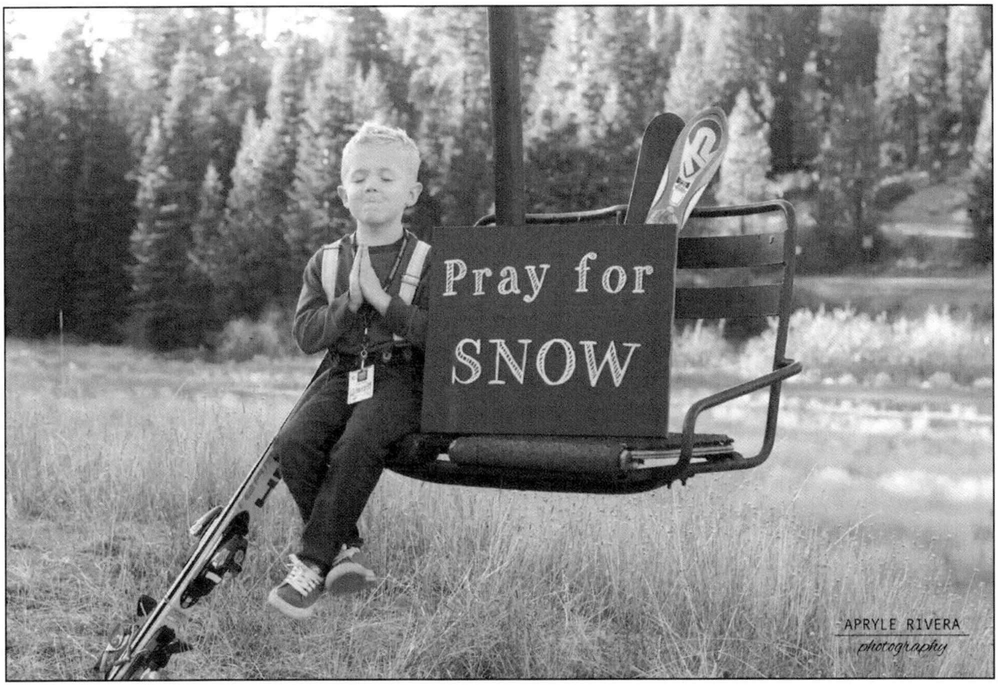

This is at the core of every snow enthusiast as the summer season ends and their thoughts turn toward the winter season. Will snow arrive in October and continue through spring? Will it be full of powder or drought? Each season is a new experience. Logan Lagarbo is doing his part to make his wishes known as he waits and wonders what Mother Nature will deliver. (Courtesy of the Hauff family.)

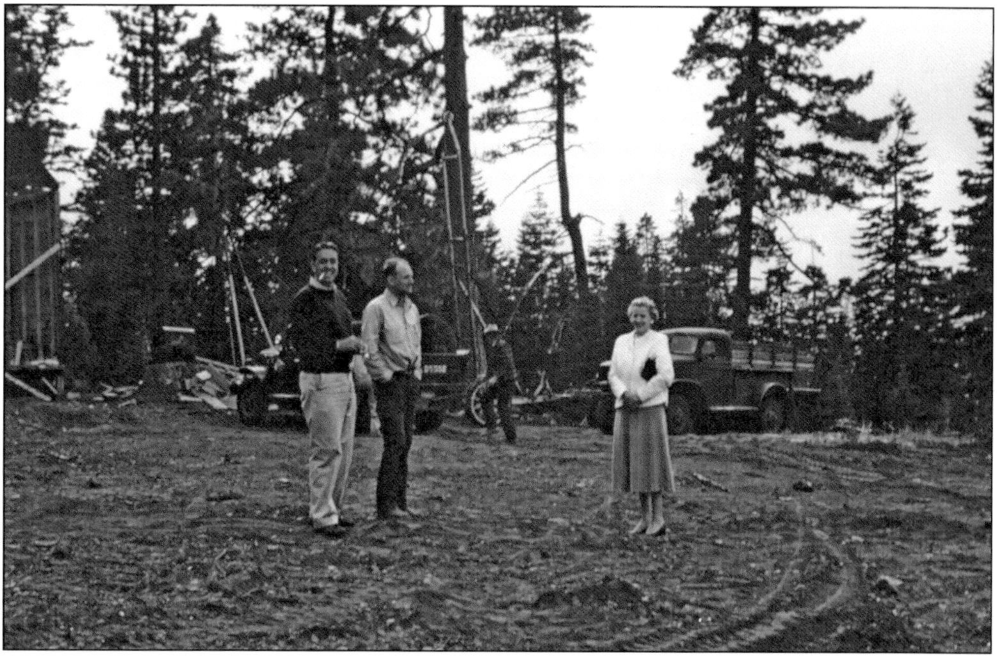

In 1956, there was still a lot of work to be done to enhance the resort. From left to right are Earl Purdy, Norman Morrison, and Allison Morrison at the top of the new T-bar. The Morrison family were investment partners in Dodge Ridge, helping make the dream a reality.

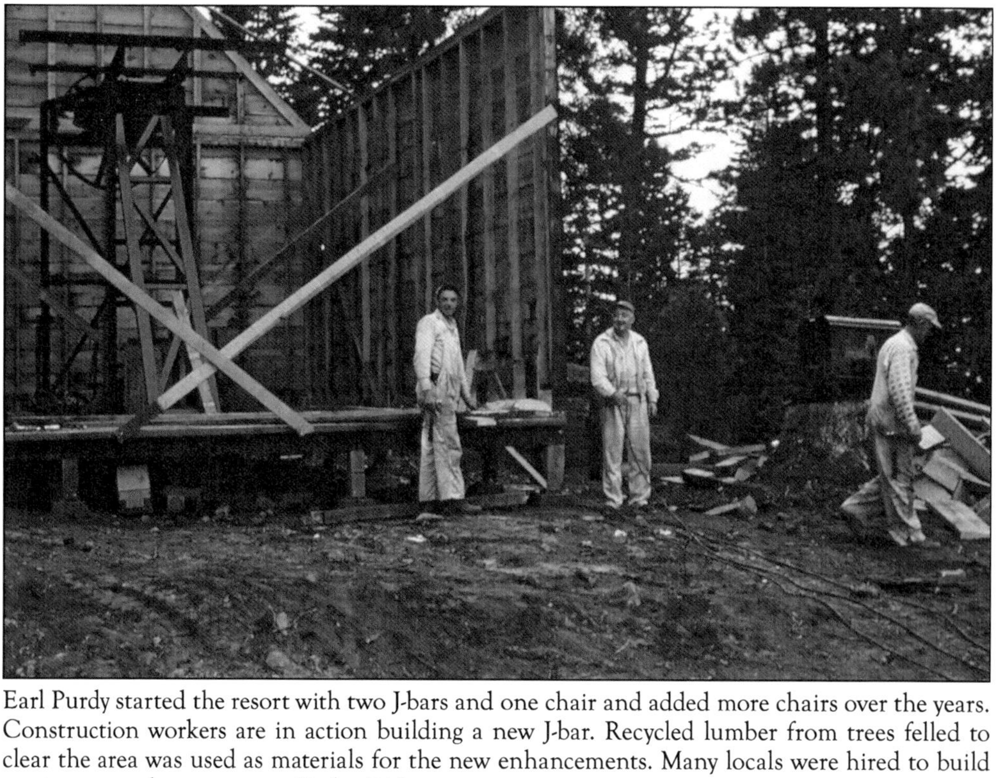

Earl Purdy started the resort with two J-bars and one chair and added more chairs over the years. Construction workers are in action building a new J-bar. Recycled lumber from trees felled to clear the area was used as materials for the new enhancements. Many locals were hired to build equipment and structures at Dodge Ridge.

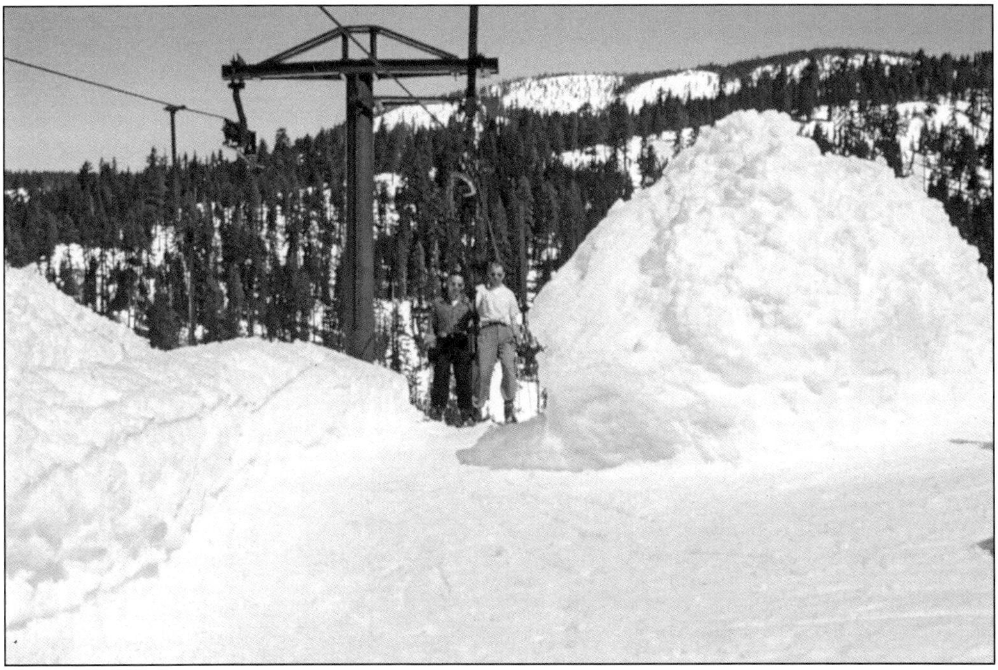

In 1955, this was a T-bar. On April 24, 2022, the new Chair One was operating at Mount Rose in Nevada. The next day, Brett Fulkerson and crew started to dismantle it and, within weeks, moved it to Dodge Ridge. It was unique to do a refurbish in-house, and it basically became a new lift because of the rebuild. On October 17, 2022, it was up and running.

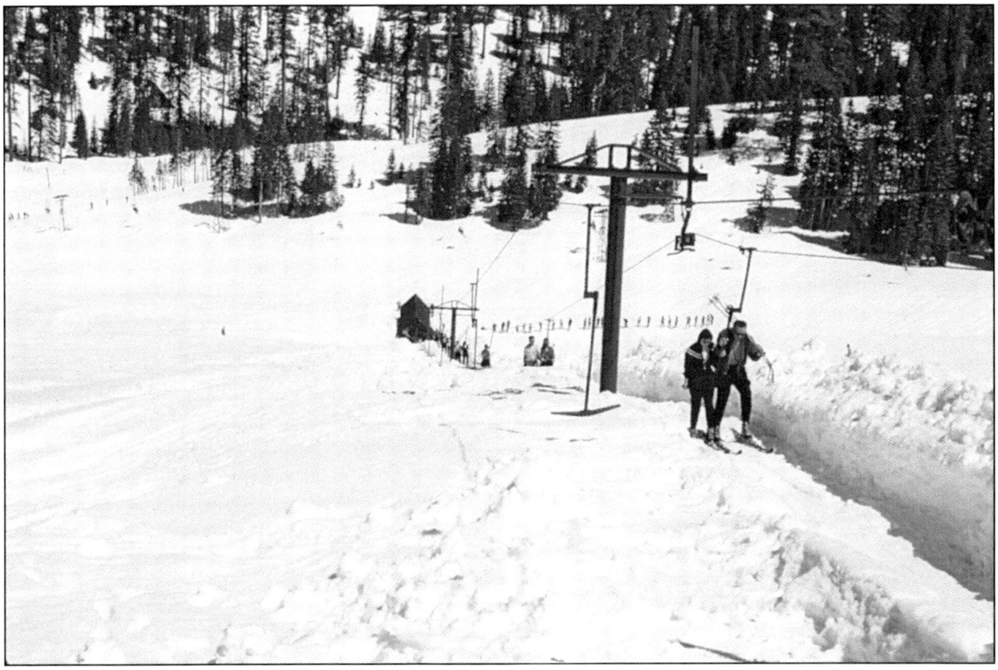

A trench had to be dug out and maintained daily to allow guests to reach the top. Skiers needed to be in sync to balance themselves, especially before releasing, so as not to fall. The T-bar was a little easier to handle as opposed to the Poma lift.

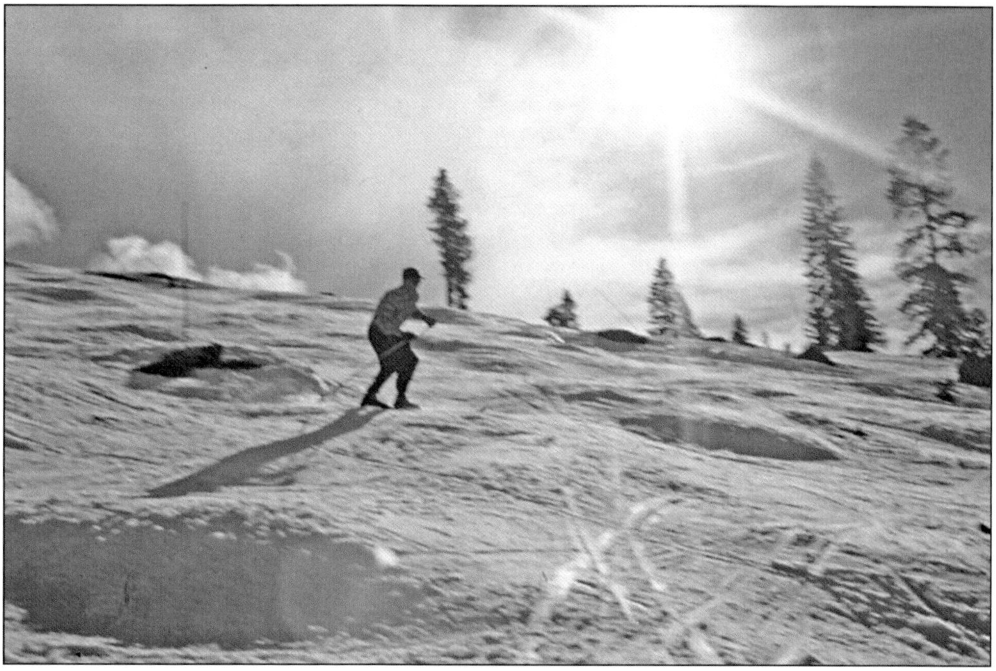

Early Purdy felt it was important to ski the slopes and be aware of changes in the weather and snow conditions for the guest experience. He is shown here skiing the East Bowl in 1957.

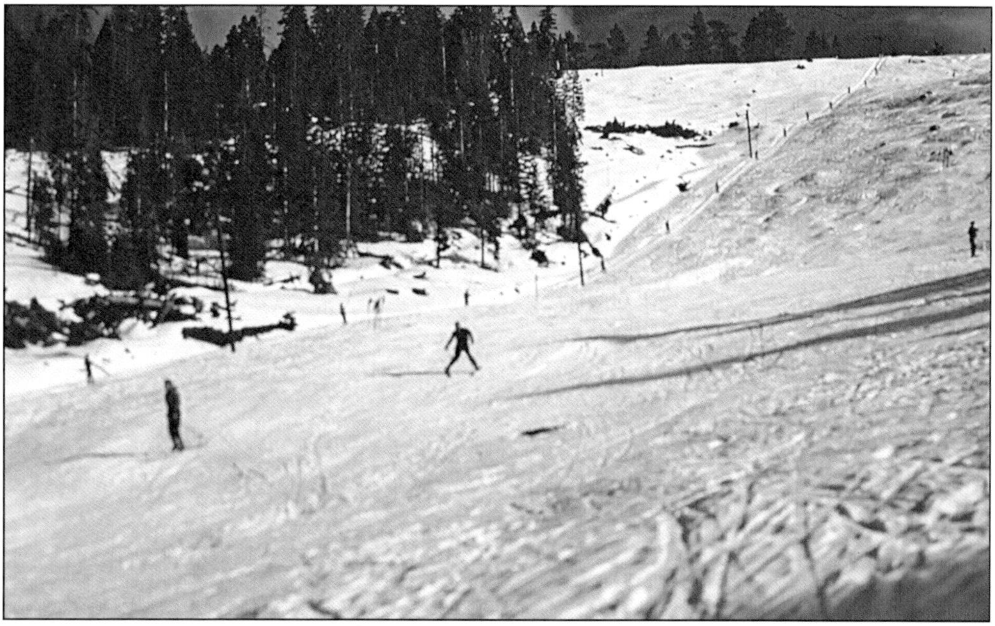

This is the original Poma lift in the East Bowl in 1957. The Poma lift was a way to pull a skier up the hill using a disc that went between the legs while holding onto a rope or pole. Some claim it launched them 30 feet forward, and if someone was still holding on and upright, it dragged them up the hill.

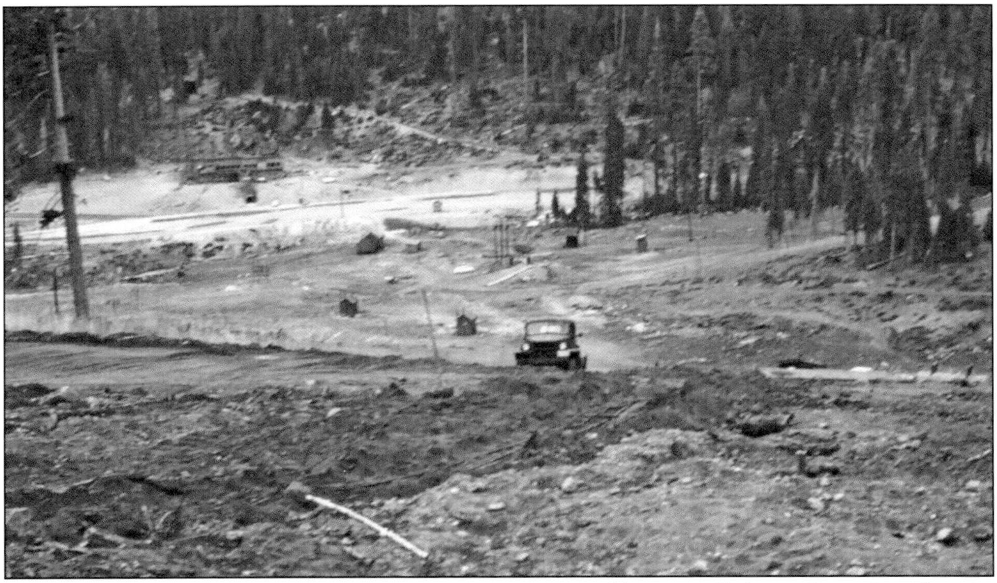

In 1957, this is the original base area where Chair Two would eventually live. The parking lot, the out road, and the original lodge are in place in the background, and now the maintenance and first aid buildings are under construction. There is quite a bit of empty space compared to the new building that currently stands in this spot.

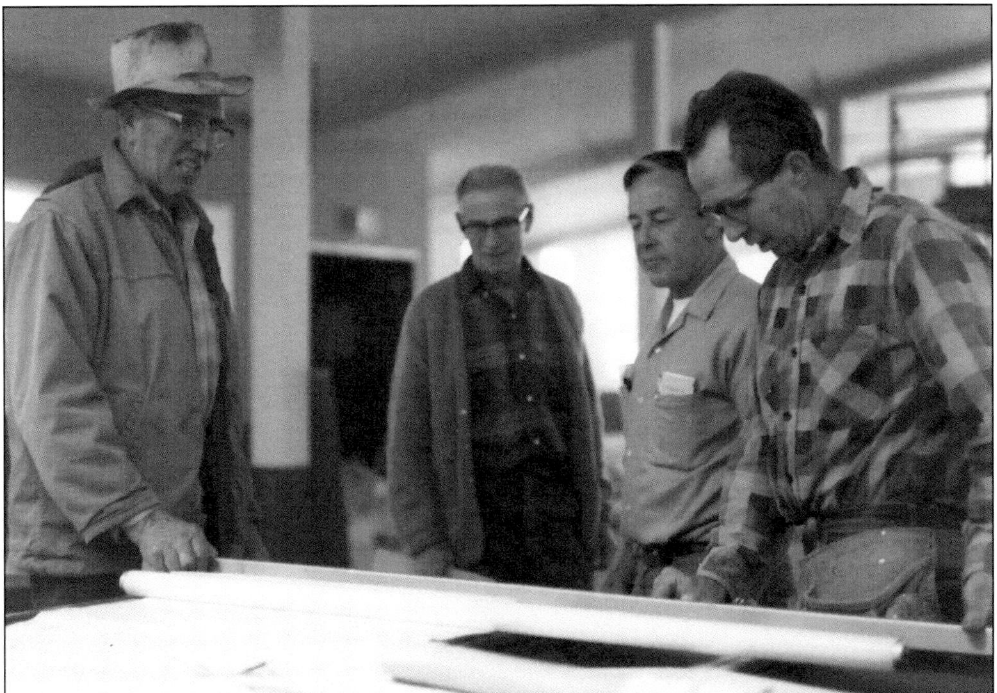

Jasper Meuli built the Cold Springs ski resort. It had a J-bar lift, which was an improvement from the rope tows. He was a hard worker who got things done. In 1952, Meuli became the assistant manager at Dodge Ridge. He also led the construction crew. Shown here on the left, Jasper reviews plans for the Creekside Lodge kitchen expansion. Ken Kessell is on the far right.

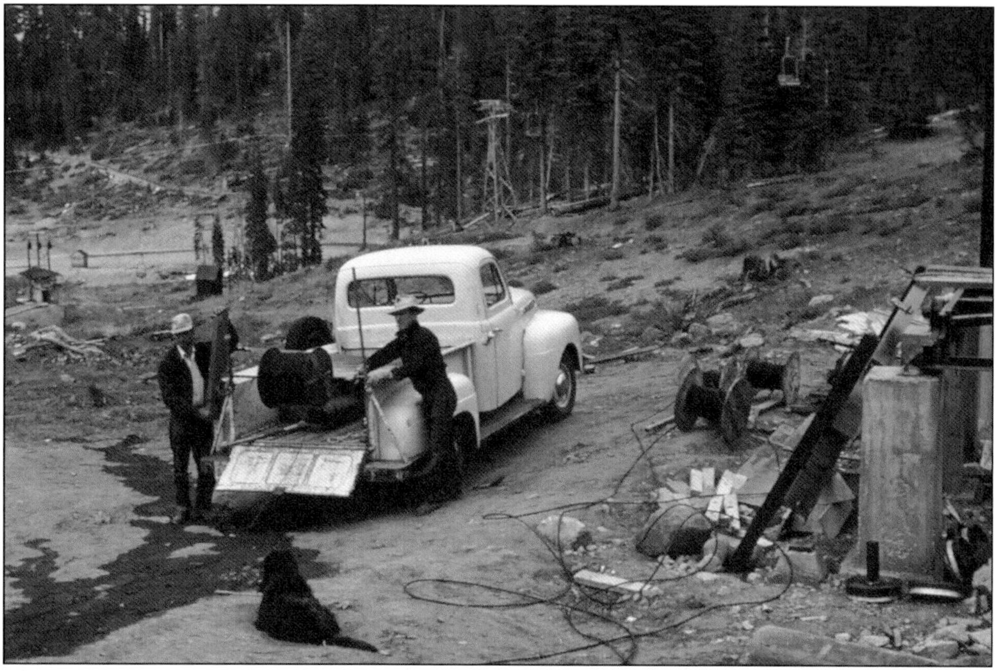

Chauncey Rometty was a bartender in Orinda, California, before coming in the 1950s to Pinecrest, where he lived in a cabin along the lake. He is shown here on the right side of the truck moving equipment at the beginning stages of the building of Chair Three.

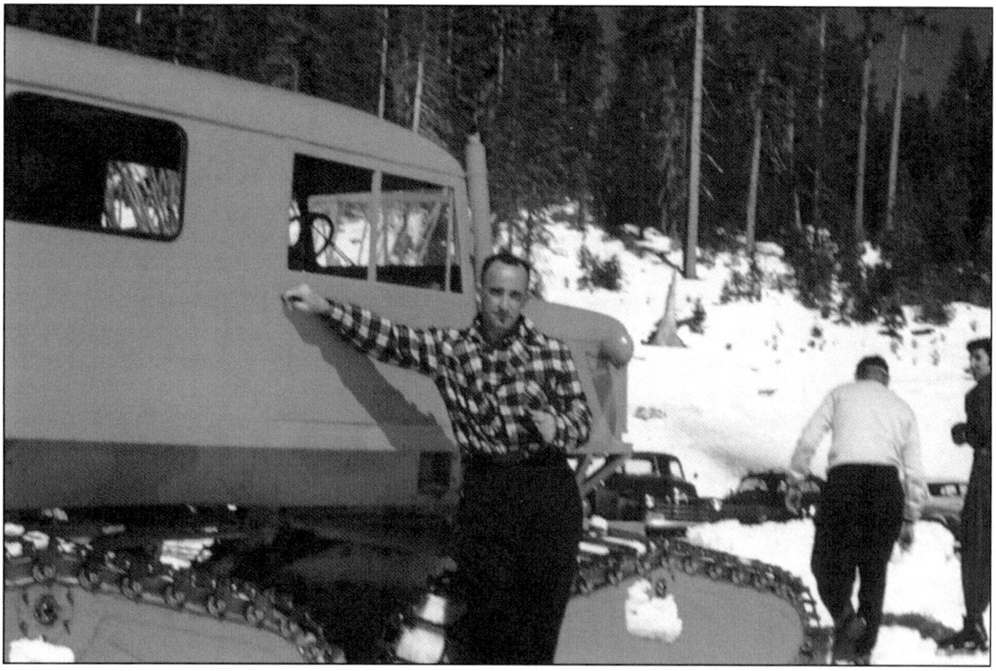

Norman Morrison, in the 1954–1955 season, stands with one of the first Tucker Sno-Cats used at the resort. It could reach terrain that was previously unreachable and was used to prepare the trails and keep them groomed. It also kicked up hard-packed snow known as death cookies that could knock out teeth if one did not stand out of the way.

In 1951, lift operator Pop Horton helps skiers on the original Chair Three, a classic double Heron chairlift. It allowed two skiers at a time and was very noisy. This chair became one of the first enhancements Frank Helm made when he took ownership.

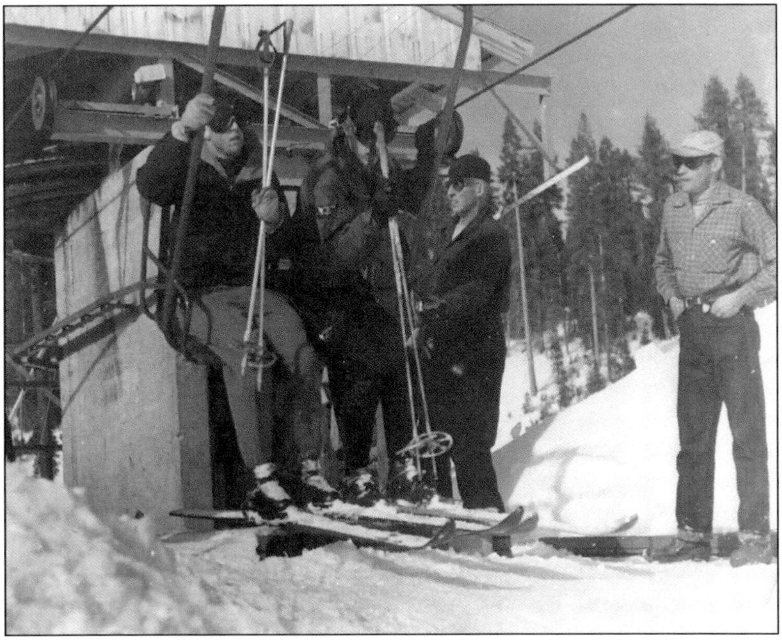

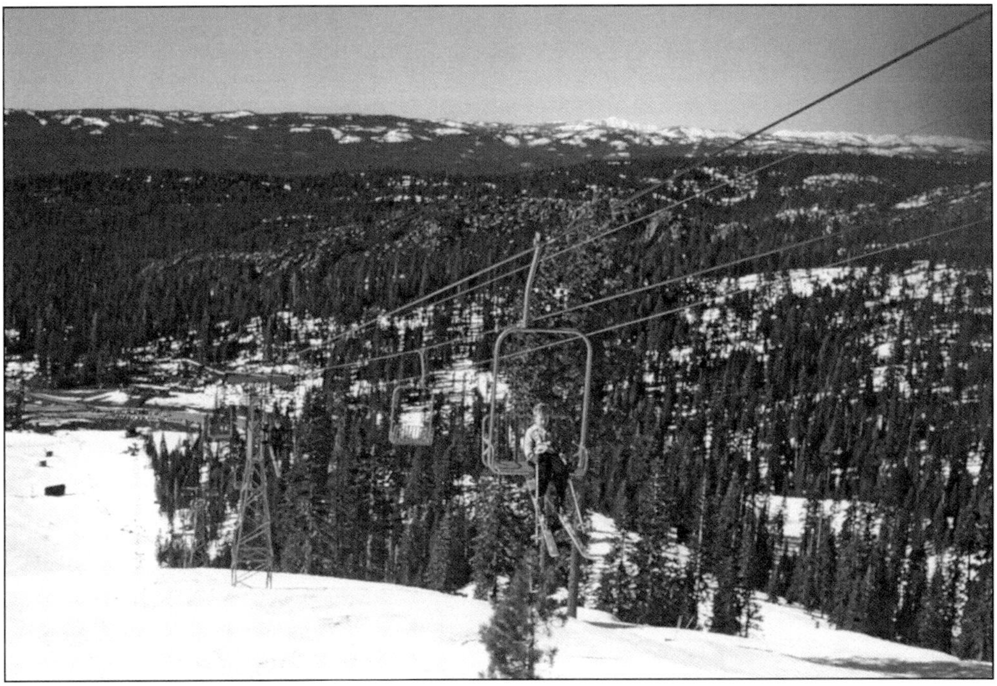

This is the original Heron lift, the only chair lift in the beginning years of the resort. It was orange in color with no safety bar. The run was rockier back then, so this was considered a more advanced run. Today, it is known as Chair Three and is considered an intermediate run.

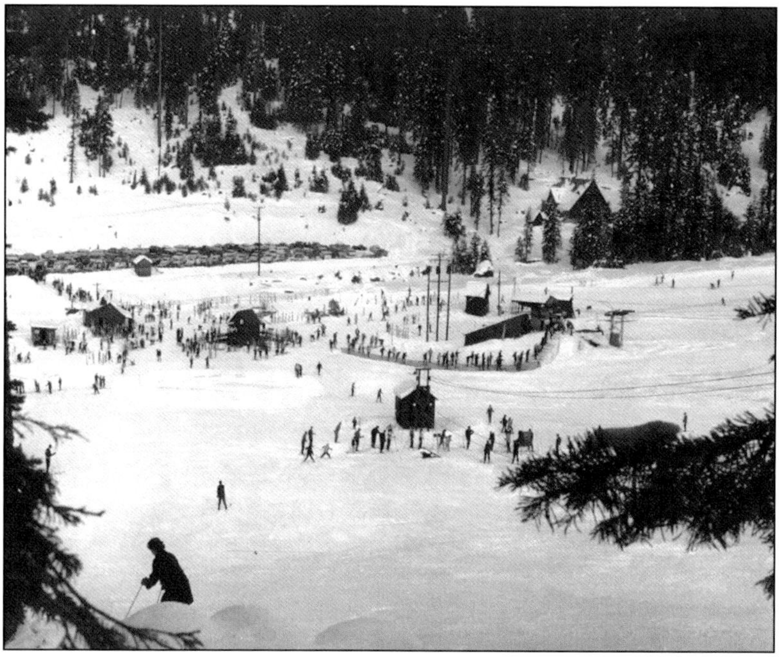

Looking down at the base area from left to right is a line for the rope tow just in front of the ski patrol building. The ski school is the next building over, then is the ticket office. The small structure in the middle is a rope tow where Chair One now lives. Next is the tunnel at the bottom of Chair Three, and the Mountain House is at the end of the parking lot.

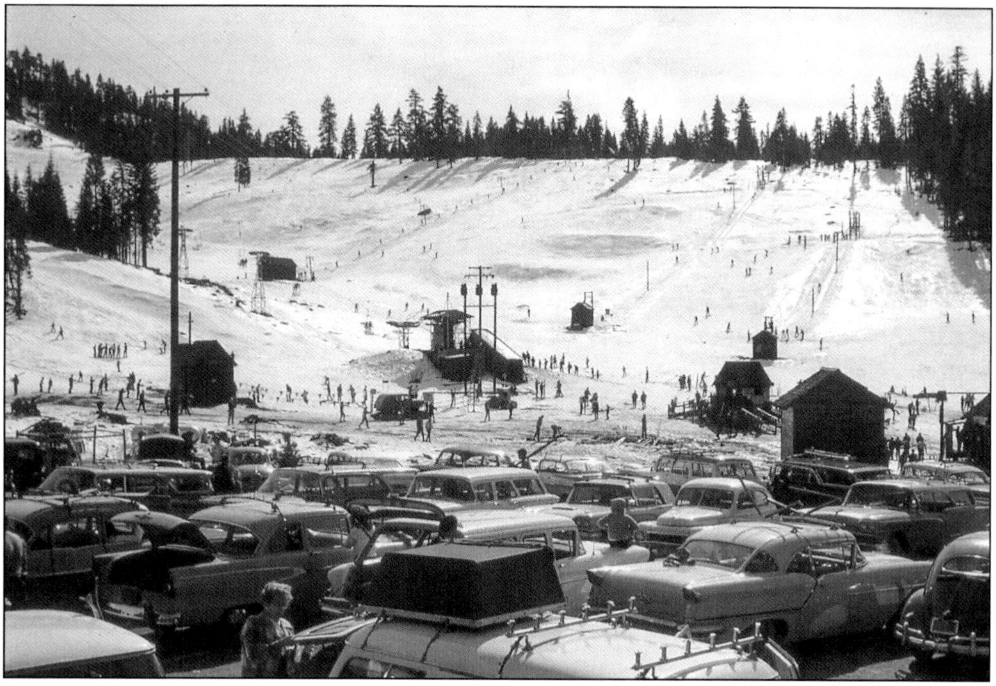

In the early days of Dodge Ridge, a tunnel was added to the line of Chair Three, shown in the center of this photograph. Skiers would hike to get in, but it provided some protection from the elements. Notice that the parking lot was much smaller than it currently is, so patience was required.

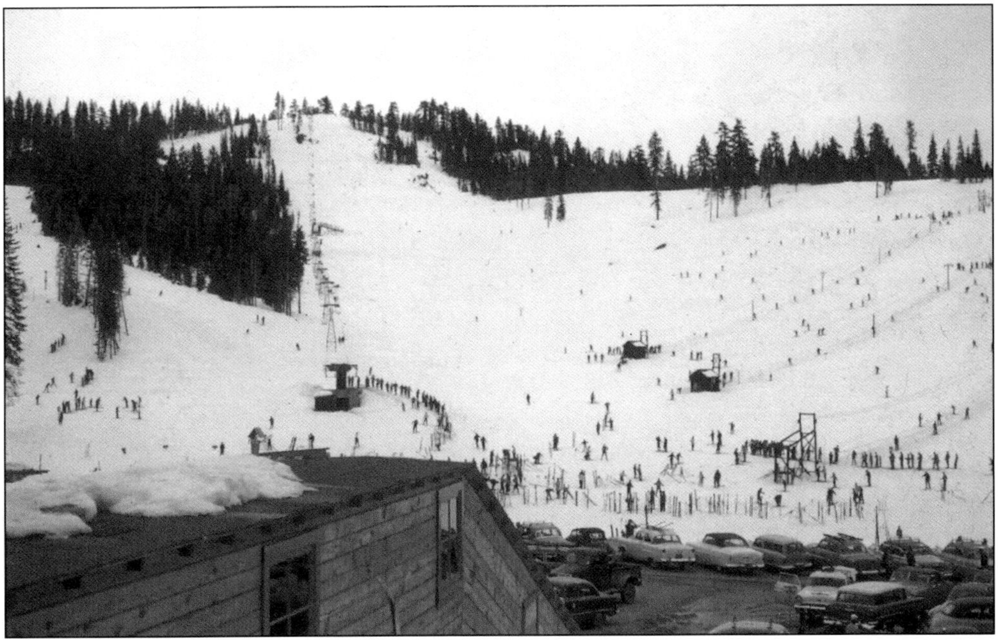

The layout required quite a bit of walking to reach the rope tows on the right side and chairs in the middle. Beginners did not do well hiking sidestep up the hill.

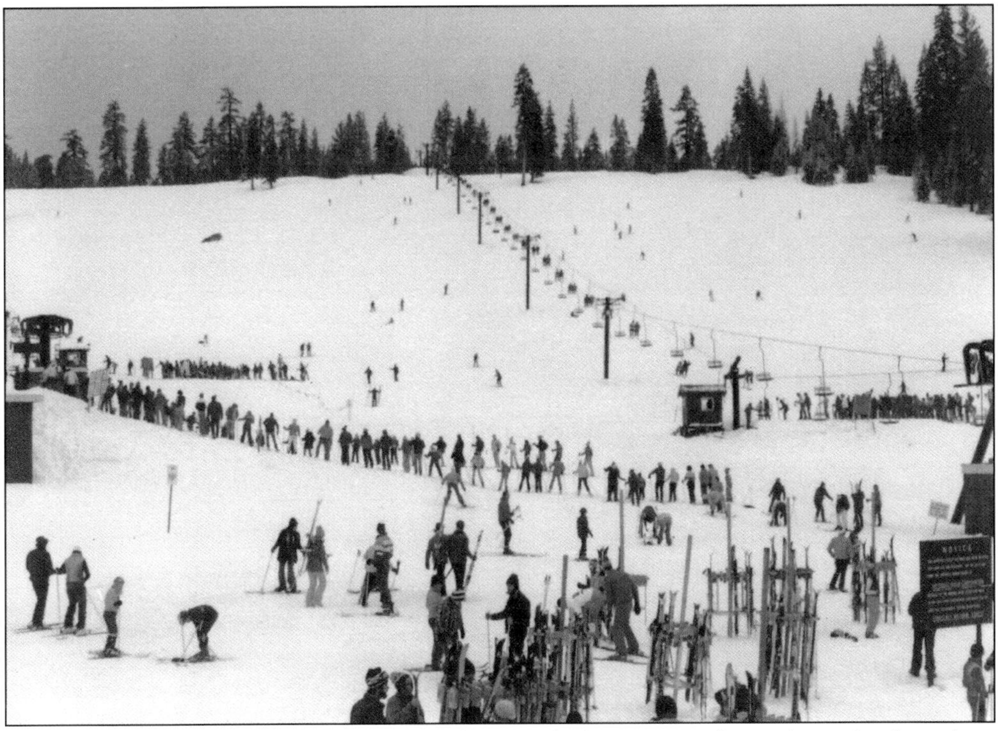

With enhancements, guests now had three chairs in the base area to choose from. On the right is Chair One. On the left is Chair Two with the shorter line, and in the left corner is Chair Three with the long line. People were very patient in line, as it was not uncommon to have a 40-minute wait outside.

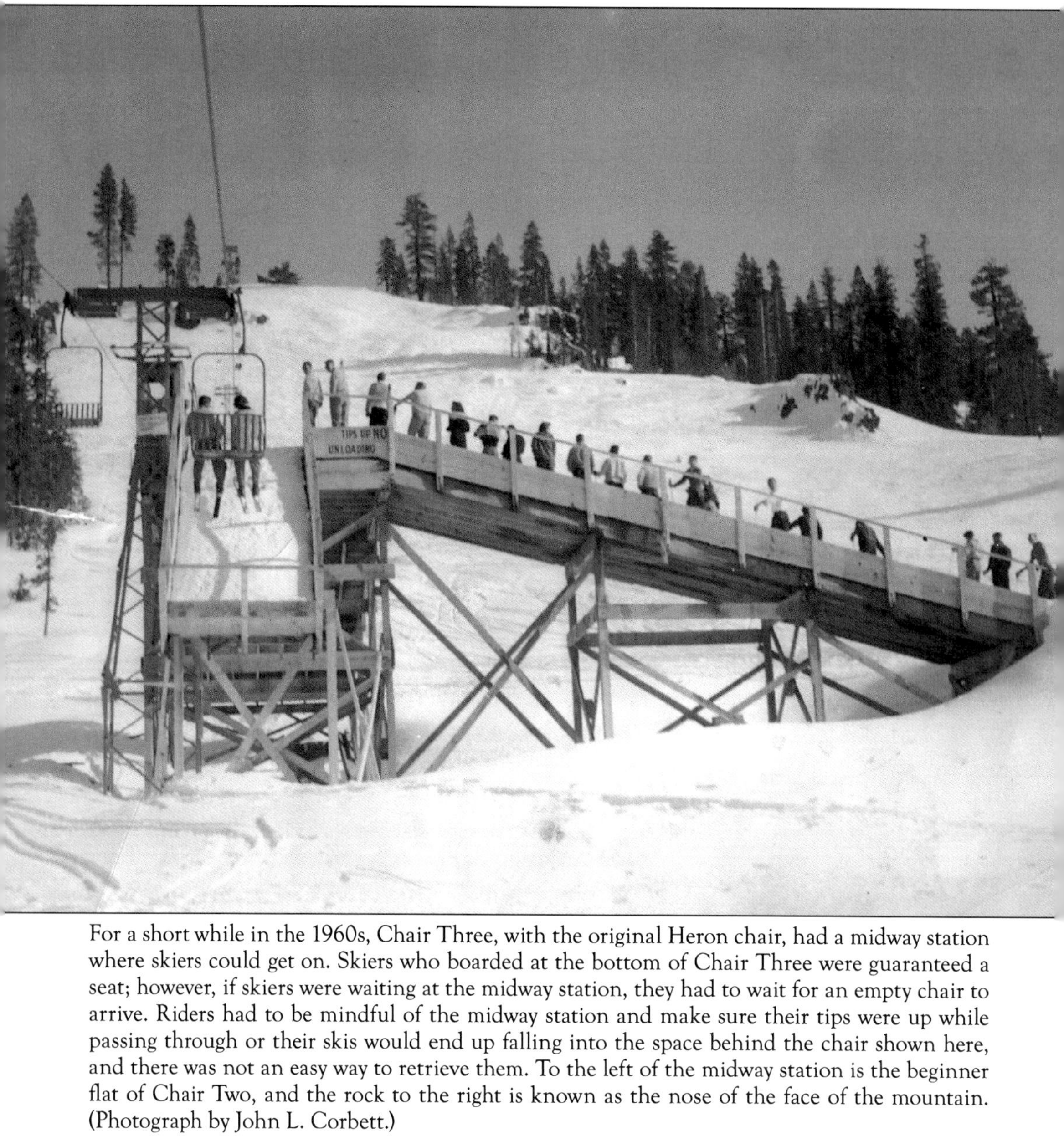

For a short while in the 1960s, Chair Three, with the original Heron chair, had a midway station where skiers could get on. Skiers who boarded at the bottom of Chair Three were guaranteed a seat; however, if skiers were waiting at the midway station, they had to wait for an empty chair to arrive. Riders had to be mindful of the midway station and make sure their tips were up while passing through or their skis would end up falling into the space behind the chair shown here, and there was not an easy way to retrieve them. To the left of the midway station is the beginner flat of Chair Two, and the rock to the right is known as the nose of the face of the mountain. (Photograph by John L. Corbett.)

Chair Two, located above the "Notice" sign, was not popular. It was a beginner chair and required skiers to walk quite a distance up to it, which was not easy, especially if someone was not proficient in skiing. On the right, barely visible is Chair One. While taking a break, skis were just leaning against a fence, as there were no lockers yet.

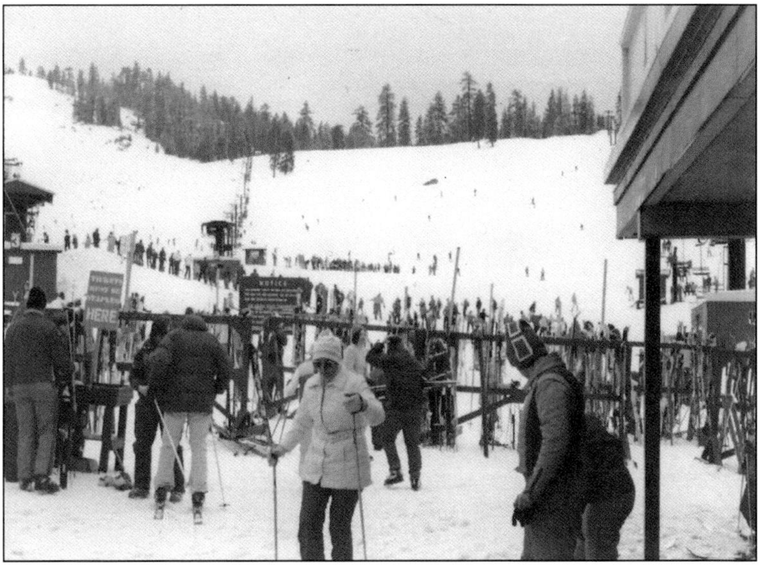

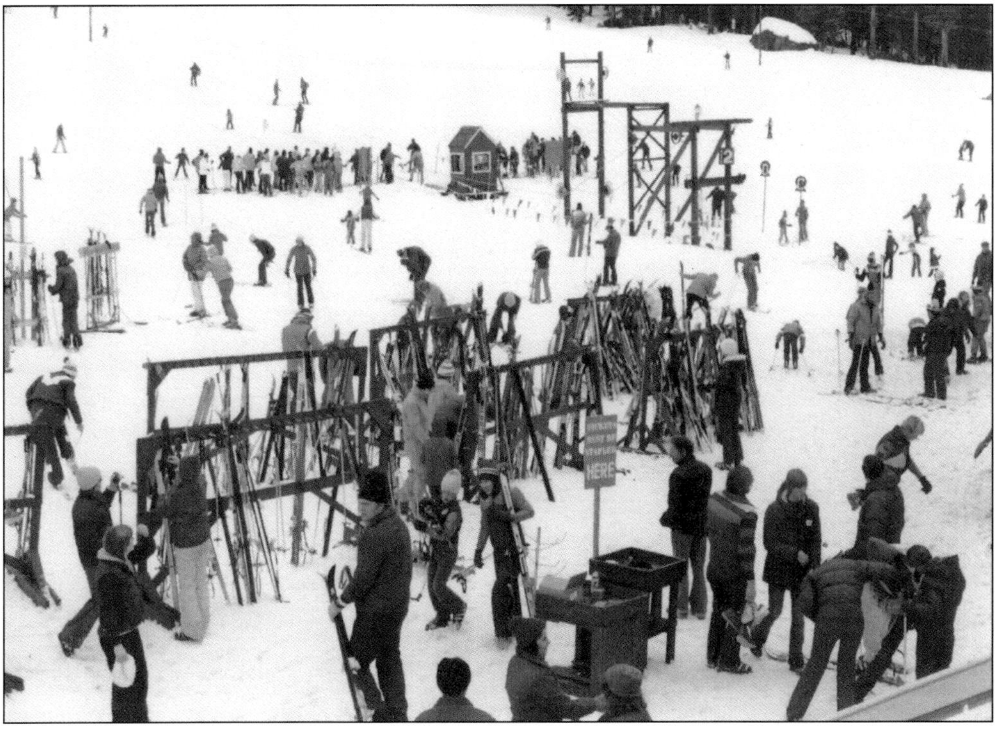

Rope Tow Two loaded from both sides of the tow structure, so there were two rows of skiers balancing their way up the mountain. This was also during the staple-the-ticket-to-clothes days and outside check-in; note the box of that day's passes and staplers in the little stand in the front of the photograph.

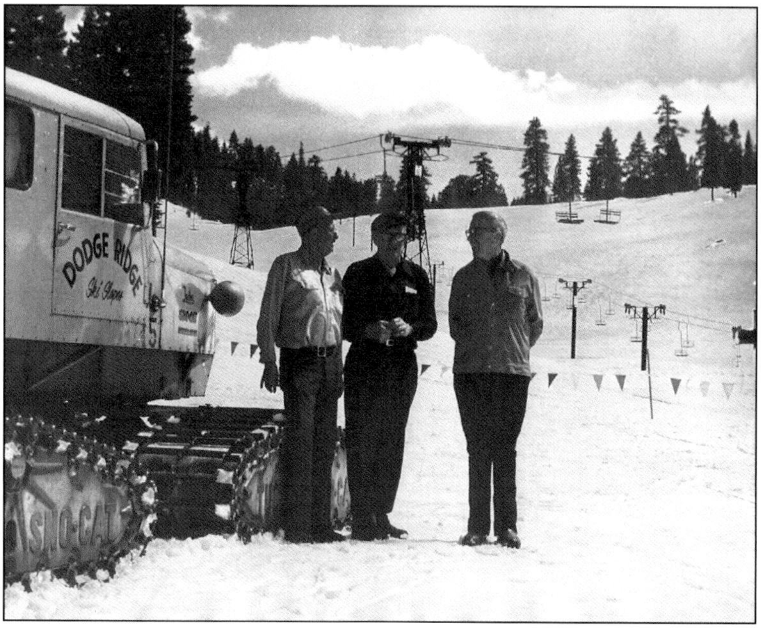

Standing next to one of the original Tucker Cats are, from left to right, Carl Williams, who made getting into the resort and having nice trails to ski possible, and Jasper Meuli, manager, mechanic, and inventor, who is also credited with designing the first T-bar in the Sierra Nevada. Earl Purdy, owner of Dodge Ridge, is on the right. (Courtesy of Calin Smith.)

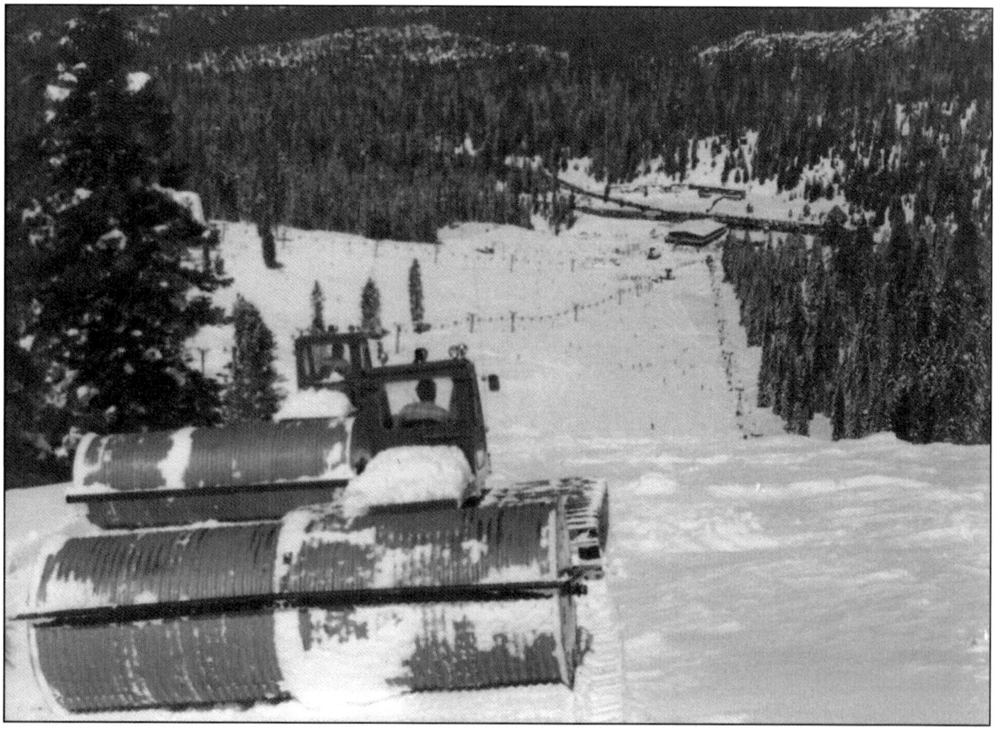

This Thycal groomer with culvert pipe on an axel is what made the beautiful corduroy lines down the face of the mountain. On the face of the mountain, from left to right, are Chairs One, Two, and Three, with the old lodge off in the distance above the parking lot, where the upper parking lot is today.

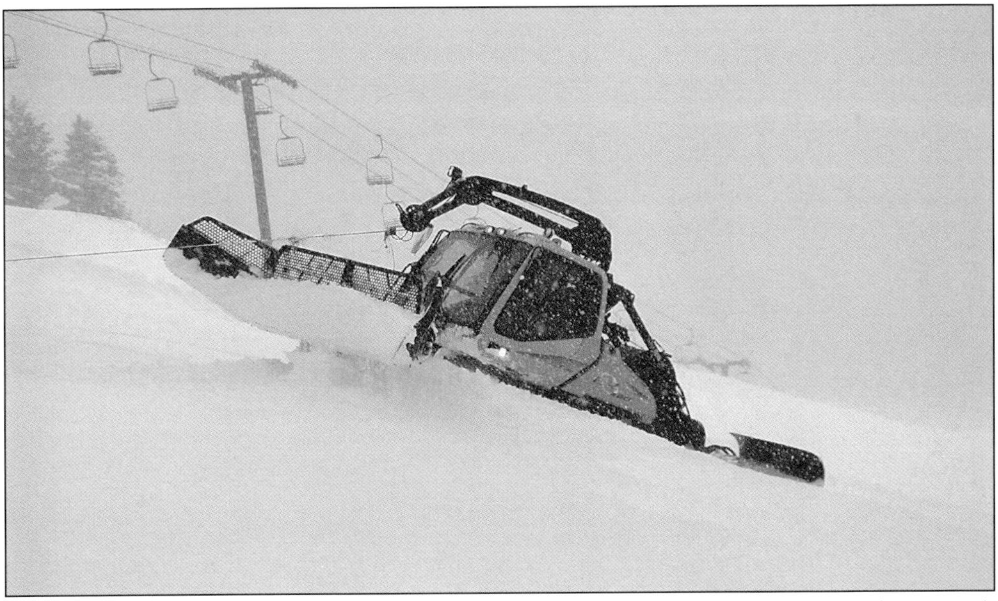

This is a Winch Cat groomer in action. It is a specialized snow groomer that uses a large winch and cable attached to something solid, an anchor tower at the top of the slope, allowing the operator to climb steep or challenging terrain without sliding down. It is a tie-up and pull-up operation, which enhanced the capability of the mountain operations team.

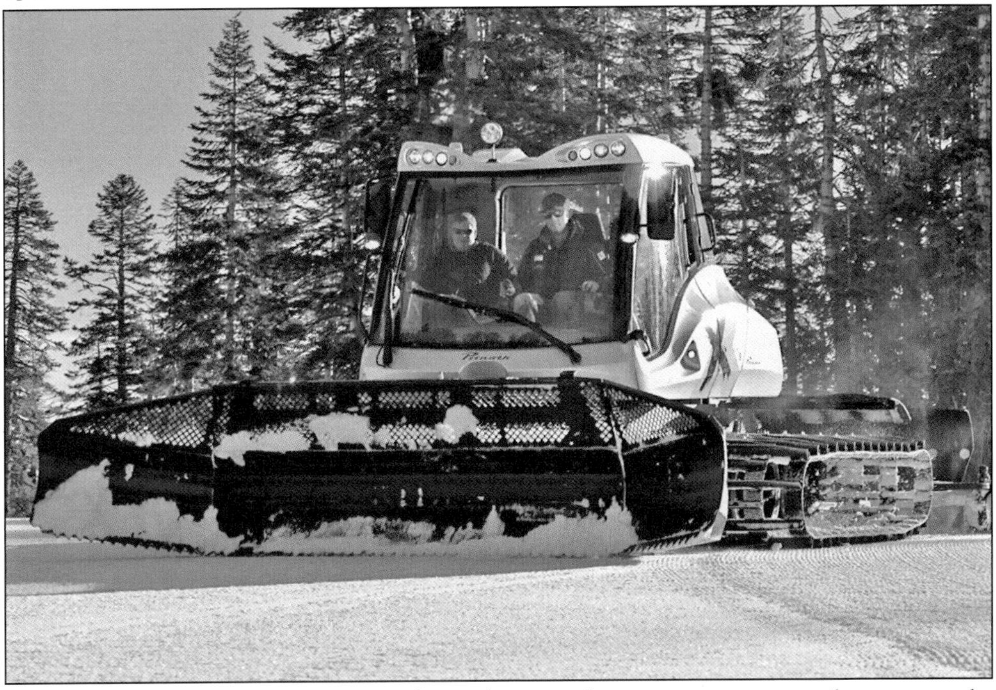

Equipment upgrades were also essential to enhancing the guest experience and increasing the efficiency of the mountain crew. Shown here, Brian Townsend (left) and Jason Smith (right) drive the Prinoth Bison snow groomer. This machine is more efficient, allowing operators to climb steep slopes, know the depth of the snow, lay smooth trails, and groom longer-lasting runs. (Photograph by Sean Waterman.)

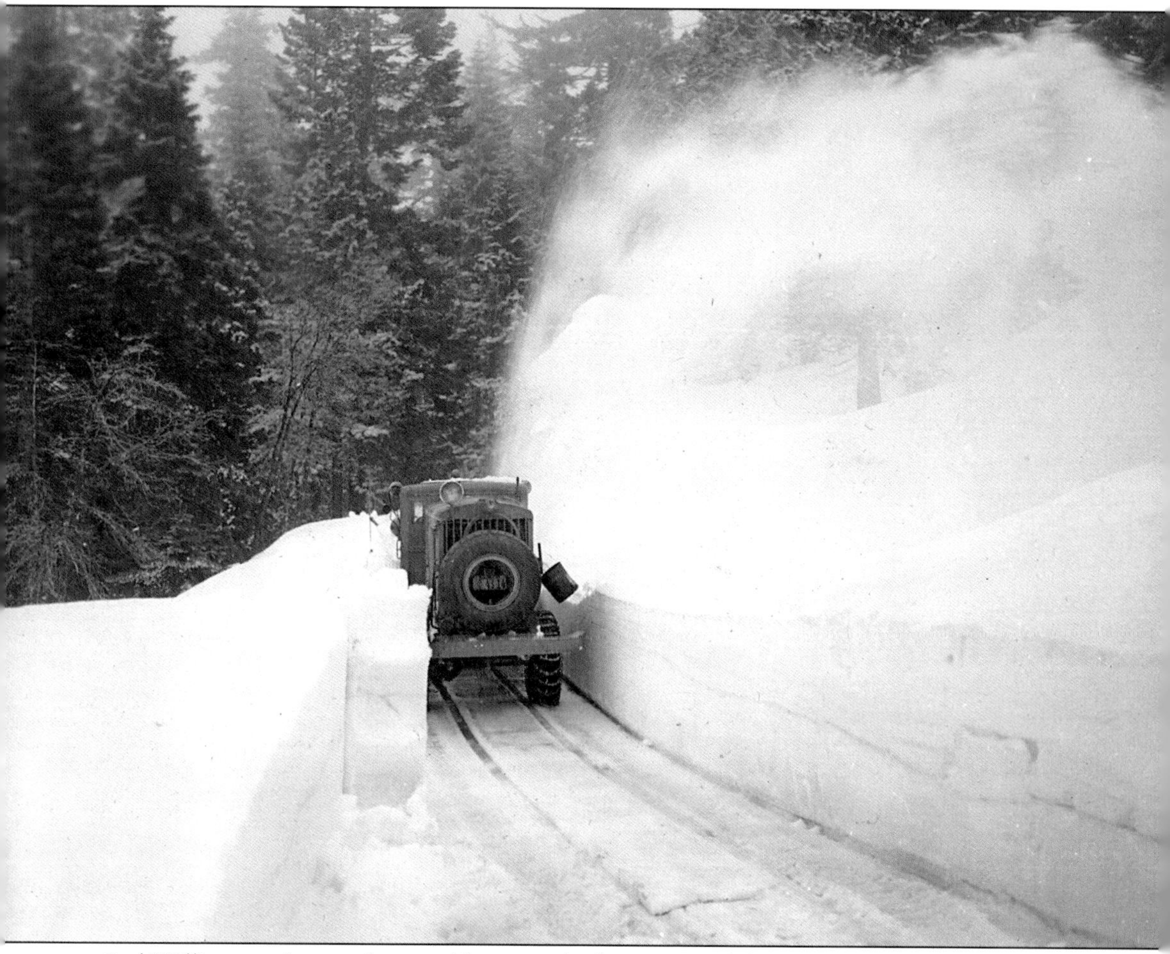

Carl Williams is driving the snowblower at the beginning of the main parking lot. He literally built the road from the Y one-way split to Dodge Ridge. Without him, the resort would be nearly impossible to reach. He constantly kept it clear every single day, no matter how much snow fell. Williams was also a county supervisor while running the maintenance shop and snow-plowing facilities at Dodge Ridge.

Compacting snow was once a big dream, but now it is common practice. Back in the day, skiers were allowed to be on the slopes at the same time as the groomers, requiring them to dodge the death cookies made of the hard-packed icy snow that could be thrown from the machine belts to snow cat tracks without notice.

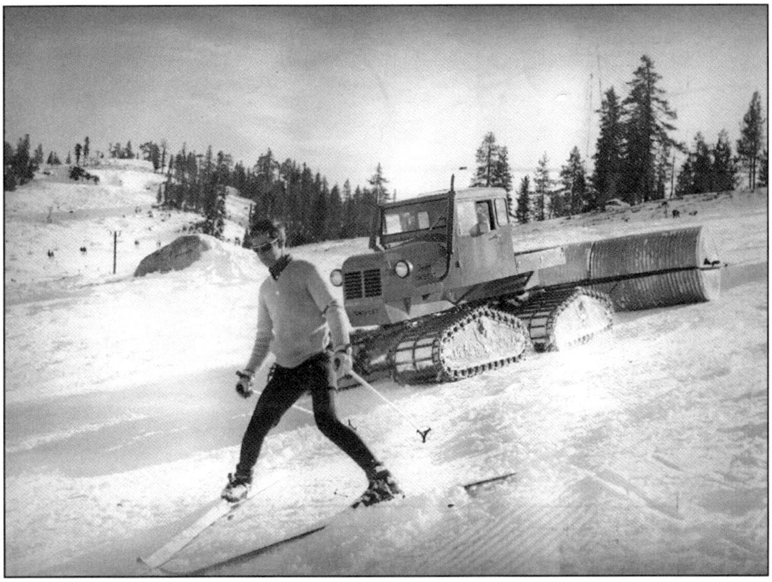

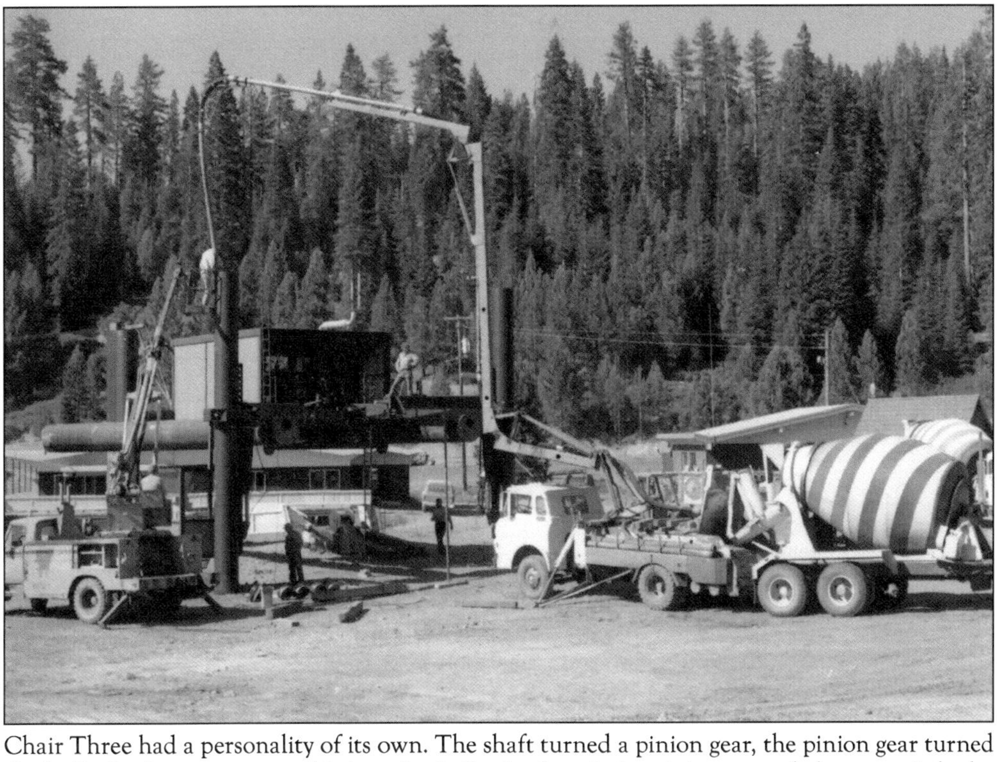

Chair Three had a personality of its own. The shaft turned a pinion gear, the pinion gear turned the bull wheel, a gear was welded to the bull wheel, and the pinion turned that gear. It had a 700-person capacity per hour and was very noisy. It needed to be updated. There was also a midway station at the end of Golly Gully.

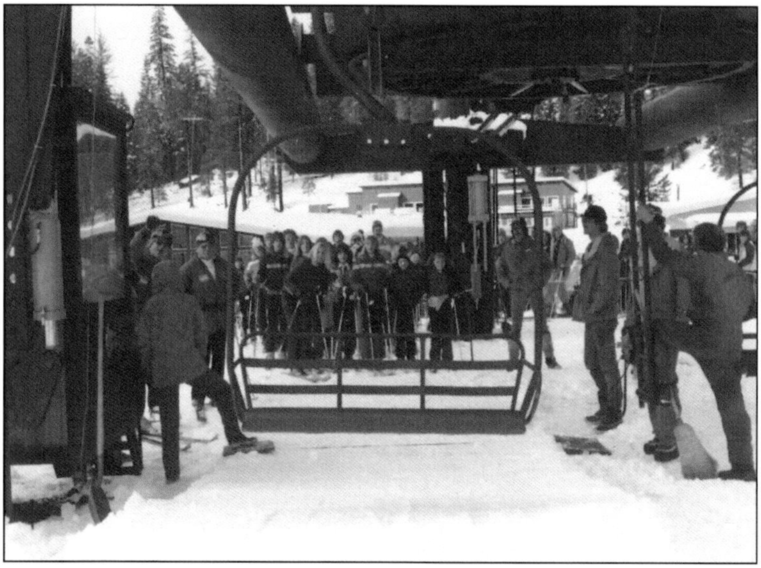

Excited skiers are waiting in line not only for the chance to be the first to cut new tracks but to also ride in the new Yon chair that Chair Three provides. Three friends in a row allowed for increased capacity.

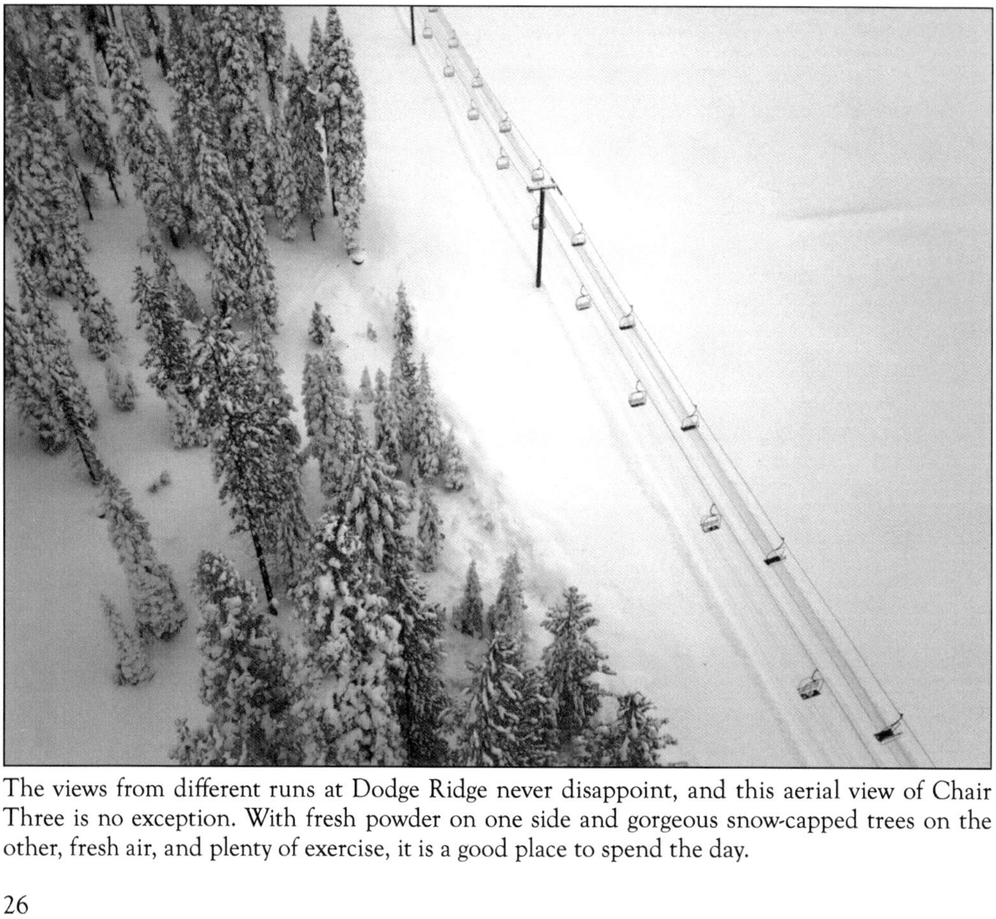

The views from different runs at Dodge Ridge never disappoint, and this aerial view of Chair Three is no exception. With fresh powder on one side and gorgeous snow-capped trees on the other, fresh air, and plenty of exercise, it is a good place to spend the day.

Frank Helm takes in the sweeping views as he replaces the Old Chair Three with the new Chair Three. This was the first major enhancement that he made after purchasing Dodge Ridge, so it holds a special place in his heart. Since making this improvement, he went on to make many more significant changes, reshaping the entire landscape of the resort.

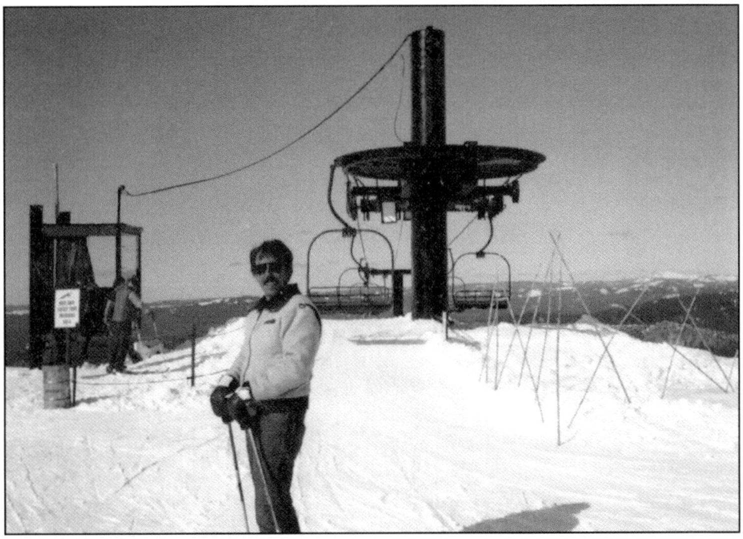

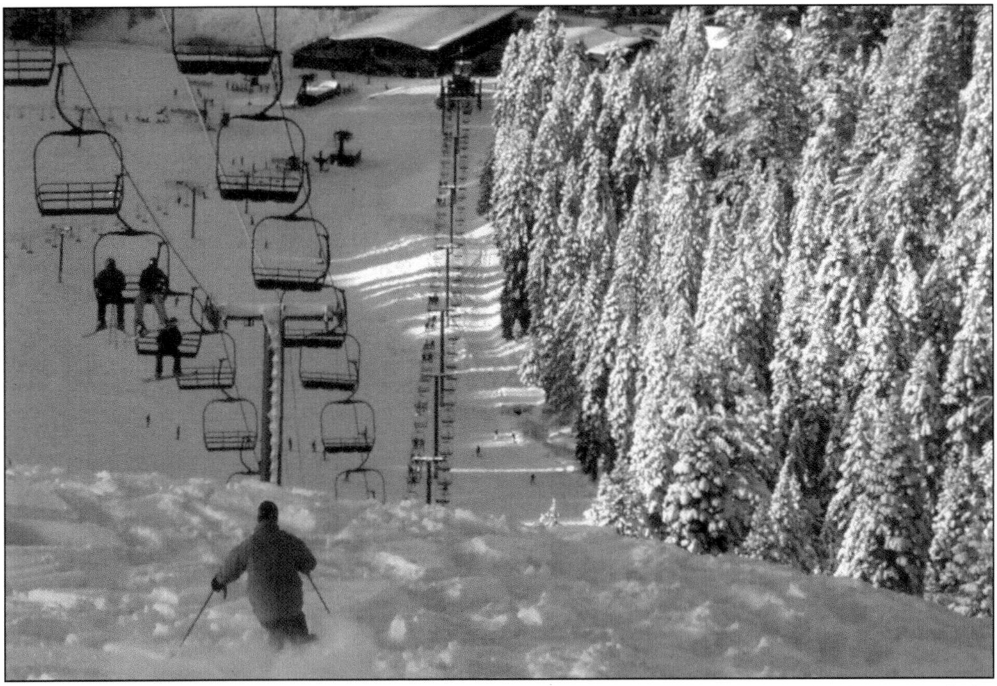

Even with the surrounding beauty, skiing can be dangerous. The skier at the bottom of the photograph is headed toward a narrow strip in between the lift and the trees on the right called Half Face. It is now affectionately known by locals as "Kline's Creek," in honor of Mike Kline, who fell in full splat and could not get out. Fortunately, he was not skiing alone and was promptly rescued with just a bruised ego.

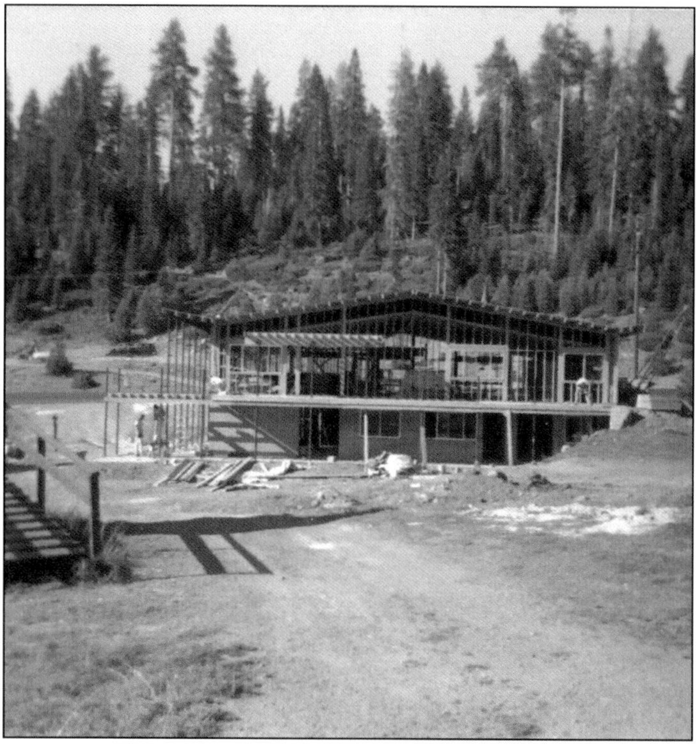

The Helms also renovated several buildings. This is the expansion of the Creekside Lodge that includes moving the ski school locker room closer to the ski school. The lodge now offers office space, a sports shop, day-use and long-term lockers, a larger cafeteria and bar, and a new deck. There is more room inside for games and live music and grilling outside in the summer.

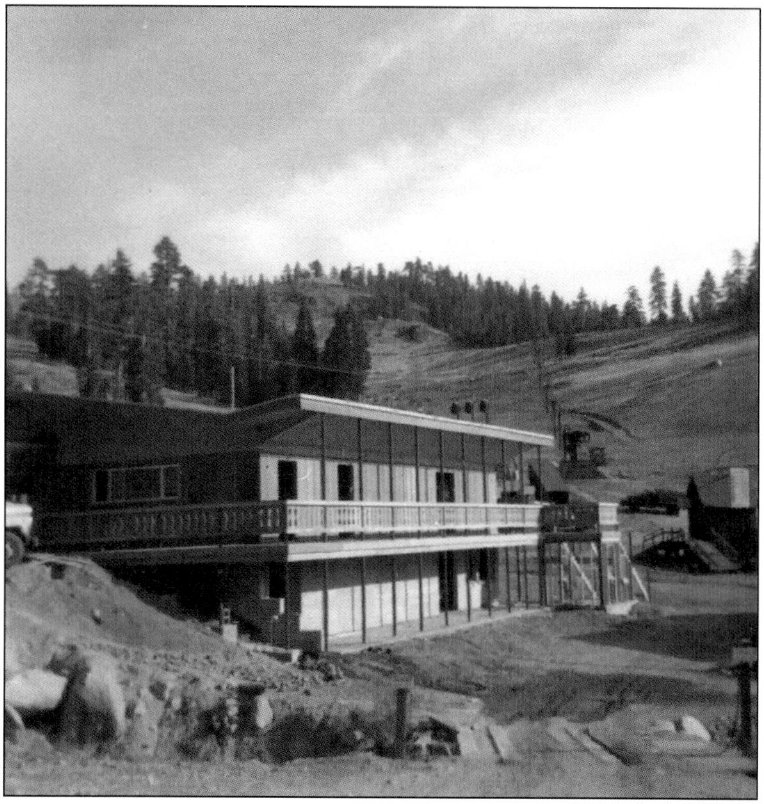

What is currently known as the Rental Building was also reconfigured for more efficient use. The ski school ticket office was moved from under the stairs and closer to the ski school, as was the ski patrol office. Now rentals and day lockers are upstairs with plenty of room to try on equipment and easily reach the lifts. Downstairs now houses the Keely Cashman Teams Room for racers.

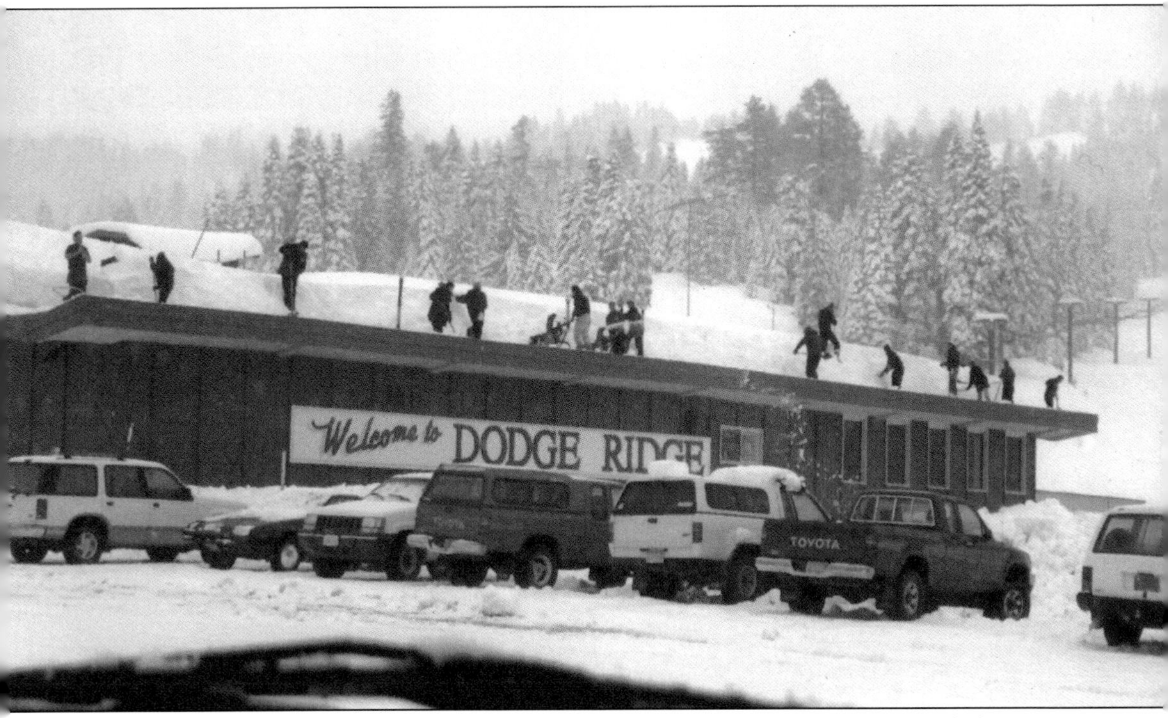

In November 1977, the biggest snowstorm in several years threatened the roof of the lodge. Signs of the roof buckling under the weight of the heavy snow were visible, so quick action was required. Instructors, maintenance staff, and anybody else that was nearby were grabbed to help shovel snow from the roof to keep it from collapsing. It was a gallant group effort to save the structure and yet another example of the ever-present and constant teamwork exhibited by the entire staff at Dodge Ridge.

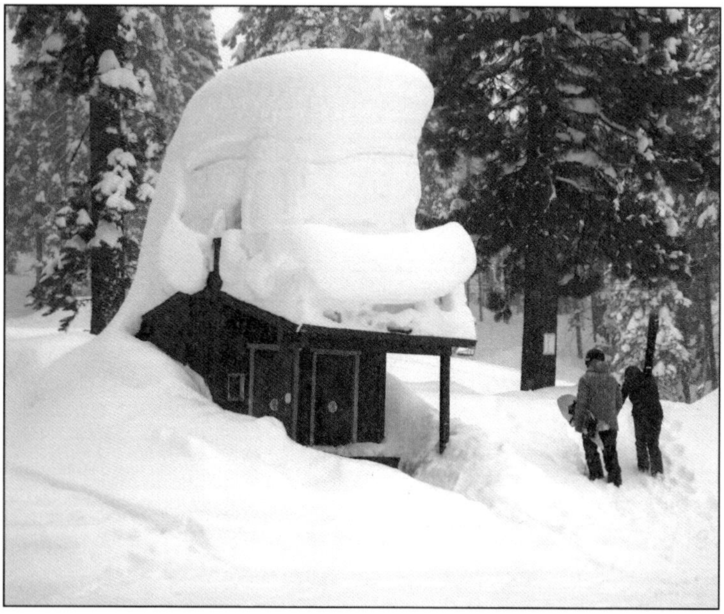

Dodge Ridge was mostly cash for a long time. Even when the systems were put in, this little ticket booth near Chair Five would lose power, and managers would run up there with sacks of cash and a roll of tickets or they would stand in the parking lot to help guests avoid the hike up and back from the disabled ticket booth. Modern technology now provides smoother transactions.

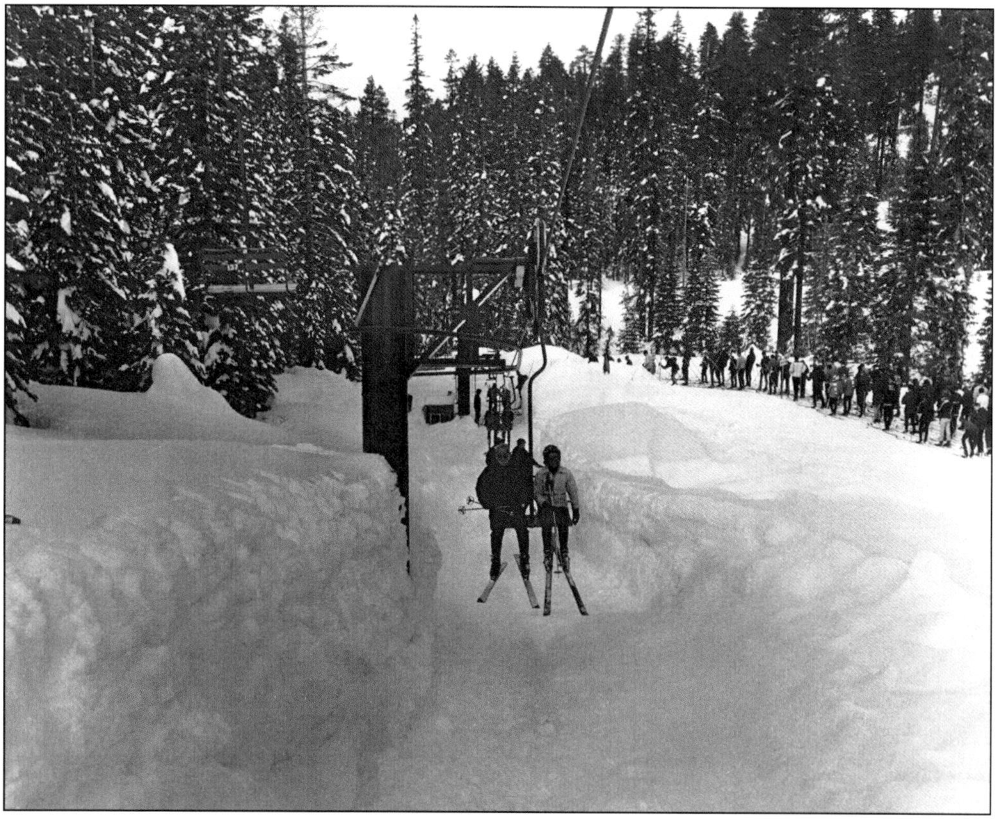

Chair Five was and still is popular with the locals, hence the long line. The chair is a two-seater with a bar in the middle and takes skiers to the summit. This photograph is from the bottom of Chair Five, where digging a trench is required for the chair to operate properly. The parking lot road was extended to provide easier access to this area.

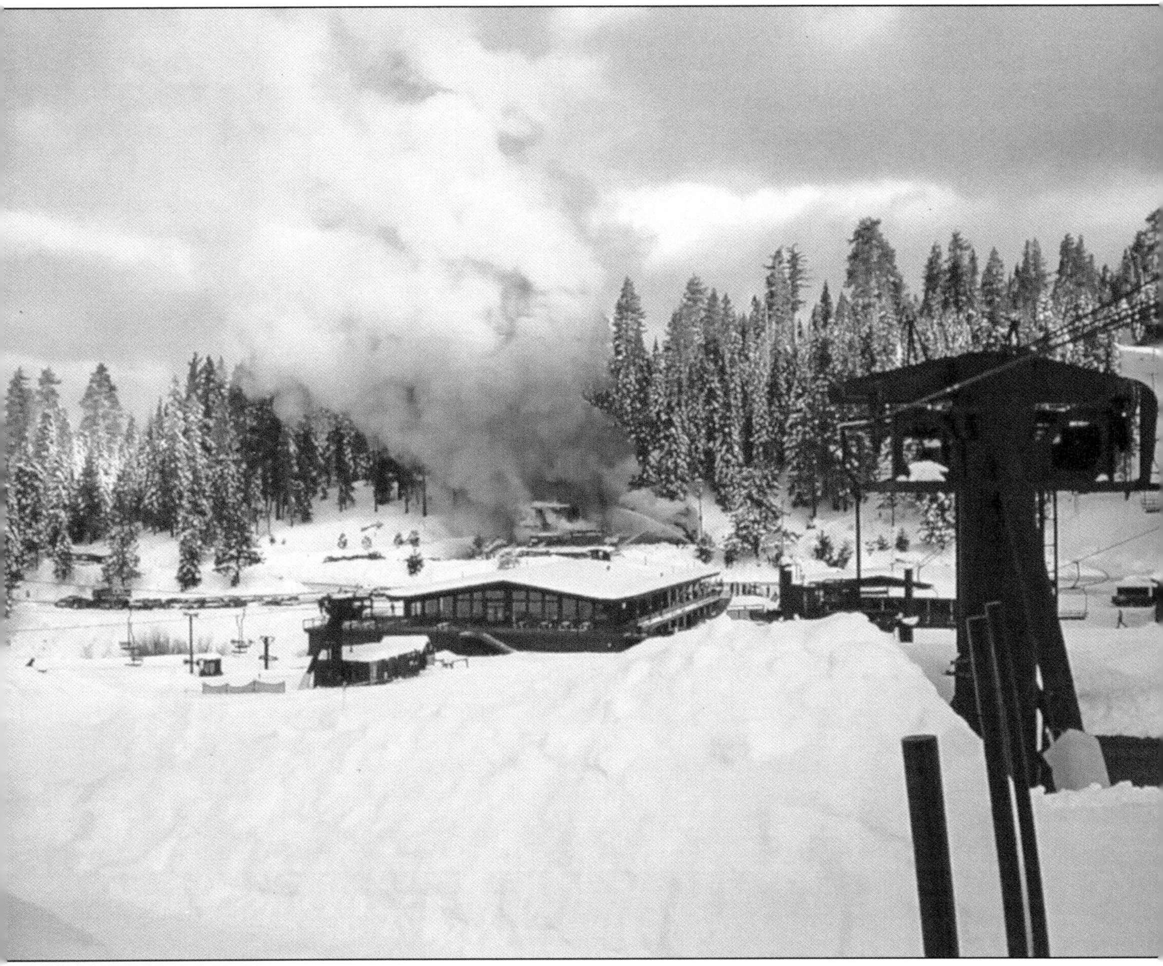

On January 6, 2005, a morning fire broke out in the Motherlode Lodge employee locker room for ski patrol, instructors, and lift operators. Employees worked to extinguish the flames, but it was a complete loss. With guests in mind, they were still able to achieve their mission to safely open the resort without disruption. Heavenly Valley Ski Resort immediately sent replacement uniforms. (Courtesy of Bruce Pedretti.)

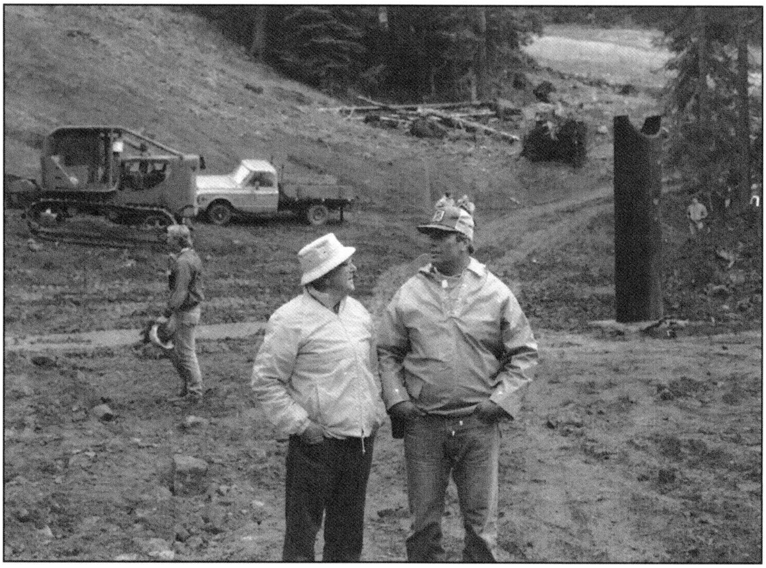

Mountain manager Preston Hough oversees the clearing and building for the new Chair Seven. This marked the initial major improvement to the resort expansion. It was part of a master plan that required approval from the Forest Service and many hoops to jump through to accomplish.

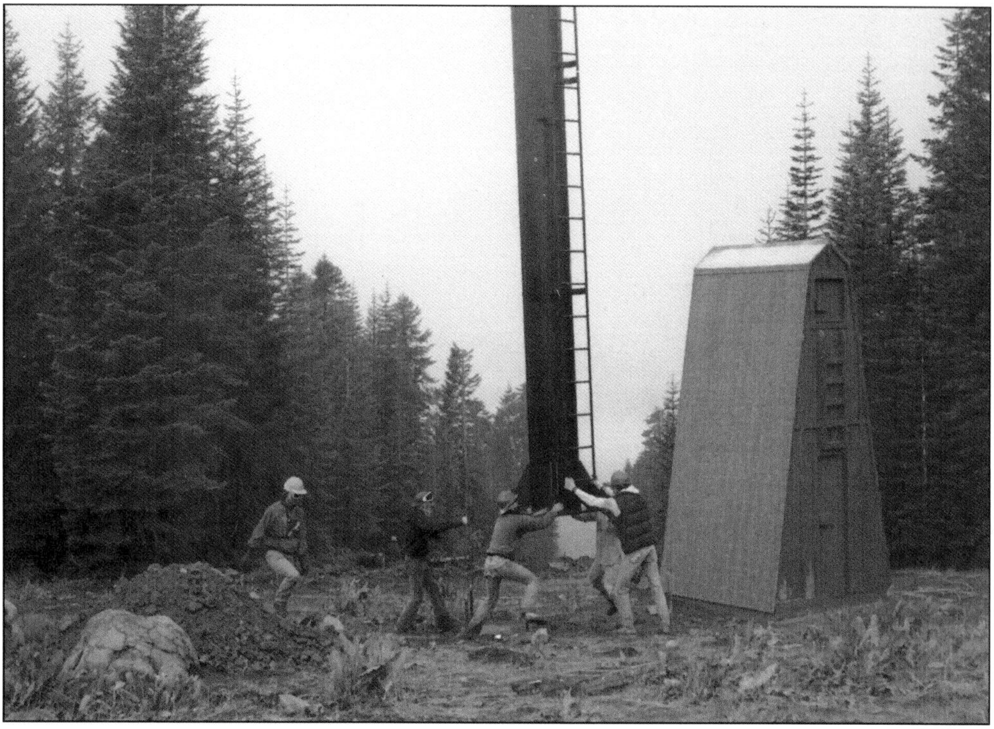

One of the most impressive enhancements to the resort was the installation of Chair Seven, which significantly expanded the skiing options for guests. It was a huge financial investment and no small feat for the crews to accomplish. Helicopter and ground crews worked closely with each other for great precision.

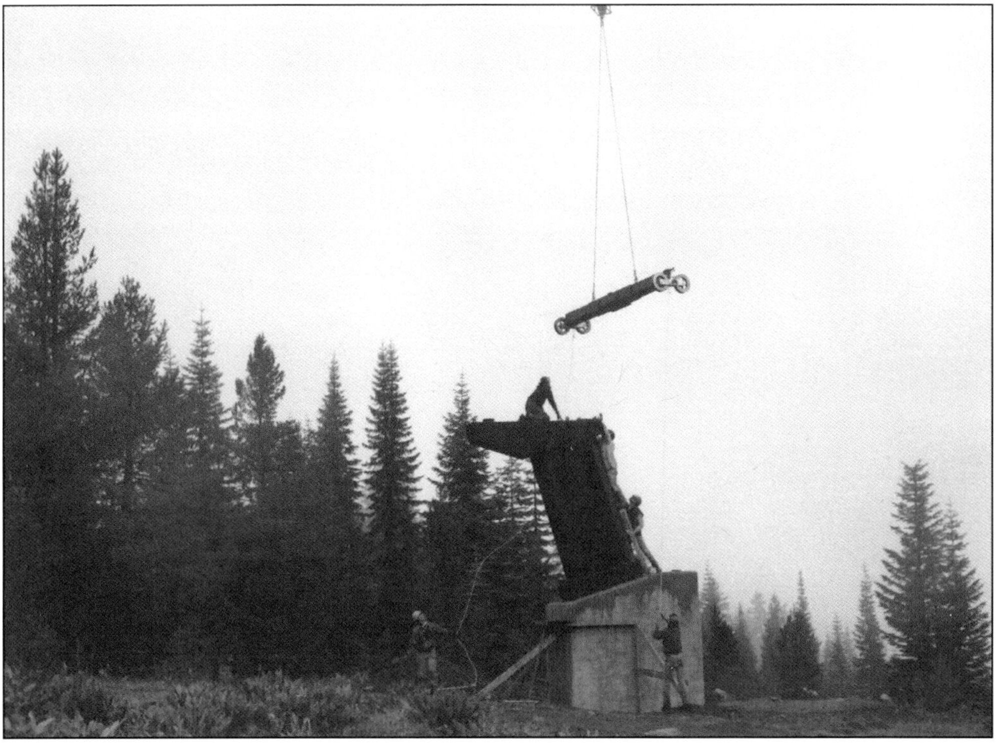

Preparing for the equipment to be placed properly required significant clearing of trees and rocks plus the digging of holes for placement of poles and towers. Environmental surveys were required, and numerous safety measures were put in place to ensure a well-rounded and successful project plan was in place.

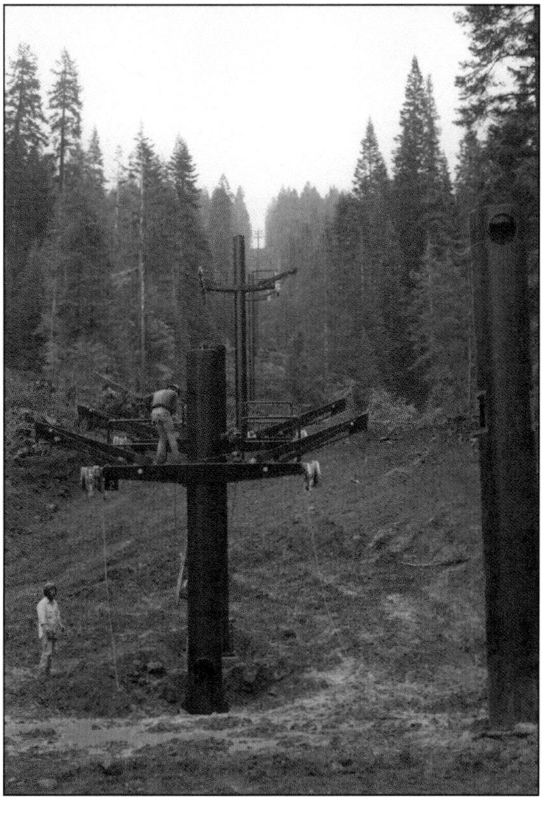

Once the towers were in place, the cables, arms, and the mechanics for each individual chair were put in place. The crew needed considerable resourcefulness to complete the large forest project. And this is just the beginning—laying the foundation for the runs came next.

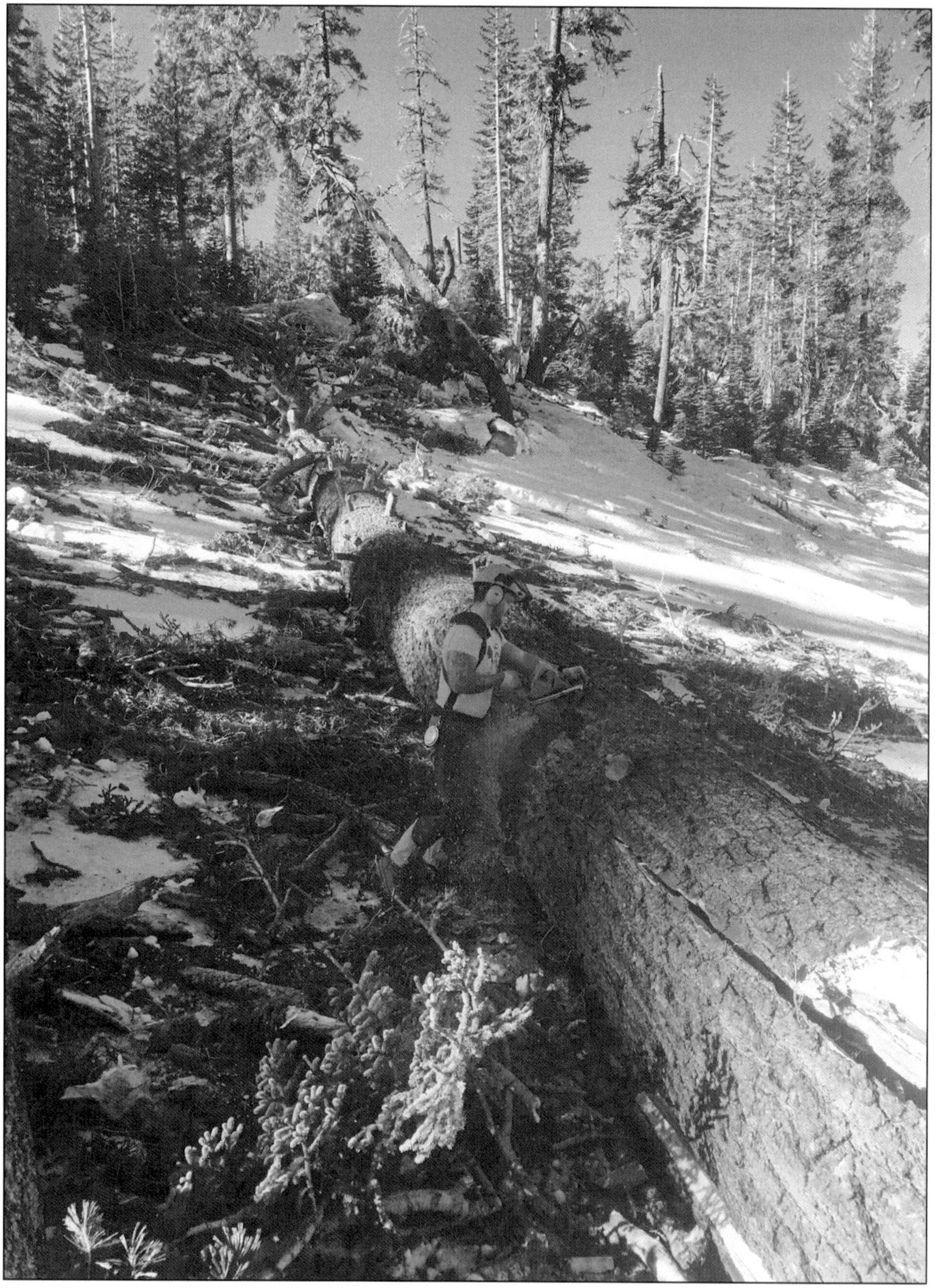

Here is some perspective on the magnitude of what it took to clear the area in order to build the chair lifts and structures at Dodge Ridge. Felling the trees was not an easy task and took time to do safely and properly. Much of the wood was repurposed at the resort.

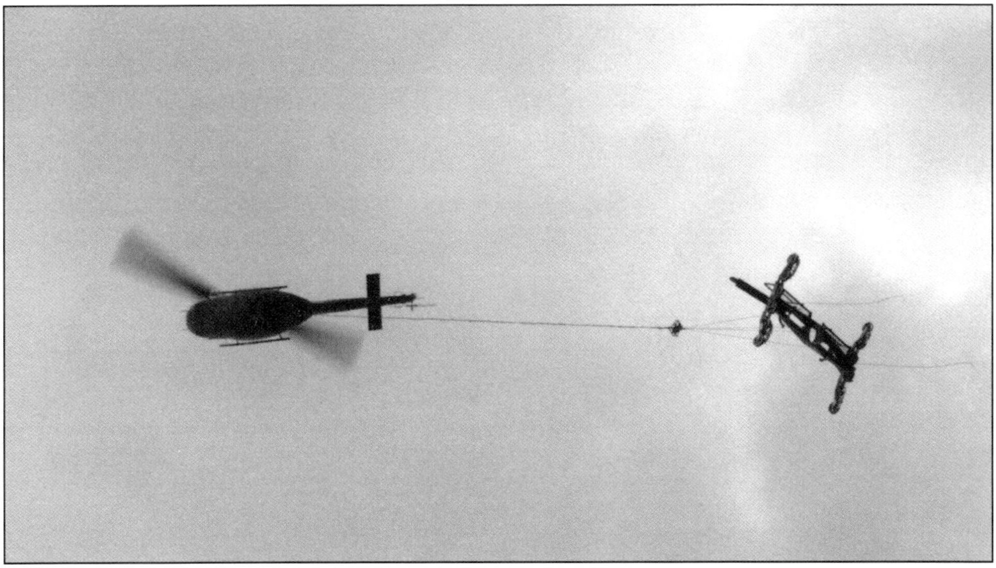

Chair Eight's installation opened the mountain's backside and tripled the skiable area. Crews again coordinated with helicopter crews to coordinate precise delivery of equipment in a forest environment.

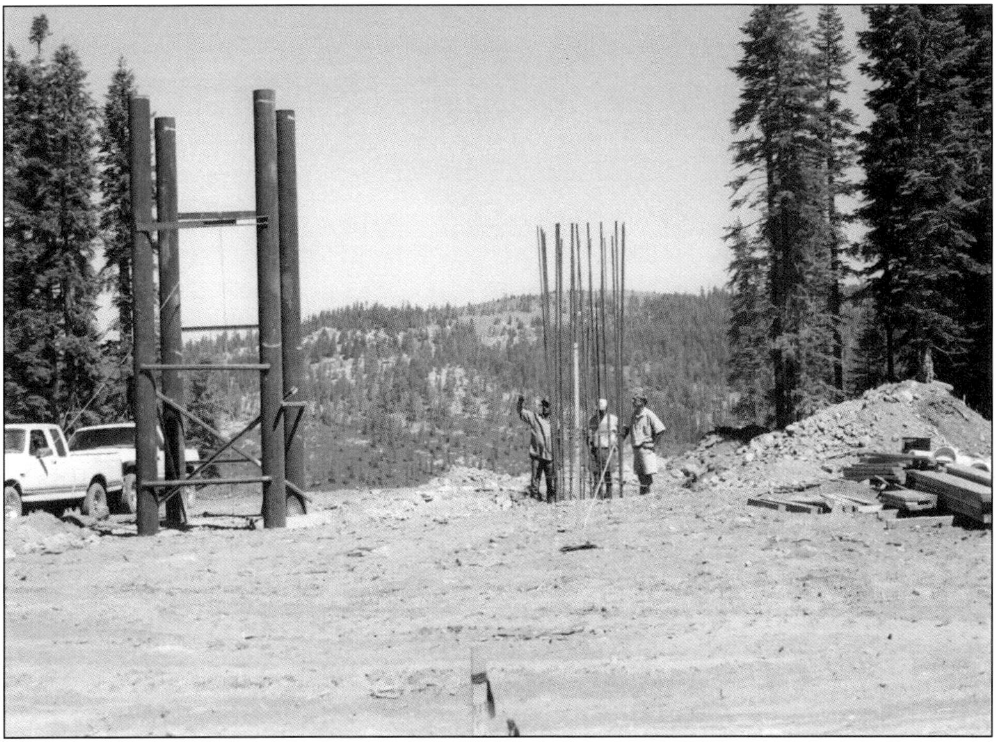

There are multiple details in play while building the chairs and runs. Aside from the mountain and construction crews, marketing manager Michael Ladinig ran the details for Chair Eight, including naming the runs and all the shots, so mountain manager Benny Hughs allowed him to jump in a cat to get a true sense of the area and come up with clever names and descriptions to share with the media.

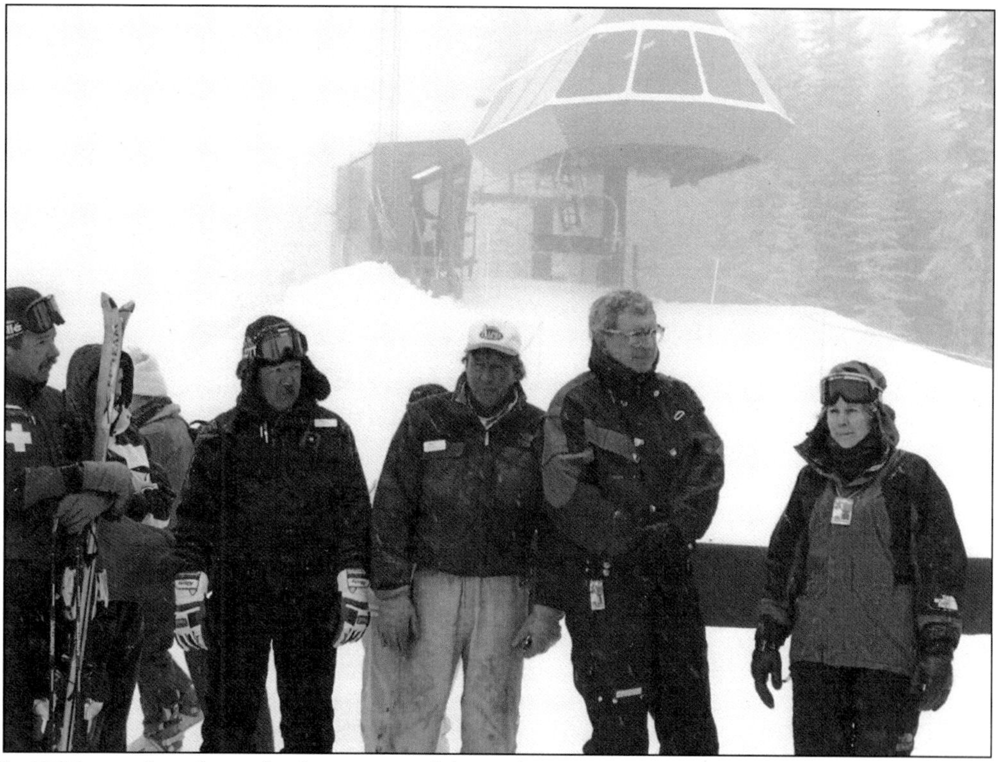

In 1998, some key players for this project celebrate the opening ceremony of Chair Eight, originally called the Prospector, which opened a whole new world on the backside of the resort, tripling the expansion. From left to right are Dave Alley, who felled trees, did snow surveys, and tested runs; Paul Mundy, behind the skis; Kevin Johnson, lift operations manager; Benny Hughes, mountain manager; Buz Carrade; and Sally Helm.

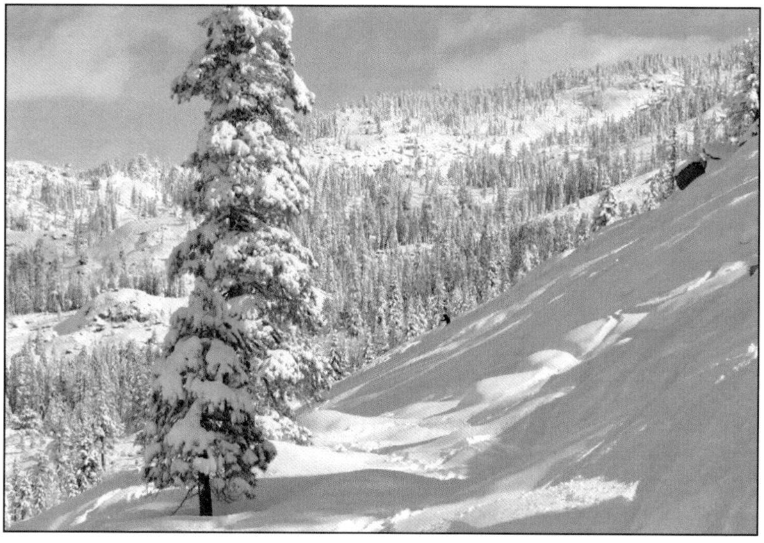

This is the glorious Granite Bowl. Some say that the best way to experience this is to take Double Shot down and then Hole Shot to ride the snow-covered boulders.

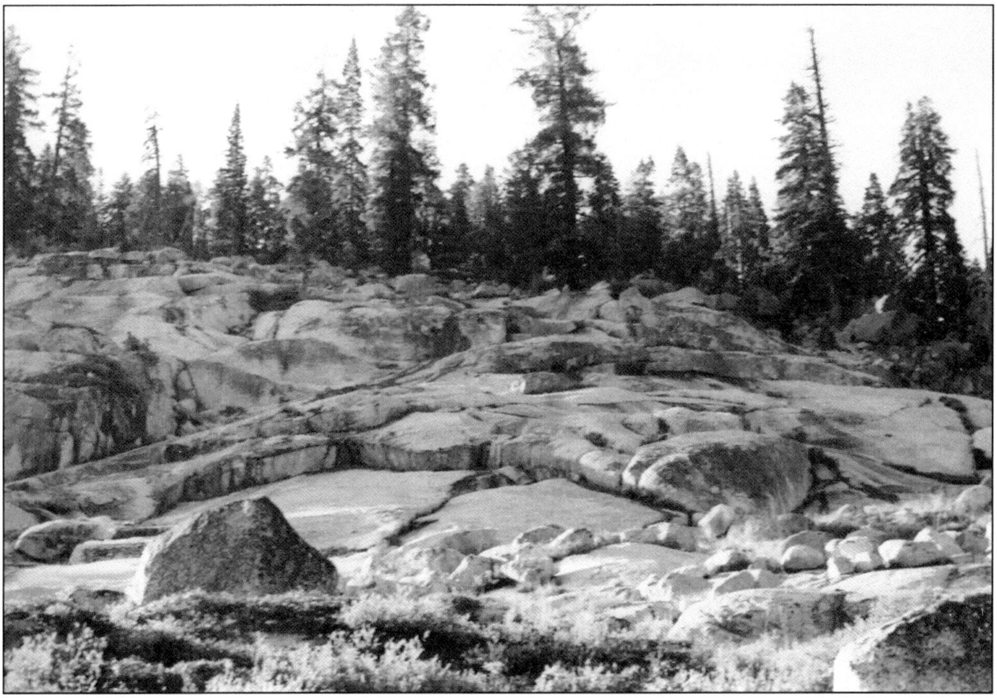

This is the original Granite Bowl. One day, the owner of the Strawberry store was flying over the Granite Bowl. Dave Alley, Ron Jensen, Al Hodges, and Mark Chan had just taken snow measurements for the new bowl and were enjoying lunch and an extra run, thinking no one would know. Suddenly, a plane swooped down through the canyon and dropped a parachute. They investigated. The parachute held four beers.

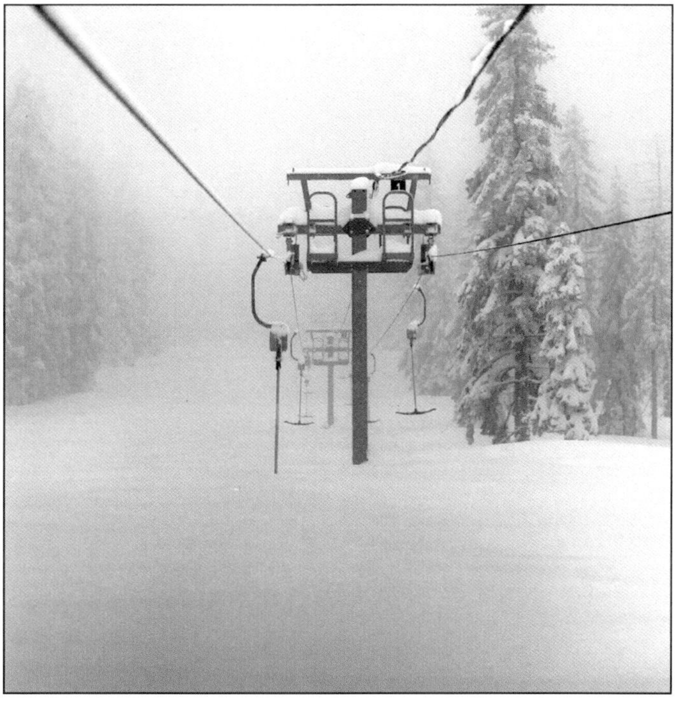

This is the new Doppelmayr T-bar T643 surface lift to reach the second summit above Chair Eight. The T-bar is designed to pull two people up the mountain with one with on each side of the upside down T. It doubled the length of three expert ski runs above the Granite Bowl and expanded accessibility to more of the mountain and backcountry. This is not a beginner run—it is advanced-to-expert skiing.

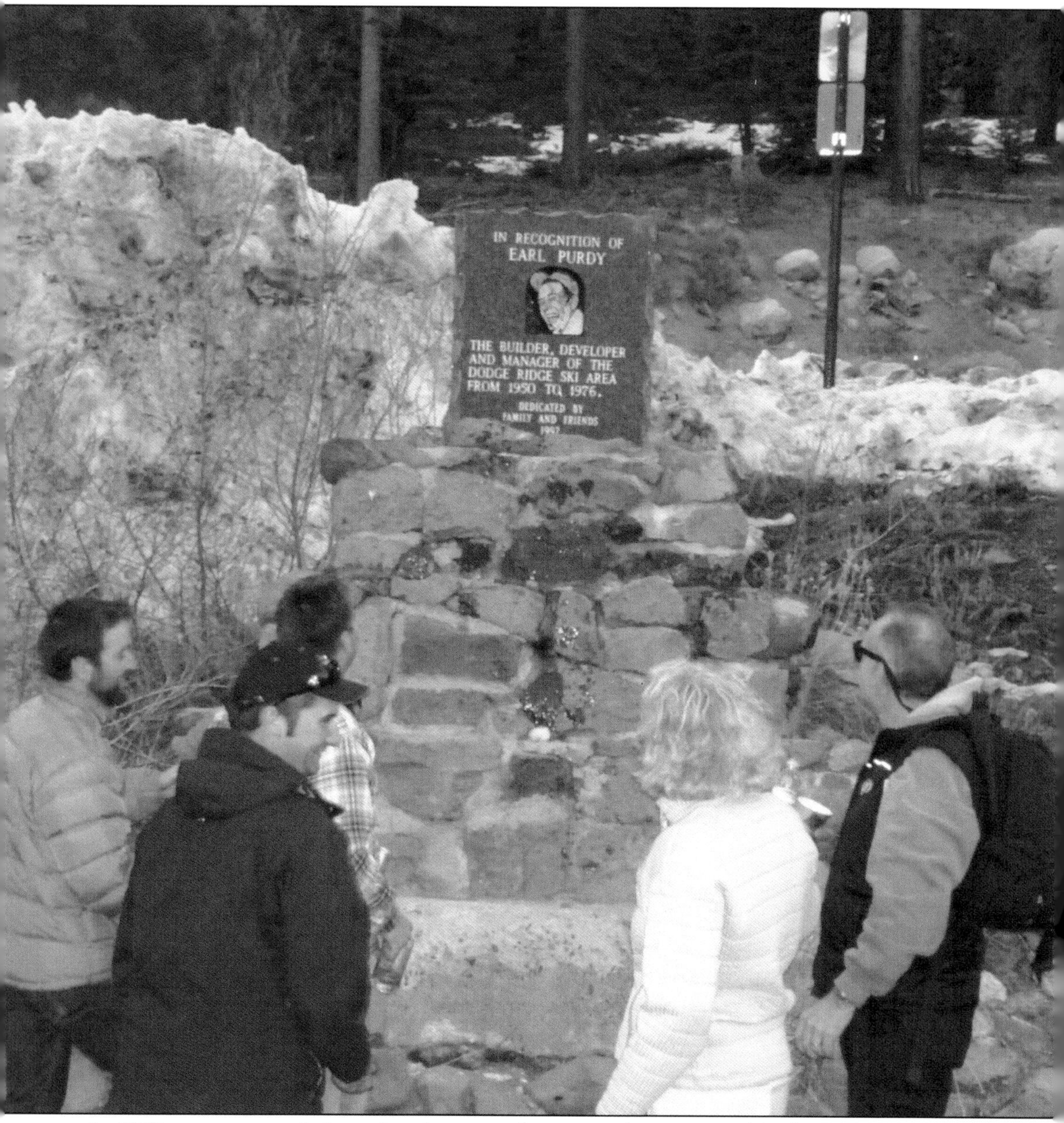

In 1997, a monument dedicated to the original owner and visionary of Dodge Ridge was erected in the parking lot near where the entrance and exit lanes meet, with the plaque turned toward the face of the mountain. From left to right are Tim McCaffrey, Jason Smith, unidentified, Sally Helm, and Sam Sells.

Two

Ski School and Racing

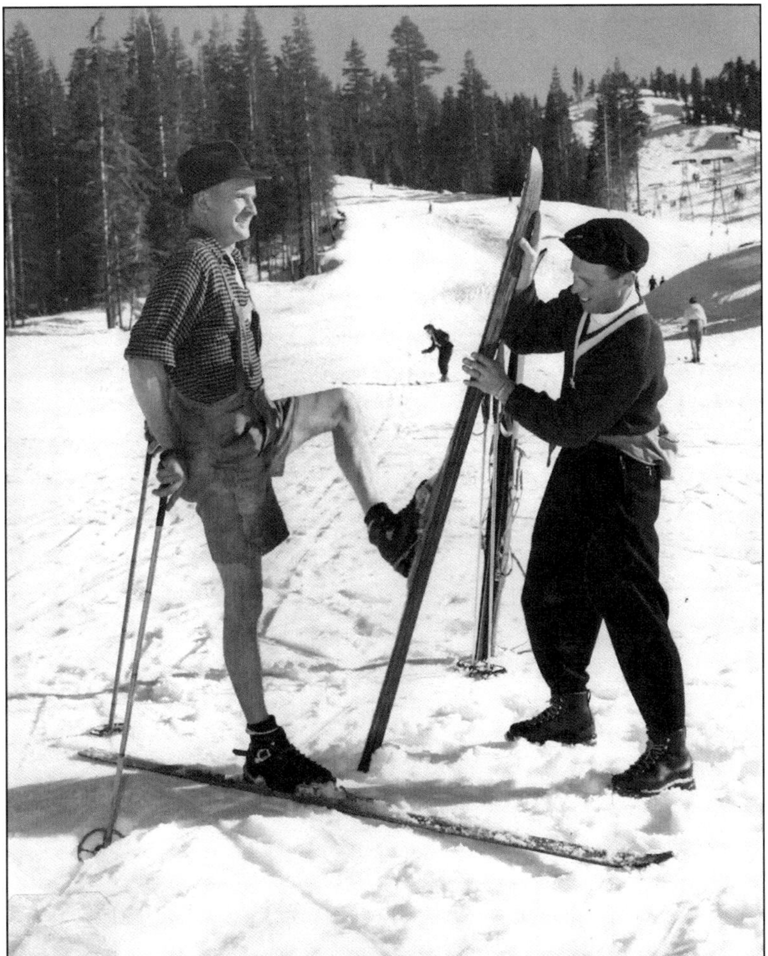

The second ski school director, Eric Johnson, prepares a student for his lesson. Wooden skis had no edges, and the bottom of the skis were painted, which required constant waxing. As a safety measure, ski instructors would inspect their students' skis prior to starting their lessons.

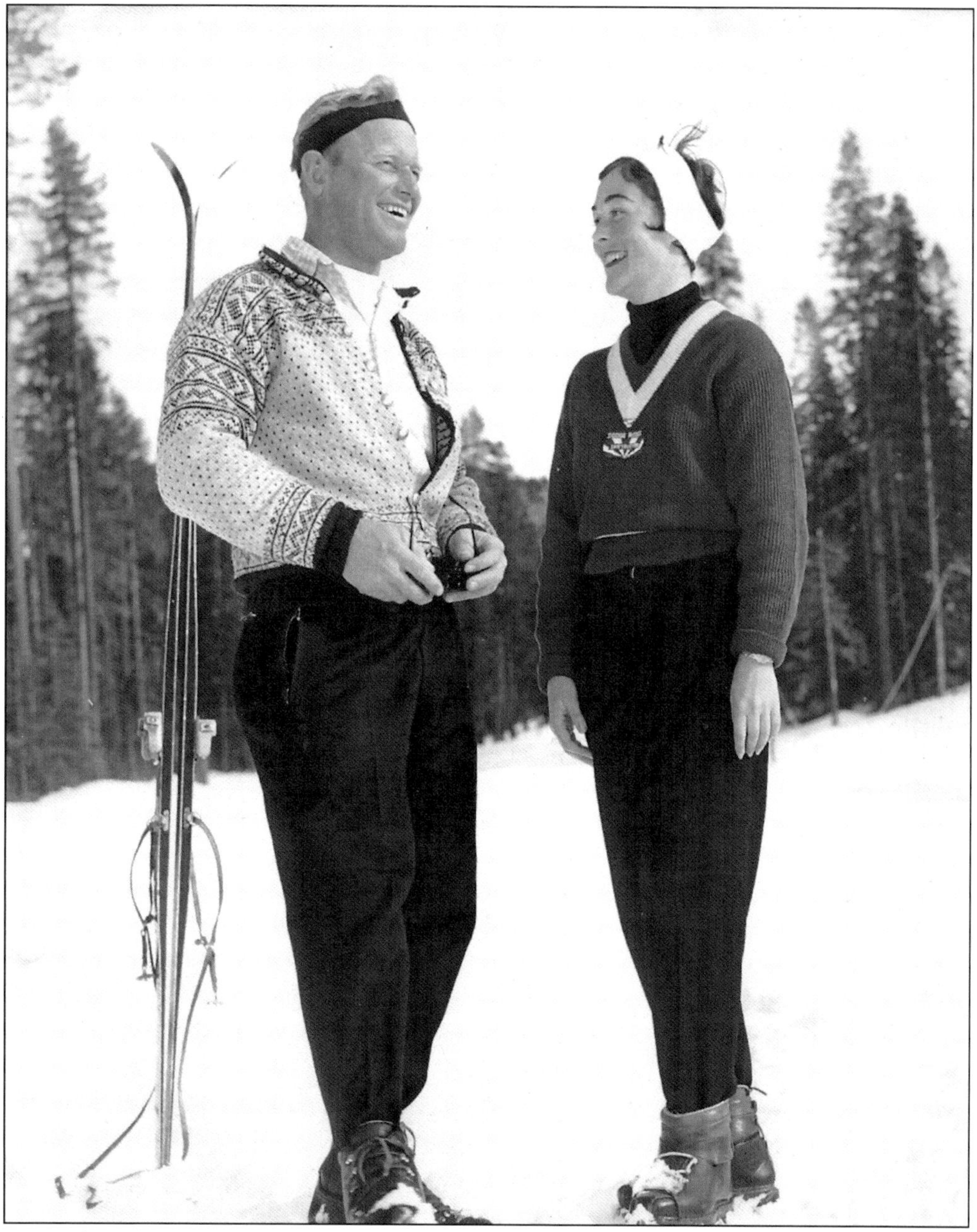

Pictured are ski school director Ray Patton and Vaux Mervy Toneff, the first woman to be certified as an instructor in Northern California. Vaux met her husband, NFL player Bob Toneff, at a charity event for the 49er ski club. She gave Bob ski lessons at Dodge Ridge before they were married and arranged to have special equipment and clothing made to accommodate his size.

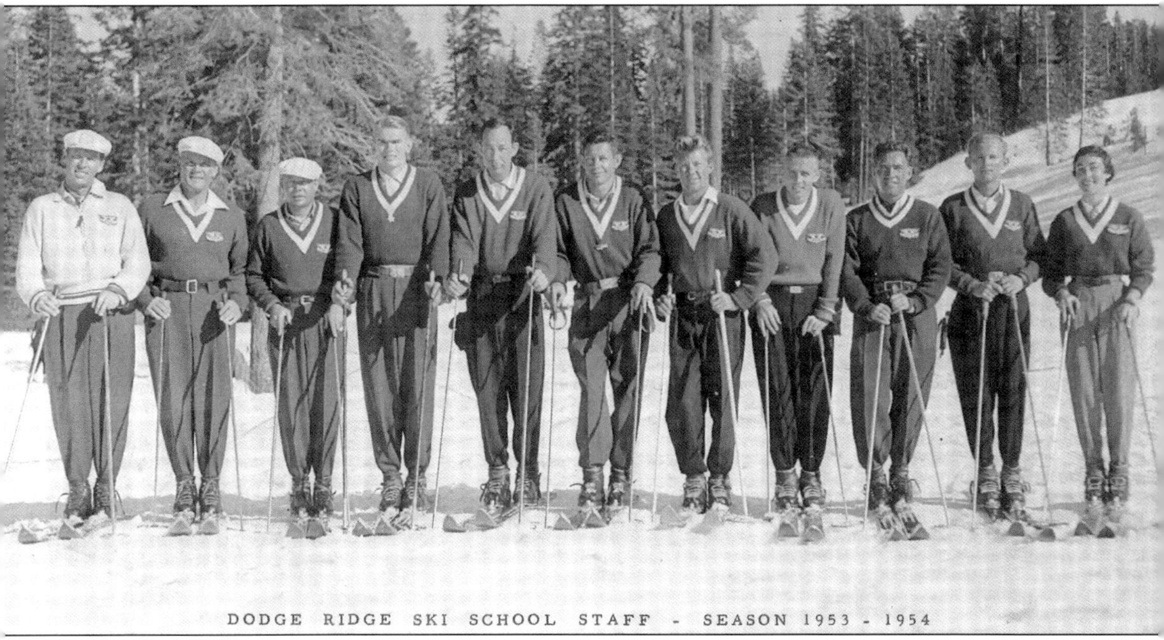

The 1953–1954 season ski school staff had very few American instructors as this was a newer sport in this country. Ken Floto was the first head of the ski school, followed by Scandinavian Eric Johnson. From left to right are Eric Johnson, Alghurdius "Al" Vokietaitis, Chuck Griffin, Gordy Soltau, John Neal, Jim Clausen, Dave Garretson, Sonny Maynard, Wayne Wissanen, Gene Thompson, and Vaux Mervy. Vokietaitis taught young Ralph and George Purdy how to ski. He would tell them to bend their knees and swing their arms with much up and down, as it took much more effort to ski in those days since the skis were very long and the boots were not very sturdy and supportive of one's ankles.

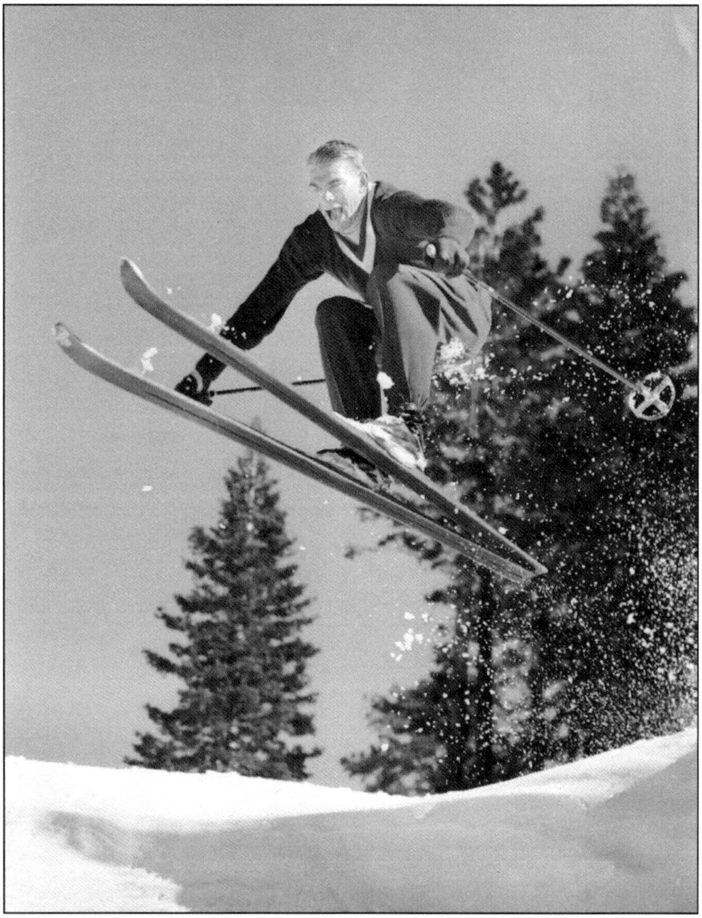

Gordon Saita had a home nearby, and his love of skiing and his skill were a good match as he became a ski instructor in the 1960s. He is shown here showing off his jumps, which was quite common amongst the instructors in those days. (Courtesy of Calin Smith.)

Ray Patton, the ski school director, is on the left, with Kristin Paragary in the middle and Pierre Futtier on the far right in the annual ski instructors team photograph. Each year, a new sweater was created by a vendor and available for purchase.

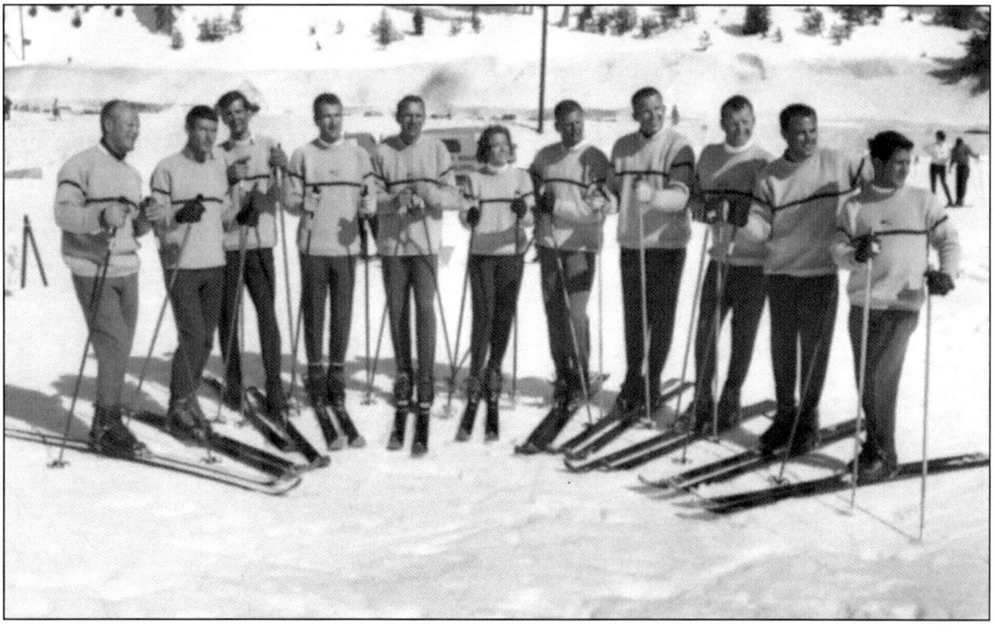

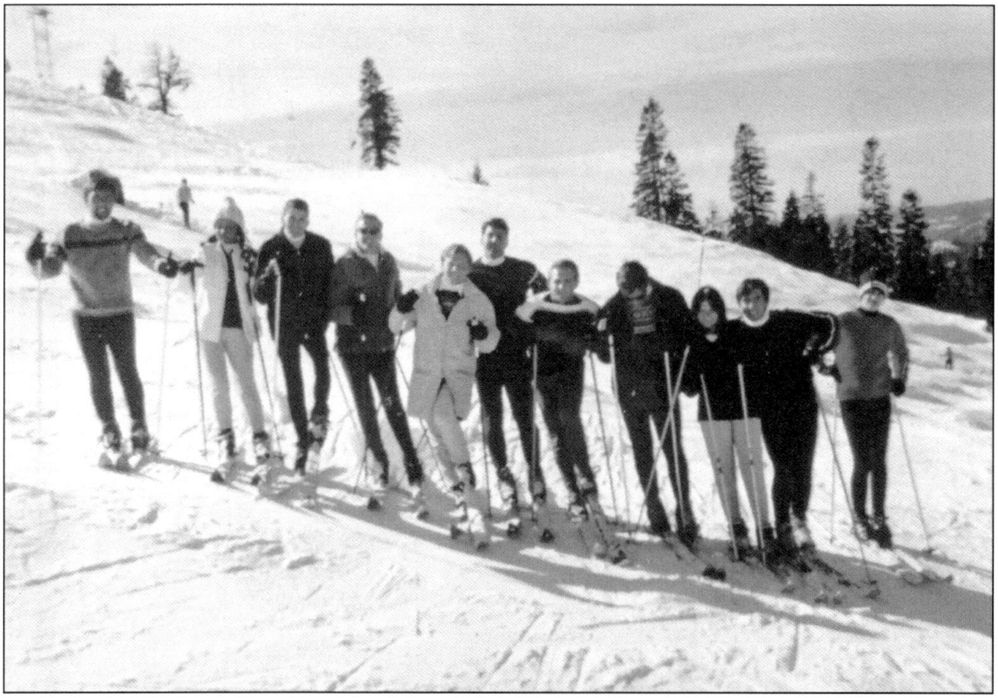

Shown here during the 1965–1966 season are friends and longtime regulars at Dodge Ridge, from left to right, Urban Gomes, unidentified, Richard Johnson, Tim Doyle, unidentified, John Casazza, Earl Hitch, unidentified, Liz Weber, Rick Saletta, and unidentified. (Courtesy of Tom McCollum.)

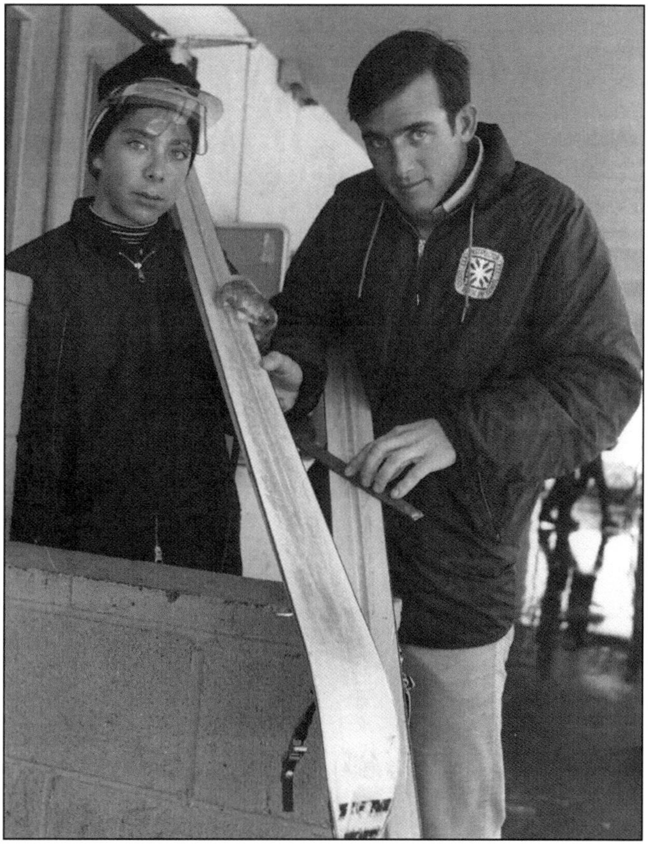

Ski instructor Pete Benson helps Nancy King prepare her skis before her lesson. Nancy's father was a ski patrolman, and her mom ran the ski patrol room at Dodge Ridge. After ski instructing, Benson and fellow instructor Urban Gomes left the mountain for the ocean and sailed around the world.

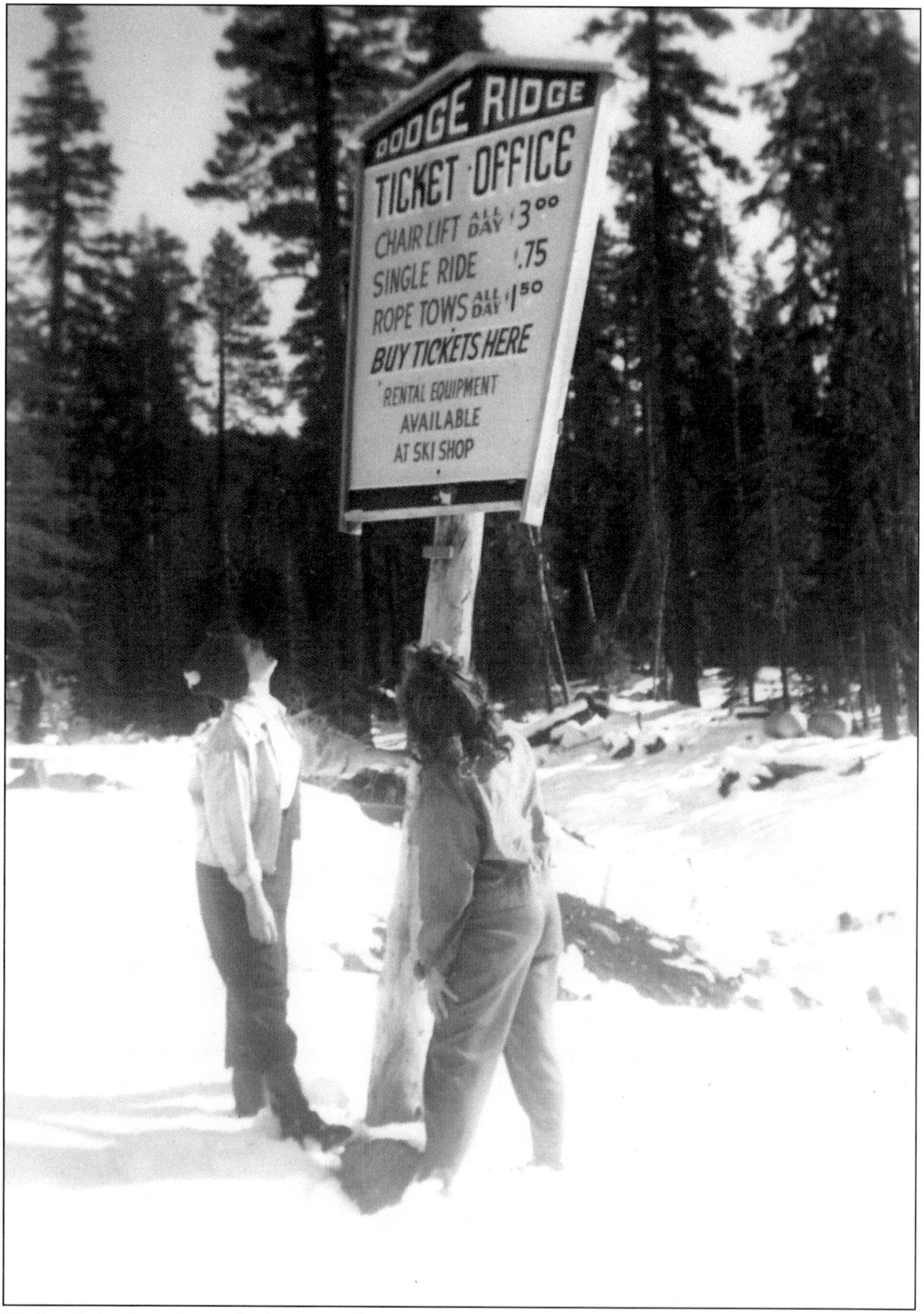

Dodge Ridge has changed a lot since this quaint sign was put up in the snow in the 1950s. Prices, the way tickets are purchased, the equipment, overall offerings for ski lessons, and variety of runs have all significantly improved, but the charm, hospitality, and familiarity of this small but mighty resort remain the same.

Figuring out how to handle ski passes was a challenge. It used to be that skiers would get a numbered ticket according to their membership so skiers could be identified. There were tear-off tickets that were handed to a lift operator, but that became cumbersome, so a more permanent solution was something that could be attached to one's clothing. Tickets were stapled to skiers' pants; however, sometimes for regular skiers, the stack would be too big, and the staples would not go all the way through. There was also the problem of ripping a perfectly good pair of pants, which upset many skiers. Eventually, tickets were hung on by a hook on a jacket zipper. Each day had a different color and stamp. Regulars who had a birthday during the ski season would get their name on a pass that day to note the occasion. It was always fun to see what the pass of the day would look like. Technology has made passes more advanced but perhaps not so creatively personal.

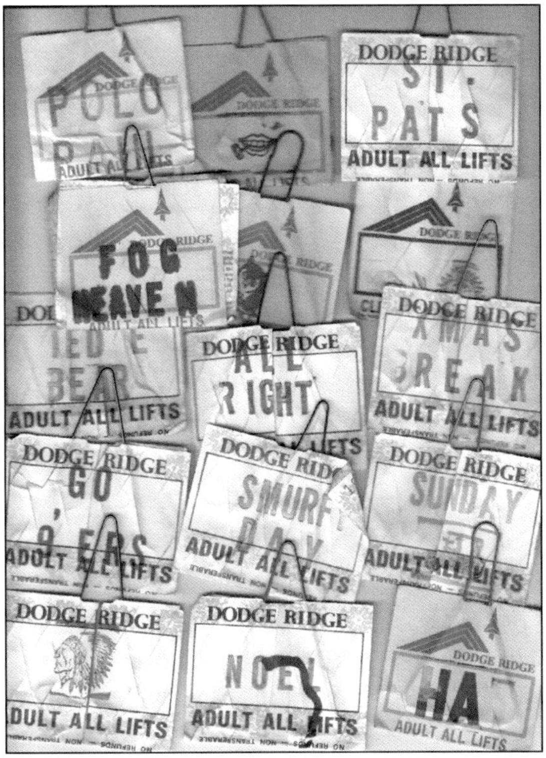

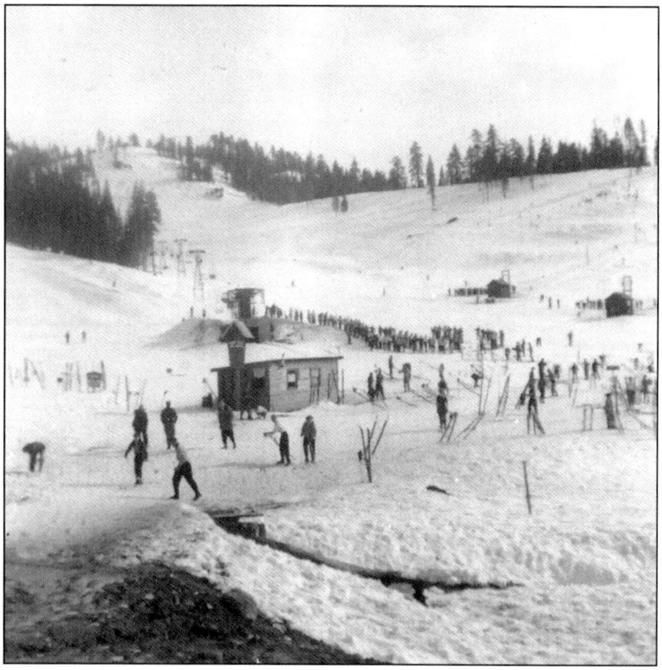

Dodge Ridge is known for being a great place to learn to ski and is considered a launching pad for racing. This picture from the 1950s shows the rope tows on the right, a chairlift in the middle, where people patiently waited their turn, and the old ski school office and ticket sales. The Ray Patton ski school sign and class bell were housed here. (Courtesy of the Twining family.)

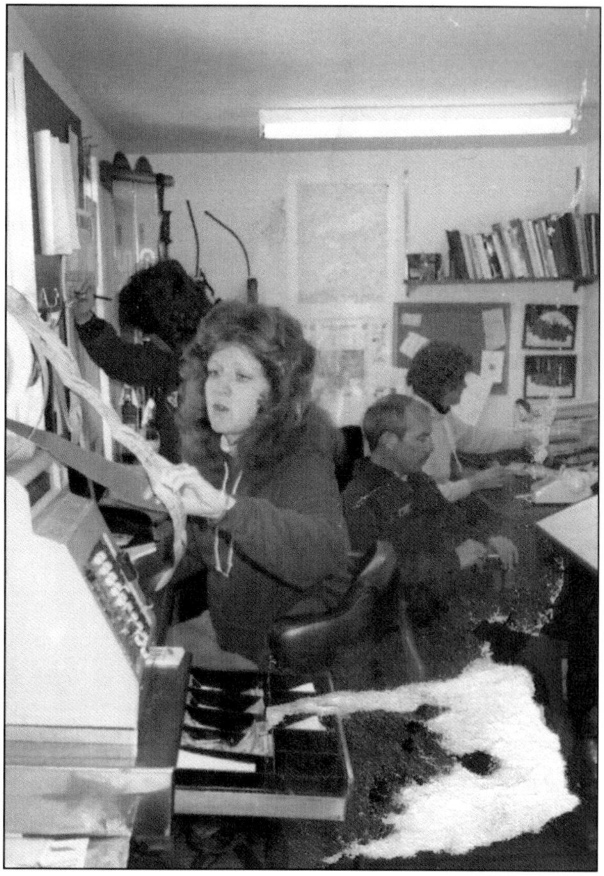

Inside, the old ski school office and ticket sales shared tight quarters. From left to right are Bobbi Hough and Sally Smith selling tickets, while Jon Mahanna and Patty Williamson handle ski school lesson planning. Eventually, Bob Hohne came on board and installed the first computer network, which allowed for increased productivity and decreased waiting times.

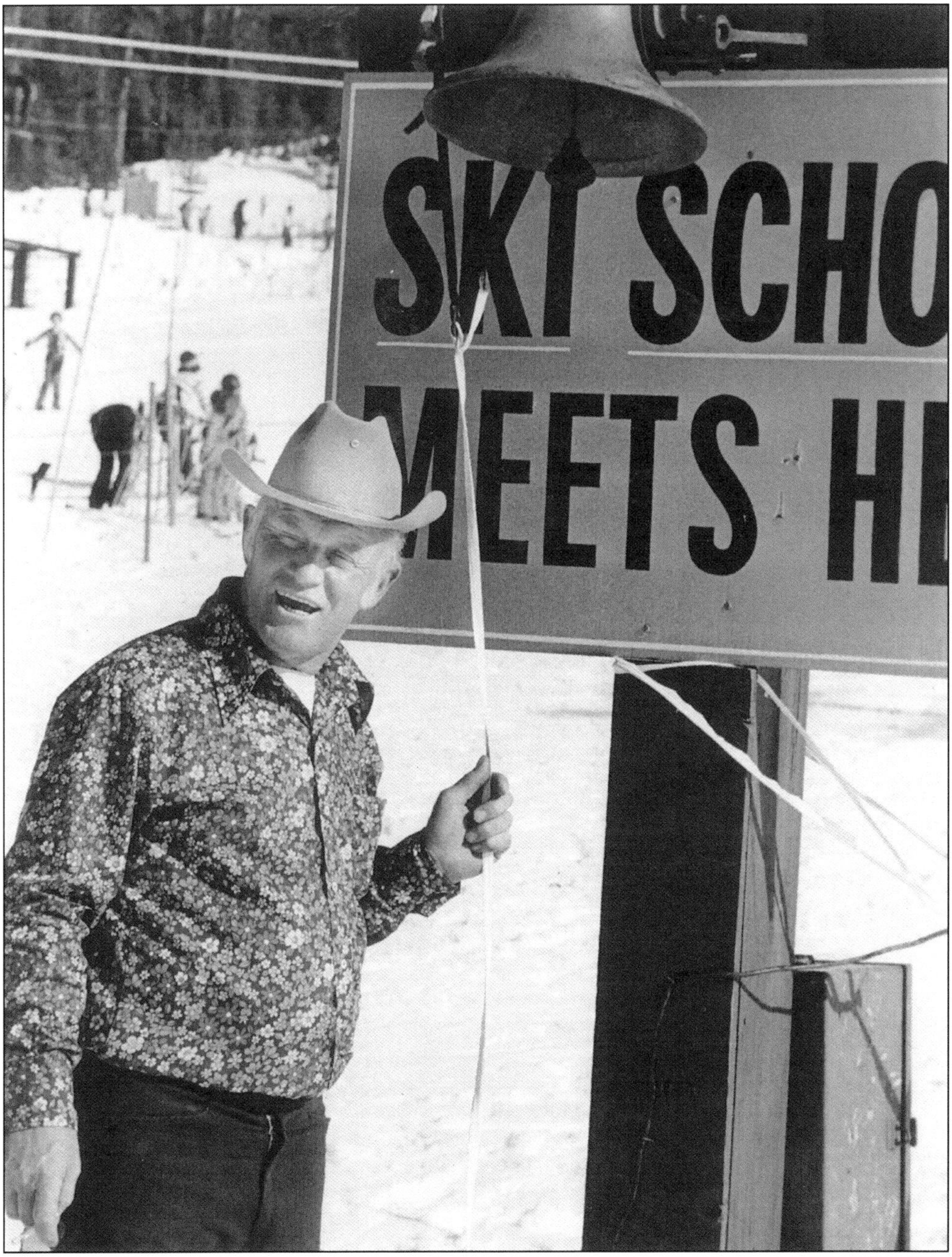

Ray Patton grew up in Idyllwild, California, where he learned to ski. He was a marine in World War II, where he got part of his kneecap blown off. He went on to get all his ski certifications and then went to Badger Pass to be a ski instructor and eventually on to Dodge Ridge as winter sports director and race coach. From 1954 to 1977, the ski school under Ray Patton operated as a separate business, which was very unusual for a ski school, so Patton had to pay a fee of approximately six percent to the Forest Service, plus a fee to Dodge Ridge. In the off-season, Patton helped Purdy out by running the soda fountain in the old lodge at Pinecrest.

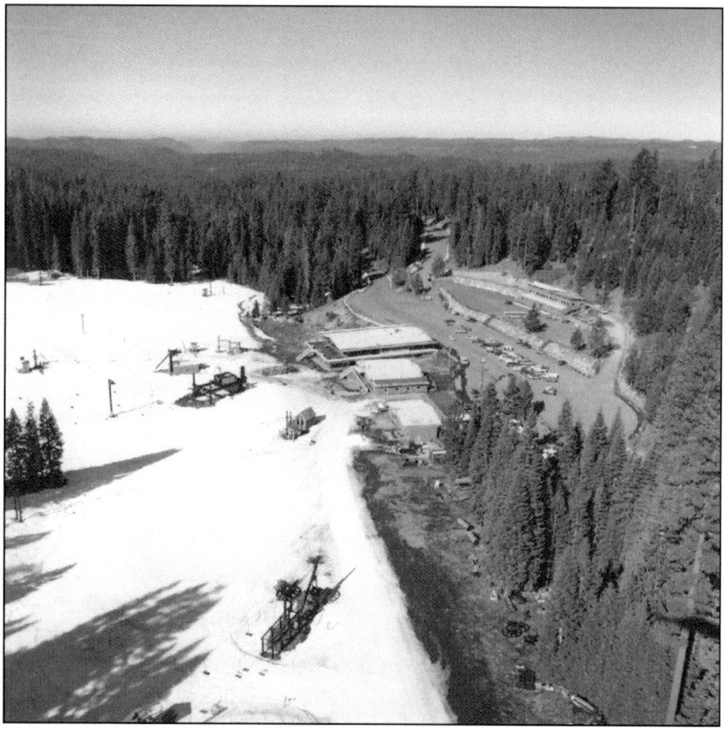

Prior to being moved to Dodge Ridge to replace a Poma lift, the current Chair Six was once the Cold Springs chair at Sun Valley Ski Resort in Idaho. Chair Six currently lives in the spot shown in the lower portion of this photograph. The crew spent five days a week for one month in Idaho moving the chair to a meadow and dismantling it with handheld torches in order to be able to move it then weld it back together once it was transported to Dodge Ridge.

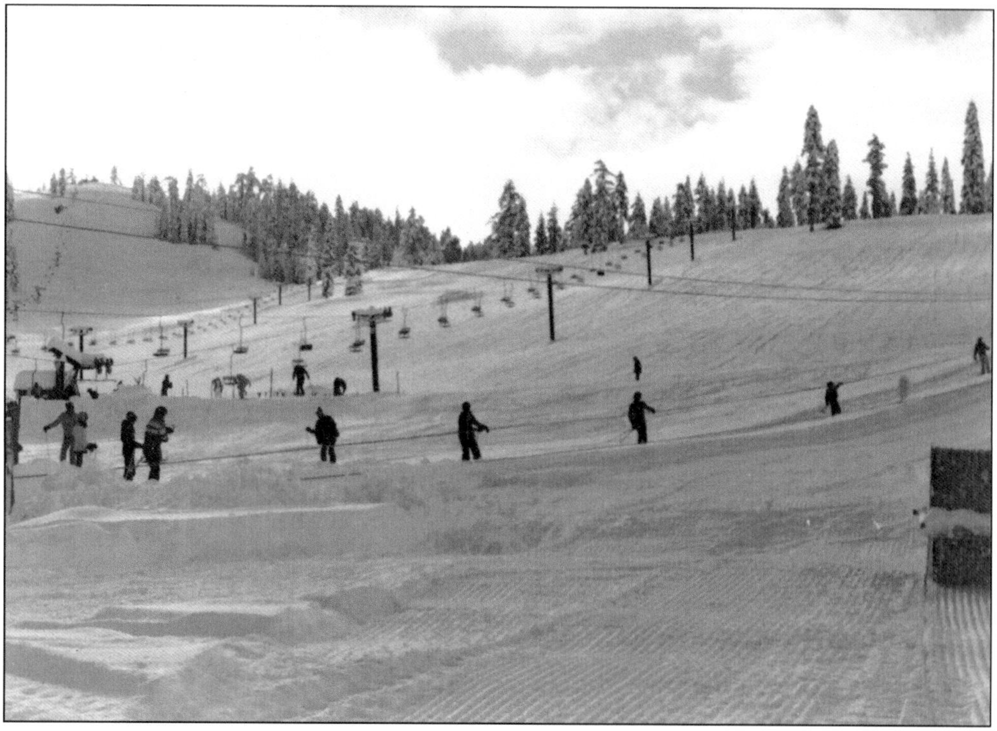

Prior to Chair Six, this rope tow was an option for beginner skiers to use to get towed up the hill, or they hiked, so Chair Six was a welcome addition for many. The old Chair One and Chair Two are also shown here.

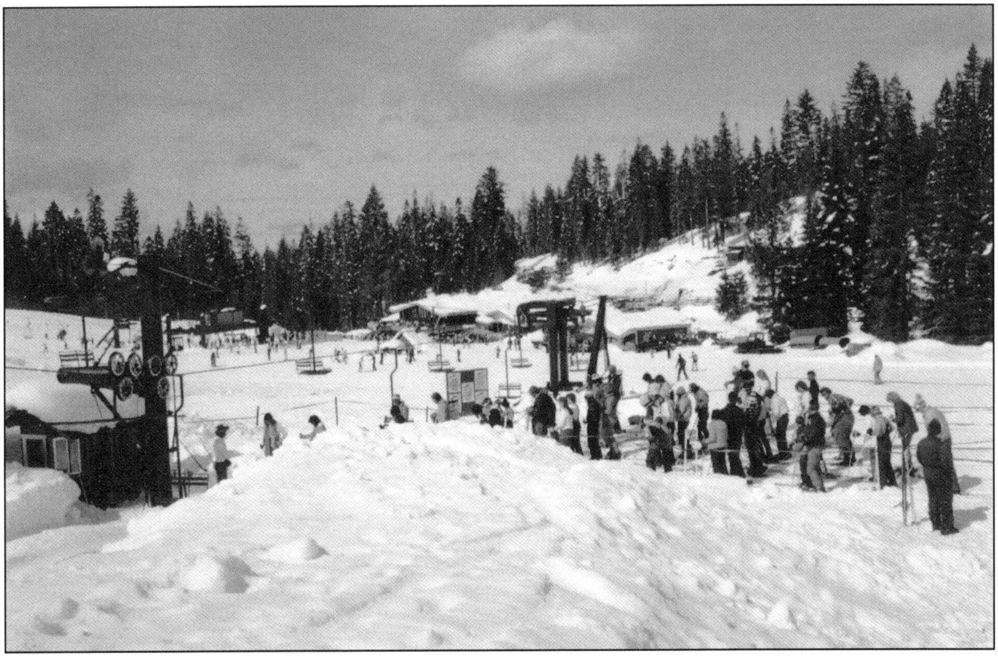

Chair Six is primarily used by beginners and ski school students but not exclusively. Depending on the conditions, it is a nice run to take if one is not up for the more challenging runs on a powder day.

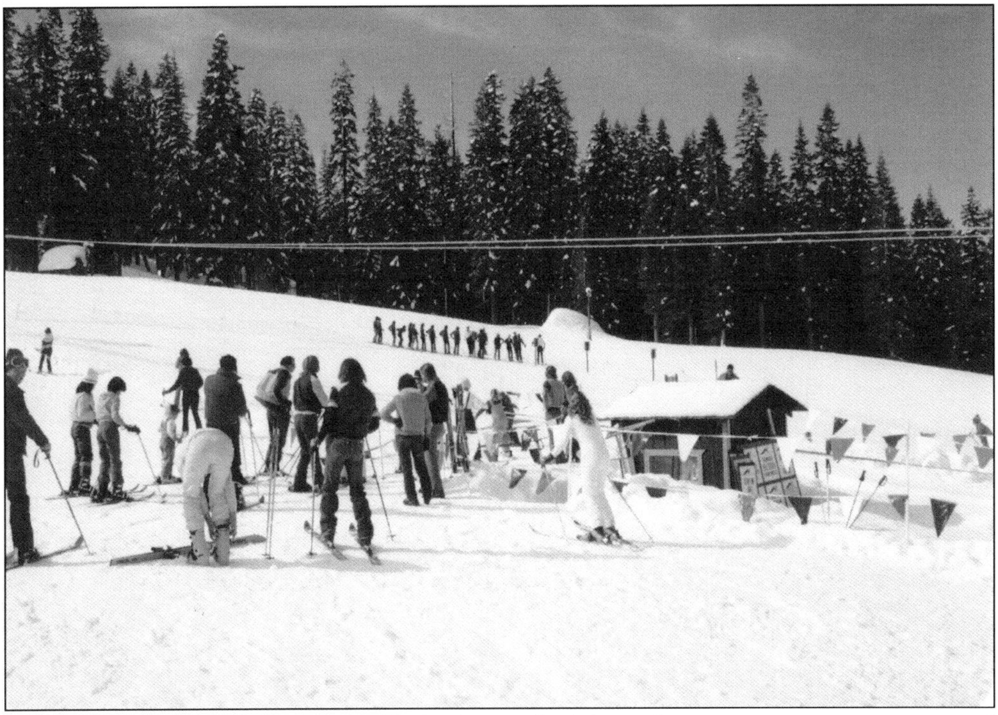

A ski school session is lined up in the background while students are starting to prepare and assemble for the next class in the foreground. Today, ski school has altered the name to snow sports to include lessons for snowboarders.

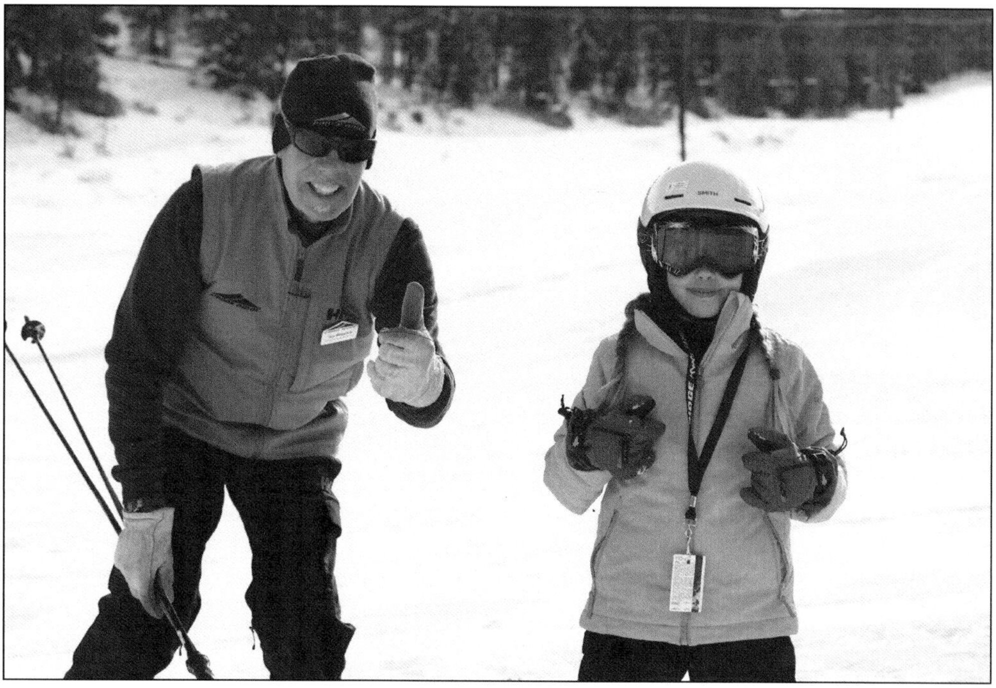

Starting in 1971, Jon Mahanna has spent the majority of his ski career in ski school or resort management. He spent two seasons on the International Freestyle Skiers Association pro circuit doing flips and other stunts and was sponsored by numerous companies. At Dodge Ridge, he was the ski school director, operations manager, and general manager. Jon is with his daughter Brittany Mahanna, who was on the Dodge Ridge Race Team.

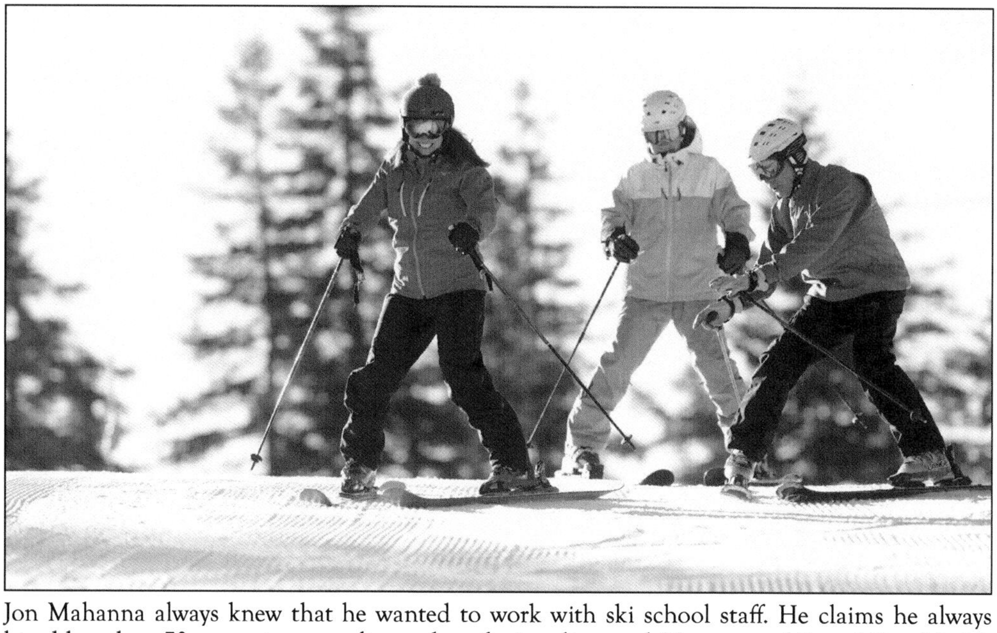

Jon Mahanna always knew that he wanted to work with ski school staff. He claims he always hired based on 70 percent personality and professionalism and 30 percent skiing ability. He felt he could improve their skiing ability to levels beyond their imagination, but they first needed the passion and personality, to be a hard worker, and to give 150 percent.

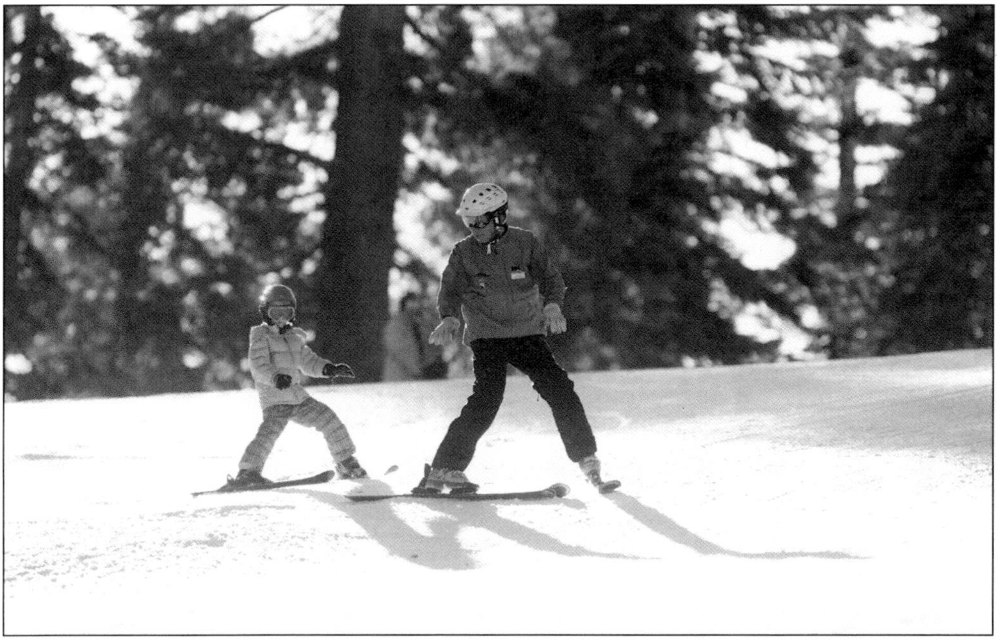

Jon Mahanna is known internationally on the slopes. At the age of 19, he watched two instructors do flips and thought he could do that. A day later, he successfully completed a flip while a photographer captured him in the air mid-flip, with skis flying off. The feat became known as "the shoot heard round the world." He continued to flip and teach skiing.

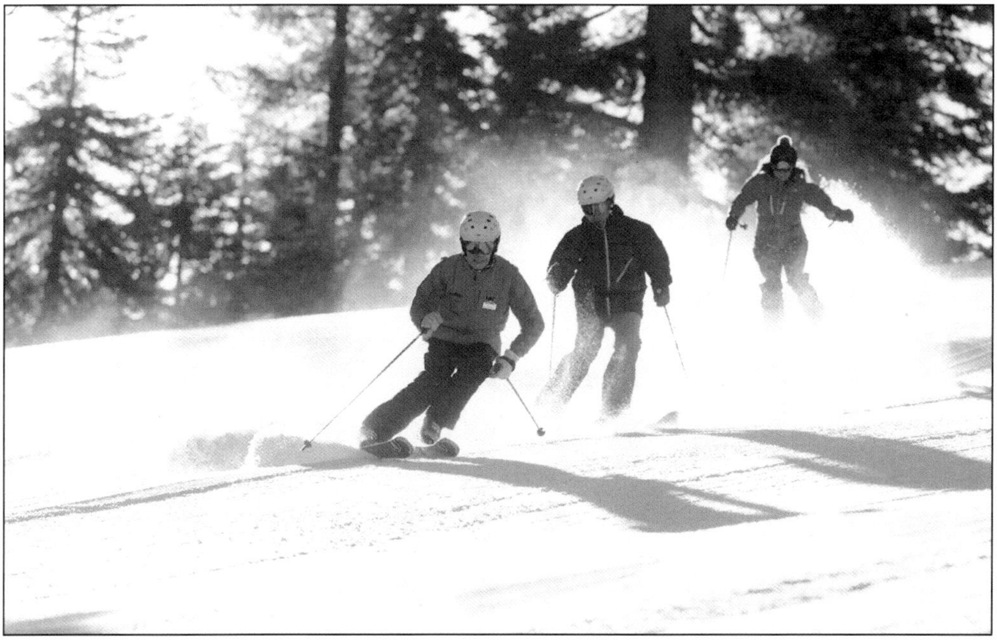

Jon Mahanna led the movement on freestyle skiing. He literally wrote the book on the Alpine guide to certification, *Prepare, Plan, Practice*. He claimed that his method could make anyone a better skier. He has received numerous awards over the years and held prominent positions all over the world, yet he always comes home to Dodge Ridge. He still runs the senior master clinic when he is up for skiing.

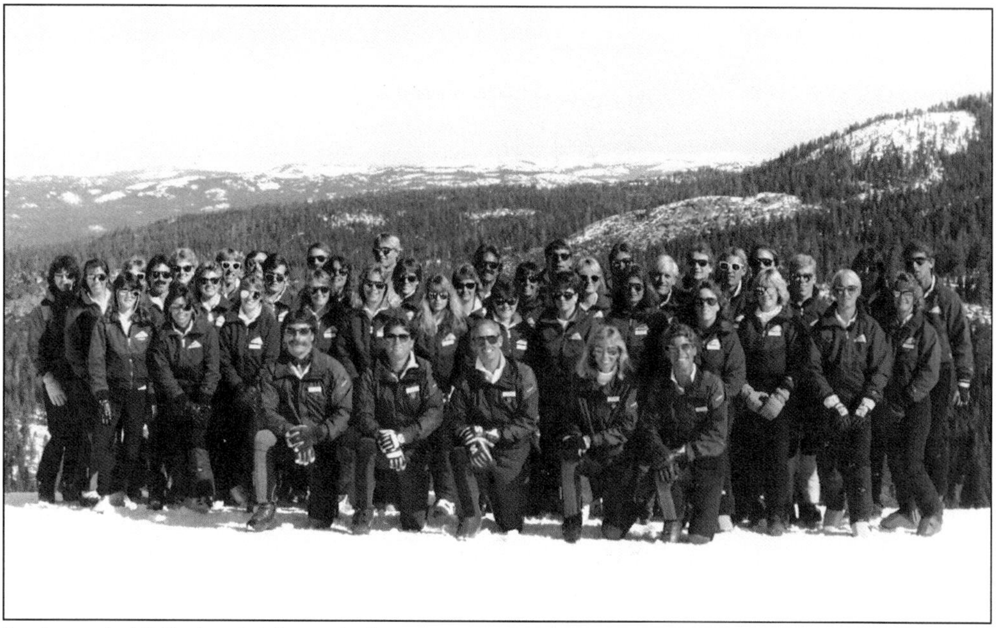

In the early 1970s, Jon Mahanna's ski instructors took their annual team photograph at the top of Chair Five. Fourth from the left with the light-colored glasses is Jamie Shock, who went on to become a US Ski Team coach.

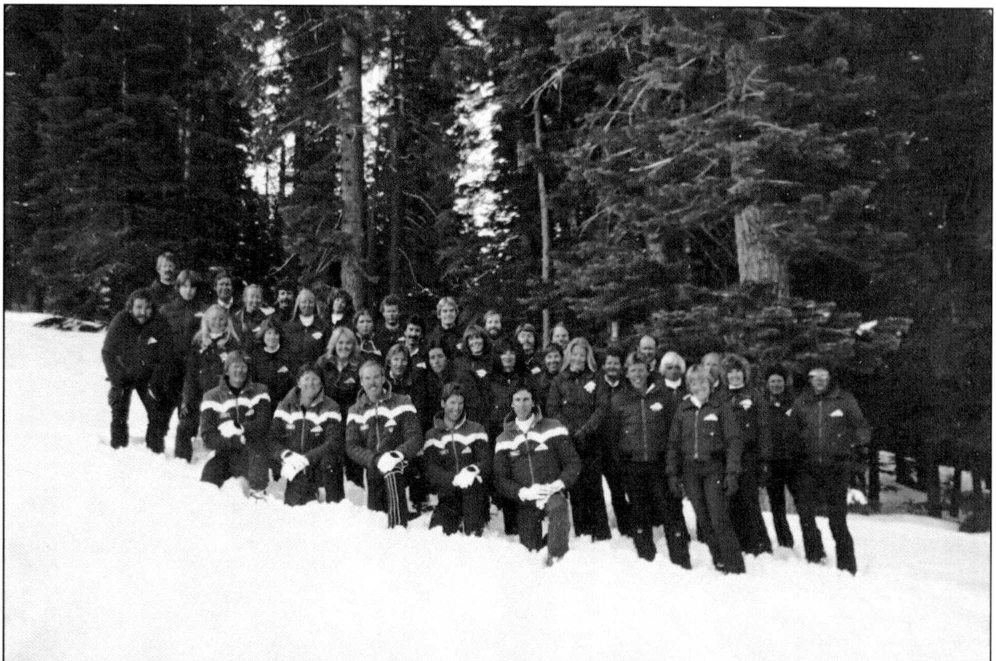

In another fun ski instructors annual photograph, the three kneeling in the middle are, from left to right, Jon Mahanna, Devon Salter, and Paul Mundy, with Susie Lavignino standing in front, off to the right. All are longtime employees, season pass holders, race parents, and friends with long histories at Dodge Ridge.

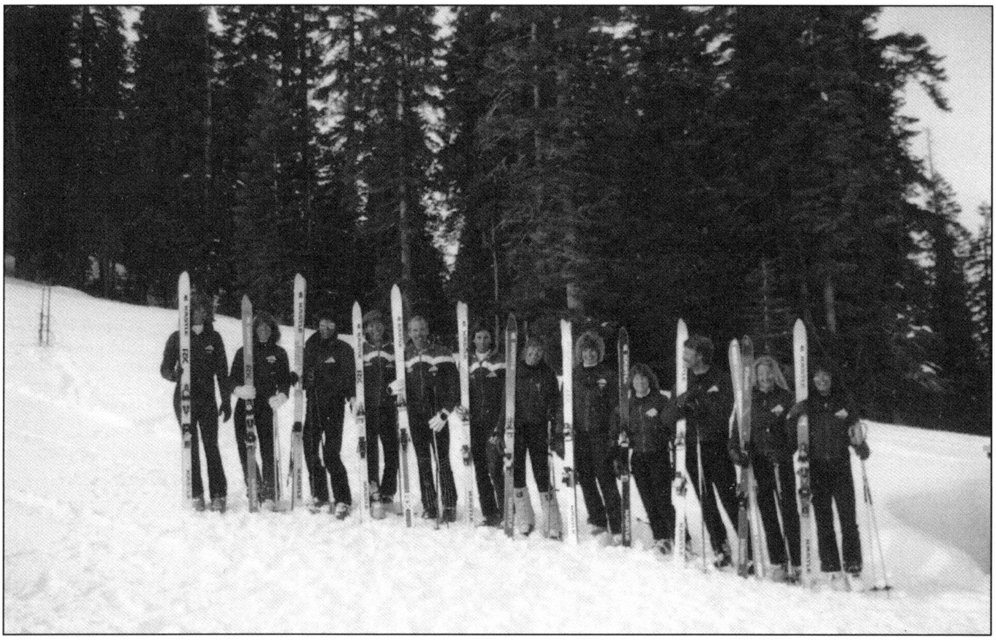

Being a known name in the ski industry, companies were always asking Jon Mahanna, fifth from the left, to demo their equipment. Each year, his instructors had access to the latest and greatest in clothing and skis, allowing them to have fancy top-notch uniforms at a discount; not every resort had this perk.

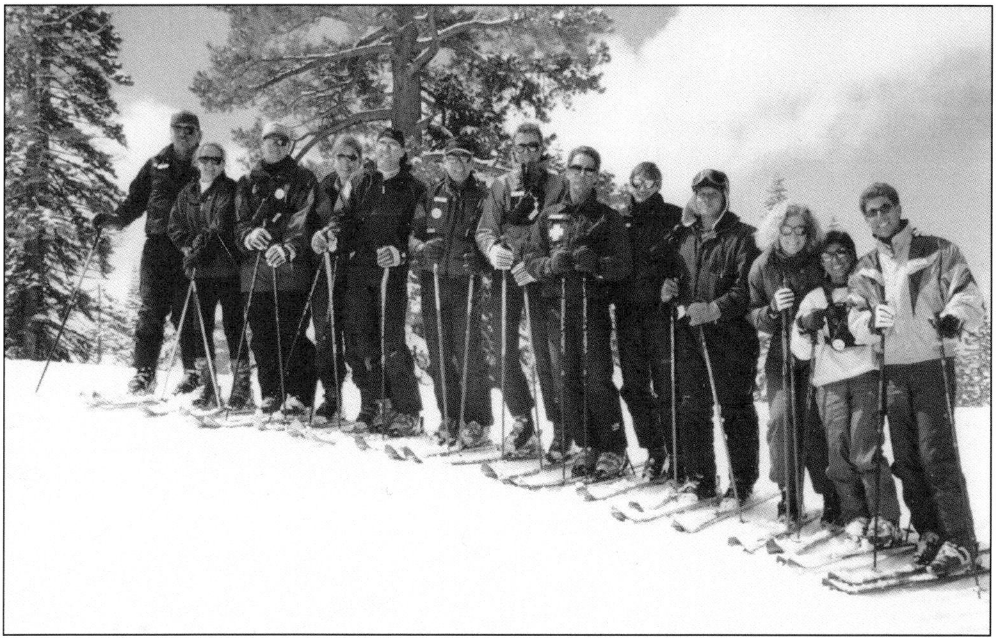

The management team for the ski school, from left to right, included three unidentified persons, Pauline Ulrey, unidentified, Jon Mahanna, Dave Alley, Dan Branch, John Getter, unidentified, Sally Helm, Carol Francisco, and Paul Mundy. Alley did not last long in this position, as he really wanted to explore the mountain more and felt confined in the beginner runs, which is probably why he was so good at building out more runs later.

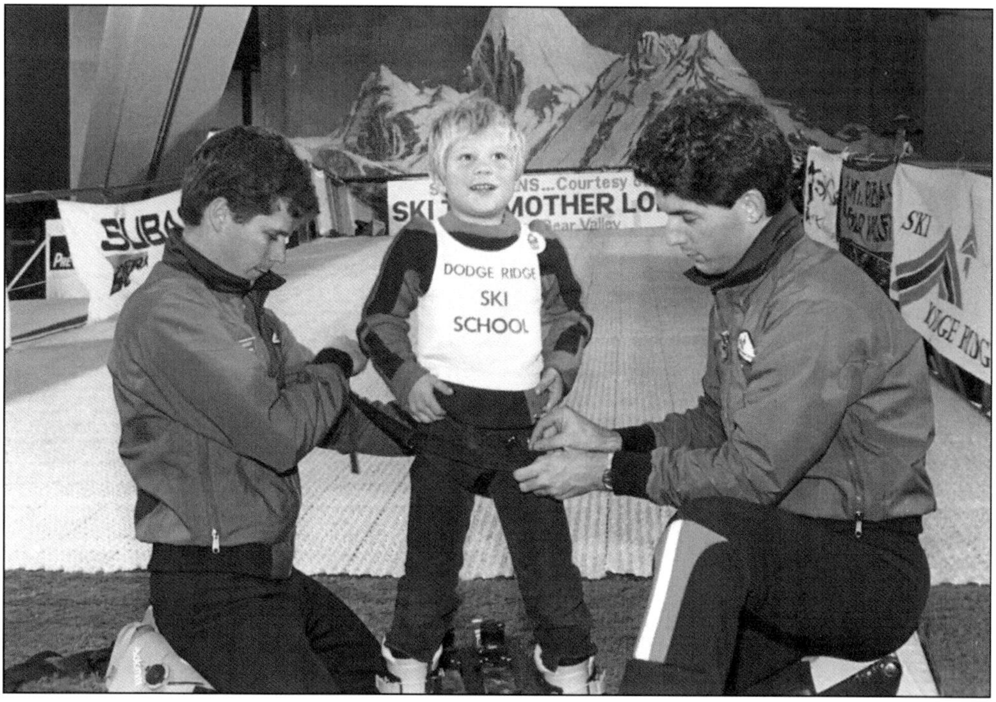

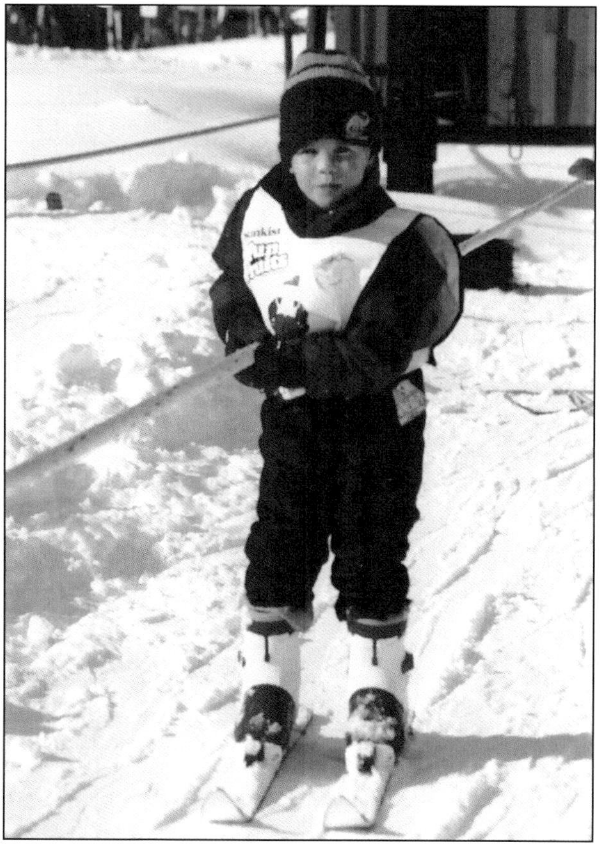

Jon Mahanna hired Paul Mundy to run the kids' program. Mundy was a founder and heavily involved with *Ski Magazine*'s SKIwee program for children ages three through eight. It was a lesson package that included classes, bibs, equipment, and snacks. Todd Lindsay (left) and Paul Mundy (right) are pictured at a ski show at the Moscone Center in San Francisco demonstrating how SKIwee works. Todd is also a pilot. (Courtesy of the Mundy family archives.)

Shown here is a SKIwee student learning how to use the rope tow. His next lesson is learning "pizza pie" and "French fries"—first, ski tips are pointed together to slow students down, and then skis are positioned parallel to gain more confidence and control.

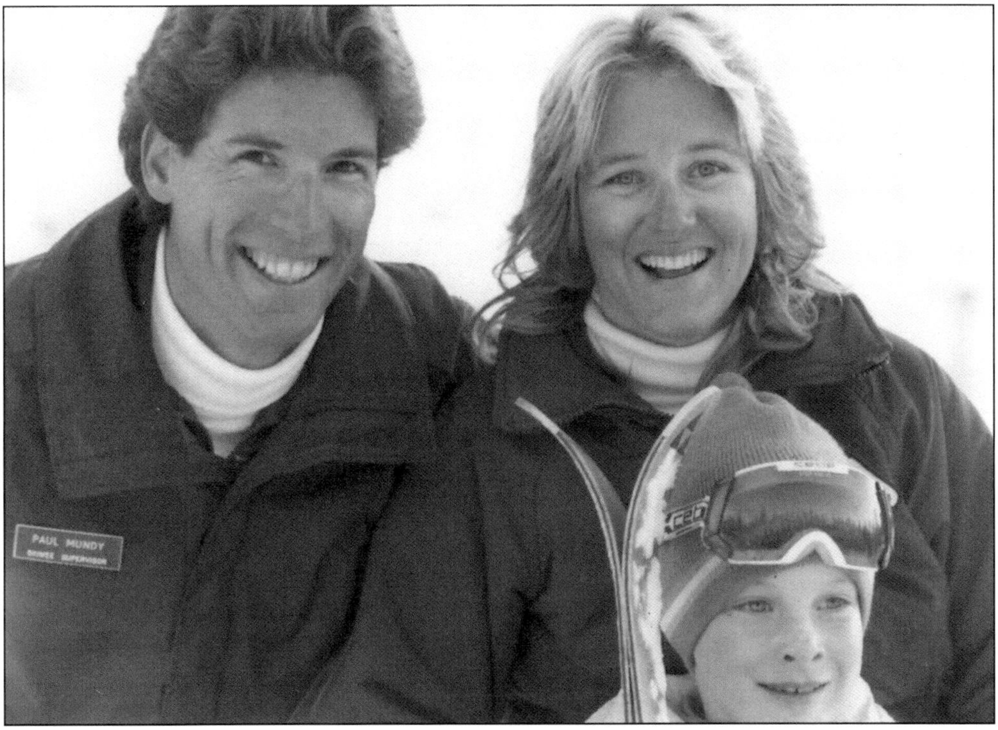

Pictured here are children's program director Paul Mundy and Katie Schwab with seven-year-old Courtney Resdon from Torrance, California, in 1984. Katie Schwab was the first instructor for kids that Mundy hired. Katie loved to ski so much that she followed winter—she would teach in Australia when it was summer in the United States, then head back to the United States for their winter season. (Courtesy of the Mundy family archives.)

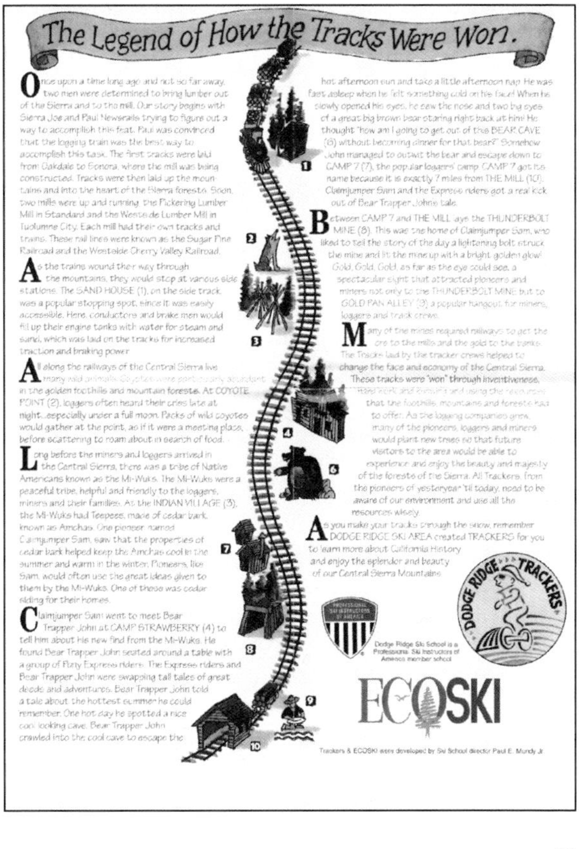

The Legend of How the Tracks Were Won.

Once upon a time long ago and not so far away, two men were determined to bring lumber out of the Sierra and to the mill. Our story begins with Sierra Joe and Paul Newsrails trying to figure out a way to accomplish this feat. Paul was convinced that the logging train was the best way to accomplish this task. The first tracks were laid from Oakdale to Sonora, where the mill was being constructed. Tracks were then laid up the mountains and into the heart of the Sierra forests. Soon, two mills were up and running, the Pickering Lumber Mill in Standard and the Westside Lumber Mill in Tuolumne City. Each mill had their own tracks and trains. These rail lines were known as the Sugar Pine Railroad and the Westside Cherry Valley Railroad.

As the trains wound their way through the mountains, they would stop at various side stations. The SAND HOUSE (1), on the side track, was a popular stopping spot, since it was easily accessible. Here, conductors and brake men would fill up their engine tanks with water for steam and sand, which was laid on the tracks for increased traction and braking power.

All along the railways of the Central Sierra live many wild animals. Coyotes were particularly abundant in the golden foothills and mountain forests. At COYOTE POINT (2), loggers often heard their cries late at night...especially under a full moon. Packs of wild coyotes would gather at the point, as if it were a meeting place, before scattering to roam about in search of food.

Long before the miners and loggers arrived in the Central Sierra, there was a tribe of Native Americans known as the Mi-Wuks. The Mi-Wuks were a peaceful tribe, helpful and friendly to the loggers, miners and their families. At the INDIAN VILLAGE (3), the Mi-Wuks had Teepees, made of cedar bark, known as Amchas. One pioneer named Claimjumper Sam, saw that the properties of cedar bark helped keep the Amchas cool in the summer and warm in the winter. Pioneers, like Sam, would often use the great ideas given to them by the Mi-Wuks. One of these was cedar siding for their homes.

Claimjumper Sam went to meet Bear Trapper John at CAMP STRAWBERRY (4) to tell him about his new find from the Mi-Wuks. He found Bear Trapper John seated around a table with a group of Pony Express riders. The Express riders and Bear Trapper John were swapping tall tales of great deeds and adventures. Bear Trapper John told a tale about the hottest summer he could remember. One hot day he spotted a nice cool looking cave. Bear Trapper John crawled into the cool cave to escape the hot afternoon sun and take a little afternoon nap. He was fast asleep when he felt something cold on his face! When he slowly opened his eyes, he saw the nose and two big eyes of a great big brown bear staring right back at him! He thought "how am I going to get out of this BEAR CAVE (6) without becoming dinner for that bear?" Somehow John managed to outwit the bear and escape down to CAMP 7 (7), the popular loggers' camp. CAMP 7 got its name because it is exactly 7 miles from THE MILL (10). Claimjumper Sam and the Express riders got a real kick out of Bear Trapper John's tale.

Between CAMP 7 and THE MILL lays the THUNDERBOLT MINE (8). This was the home of Claimjumper Sam, who liked to tell the story of the day a lightening bolt struck the mine and lit the mine up with a bright golden glow! Gold, Gold, Gold, as far as the eye could see, a spectacular sight that attracted pioneers and miners not only to the THUNDERBOLT MINE but to GOLD PAN ALLEY (9) a popular hangout for miners, loggers and track crews.

Many of the mines required railways to get the ore to the mills and the gold to the banks. The Tracks laid by the tracker crews helped to change the face and economy of the Central Sierra. These tracks were "won" through inventiveness, hard work and [illegible] and using the resources that the foothills, mountains and forests had to offer. As the logging companies grew, many of the pioneers, loggers and miners would plant new trees so that future visitors to the area would be able to experience and enjoy the beauty and majesty of the forests of the Sierra. All Trackers, from the pioneers of yesteryear 'til today, need to be aware of our environment and use all the resources wisely.

As you make your tracks through the snow, remember DODGE RIDGE SKI AREA created TRACKERS for you to learn more about California History and enjoy the splendor and beauty of our Central Sierra Mountains.

Dodge Ridge Ski School is a Professional Ski Instructors of America member school

DODGE RIDGE TRACKERS

ECOSKI

Trackers & ECOSKI were developed by Ski School director Paul E. Mundy Jr.

In 1989, Tuolumne County Schools decided to stop school ski trips to Dodge Ridge for physical education classes because the superintendent said there was no educational component. In response, Paul Mundy worked with the Forest Service to create a program called Eco Ski Trackers, which provided educational information about the railroad, animals, vegetation, and more about the area. (Courtesy of the Mundy family archives.)

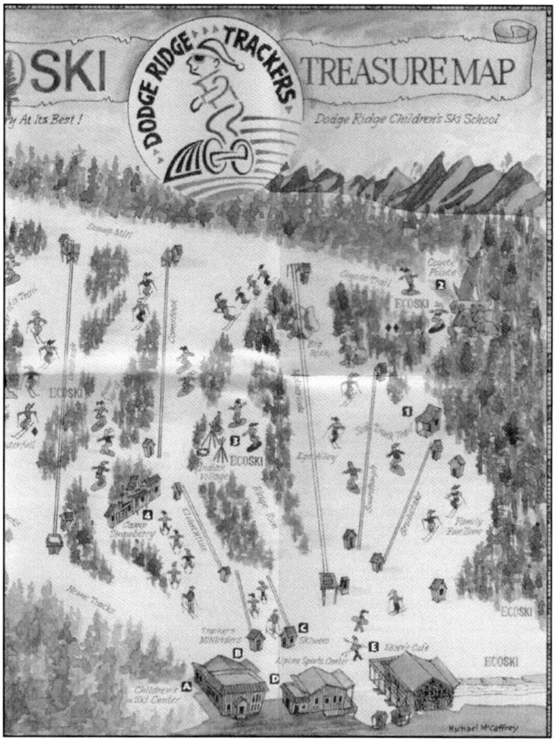

Paul Mundy also created Eco Ski Trackers Ski Map, an interpretive program that included structures that kids would visit and learn about the ecology and history of the mountain while skiing. It was more detailed than Trackers and included a treasure map. There are still a few signs around the mountain, but some have been eaten by porcupines. (Courtesy of the Mundy family archives.)

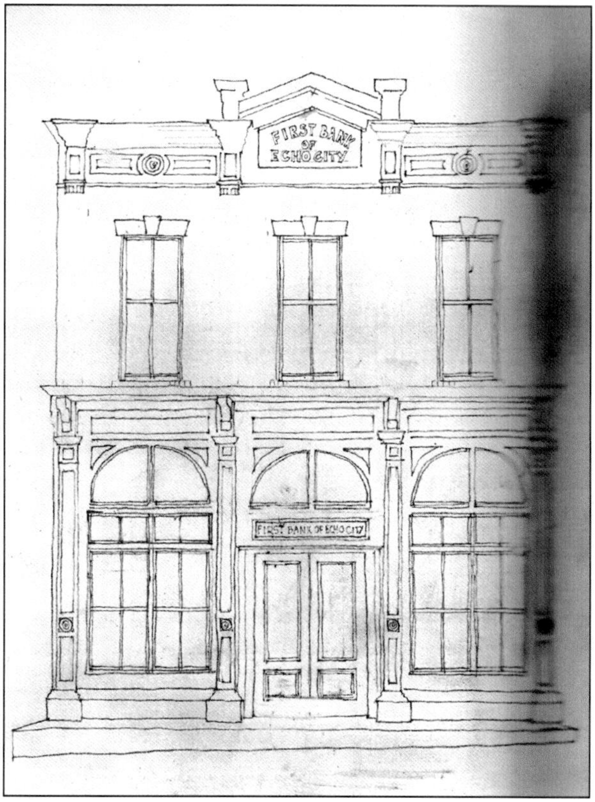

To create an educational environment on the mountain, Paul Mundy created a program that qualified as an outdoor classroom. He hired the crew from the movie *Back to the Future* to build the town, replicating the buildings on the hill at Chair Six. Using the educational maps and materials, students skied and looked in the windows to learn about the history of the town. (Courtesy of the Mundy family archives.)

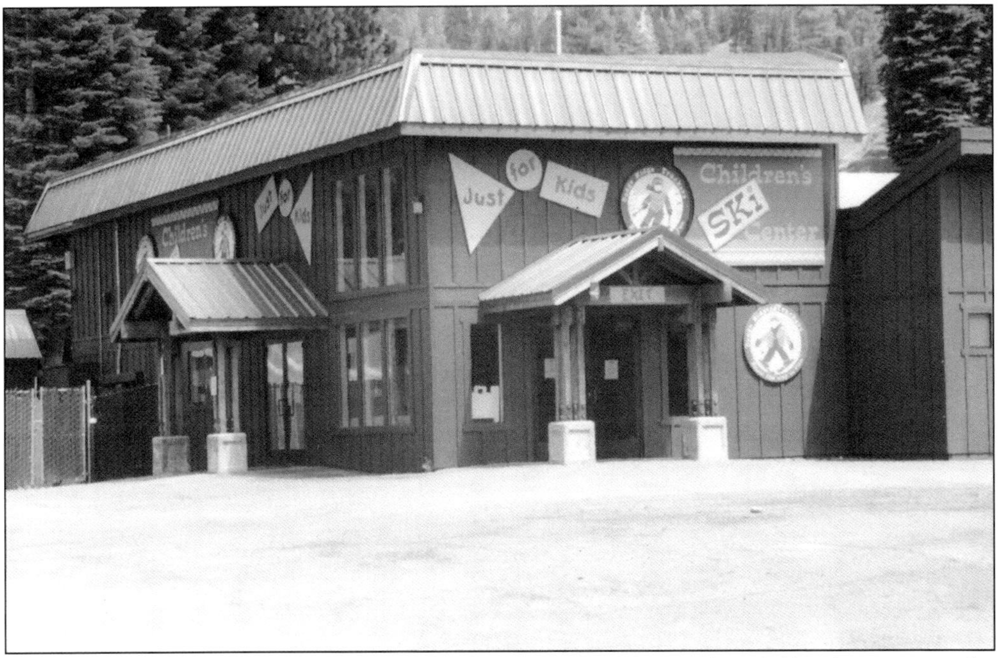

In 1992, a new machine shop was built, and the old shop became this children's center until it moved to the bottom of the new Family Lodge, along with ticket sales and guest services. Paul Mundy averaged 350 children there on a Saturday, so he needed more room and easier access. The ski school put Dodge Ridge on the map. (Courtesy of Dee Martin.)

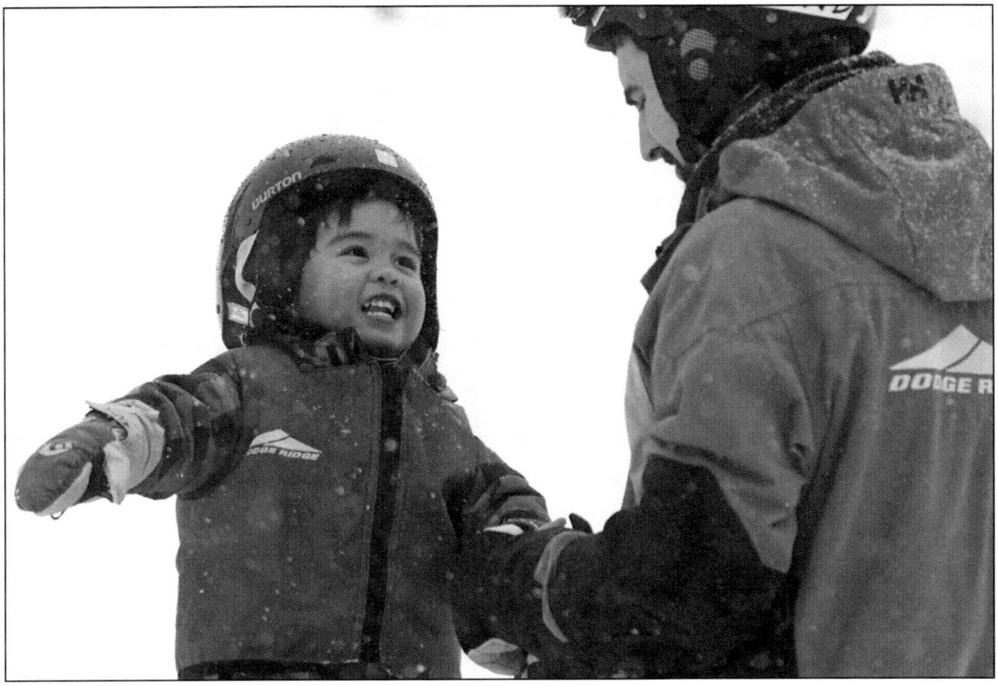

Malakai Fromm is following in the footsteps of his mother, Katie Fromm, and his grandparents Frank and Sally Helm by learning to ski at Dodge Ridge. He started skiing as soon as he could walk and eventually became a member of the race team. Dodge Ridge is home to him.

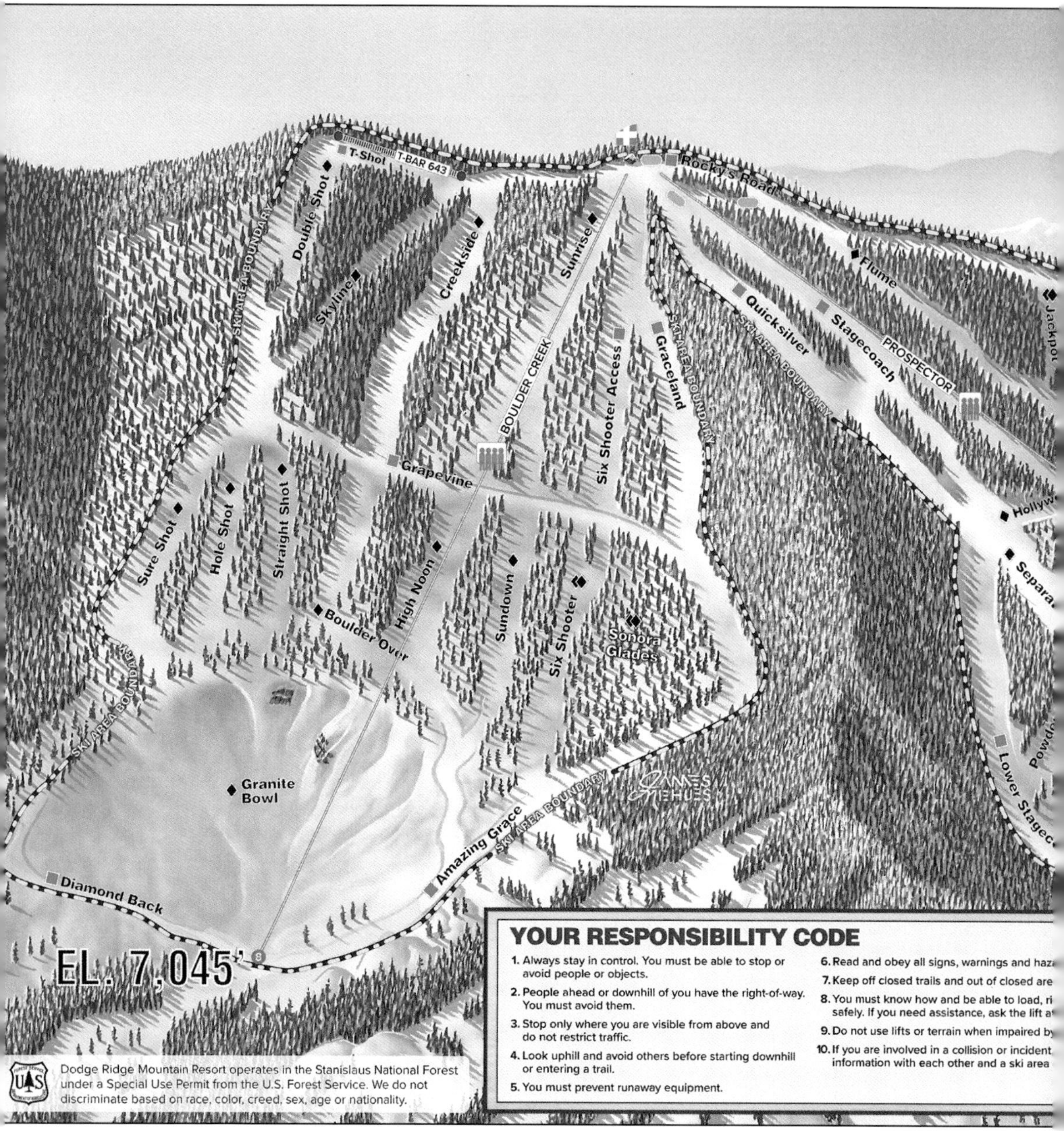

Here is a sweeping view of the Dodge Ridge Mountain Resort map showing the locations of every run and the chairs that access them. There are runs for beginner, intermediate, and advanced

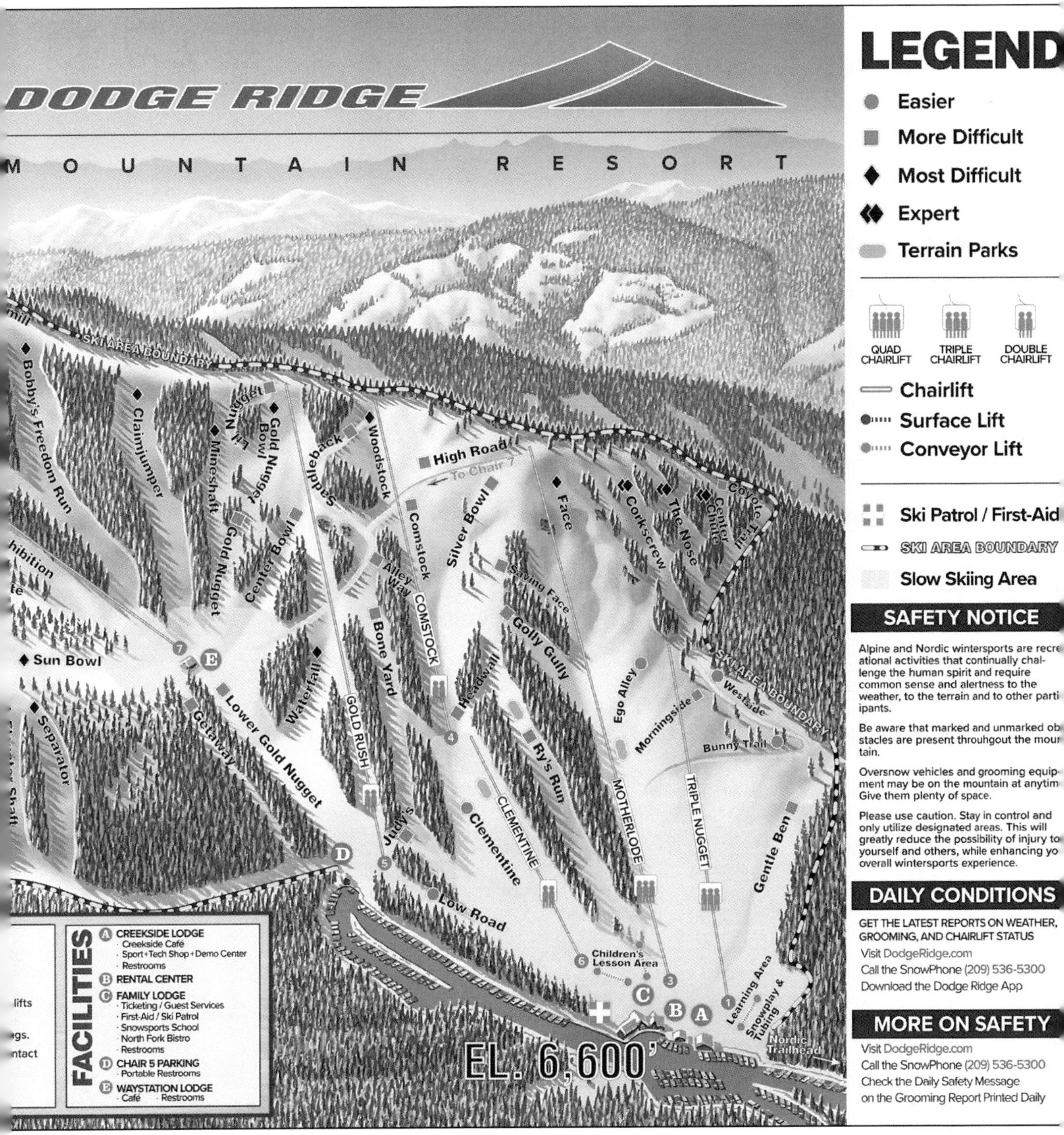

skiers throughout. This map was painted by legendary artist James Niehues.

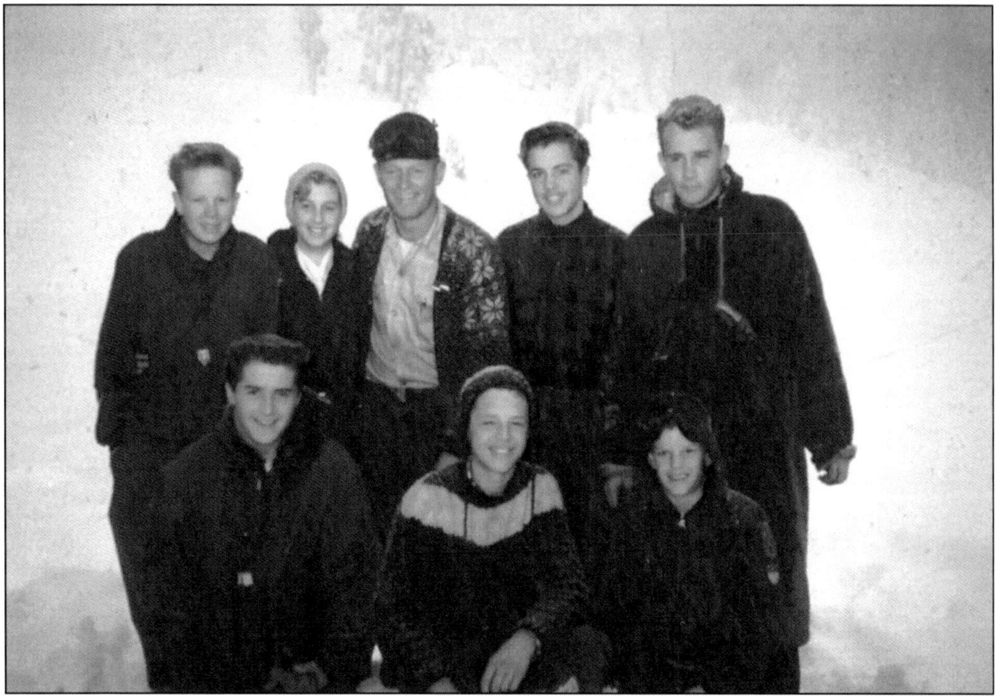

Above from left to right are (first row) Earl Hitch, Jim Reveal, and Jon Reveal; (second row) two unidentified persons, Ray Patton, Don Morrison, and unidentified. Jon Reveal started skiing at the age of three, and Patton sponsored him racing on the National Ski Team. He trained and taught in France, where he met Warren Miller and appeared in 15 of his films. In 1983, he climbed 24,000 feet of the West Ridge of Mount Everest without Sherpas or oxygen as part of the American Everest West Expedition Throughout his storied career, he managed and developed numerous resorts around the country, ending as president at Tamarack Resort, Idaho, where the ski school is now named for him. Below are the 1954–1955 race team members, from left to right, Carolyn Coleman, Jim Reveal, Jerry Weirick, and Don Morrison. (Both, courtesy of Bob Patton.)

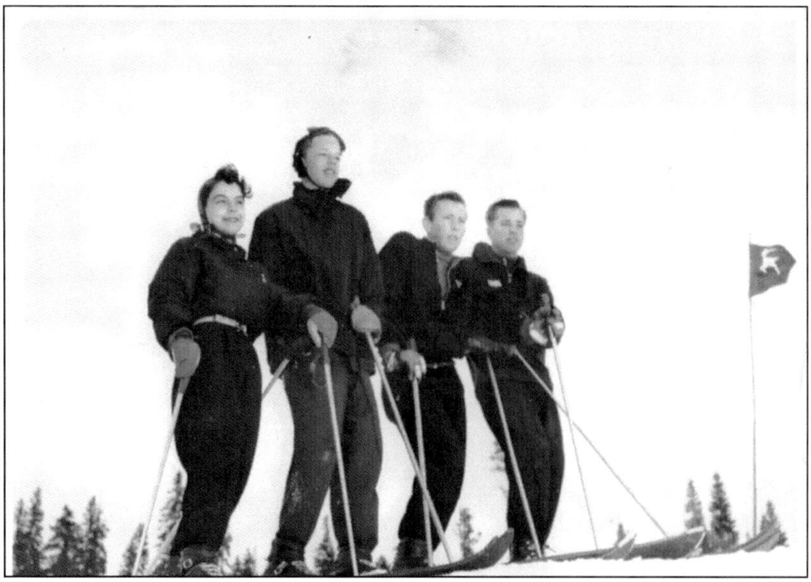

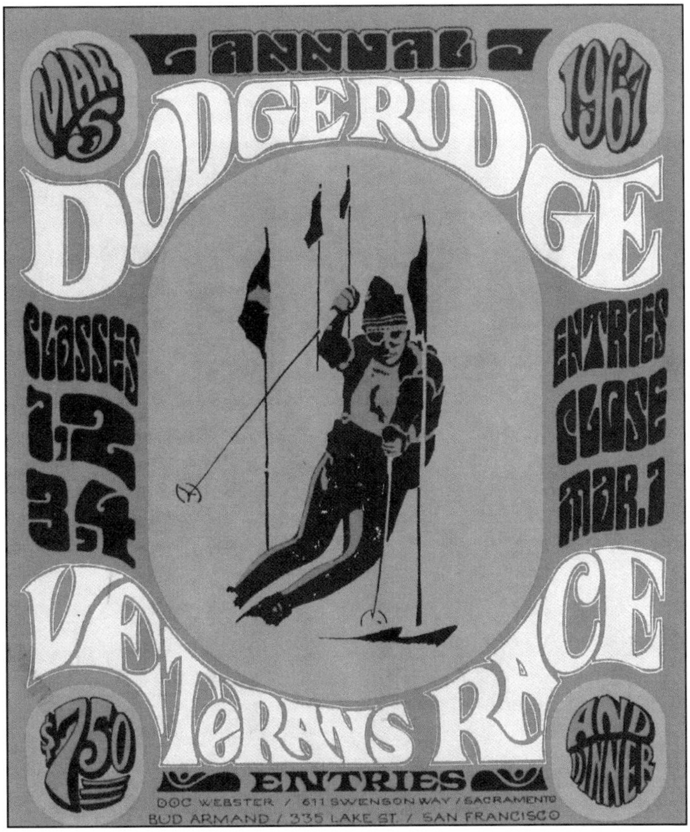

Dodge Ridge sponsored the annual Veterans Race starting in the early 1960s through the early 1980s. The age requirement was 27 years or older and then switched to 30 years or older in 1980. There were different categories for the races, and prizes for each category were presented at the after-party. (Courtesy of Andre Armand.)

Pictured is Ray Patton participating in the Giant Slalom Race during the Veterans Race at Dodge Ridge in 1968. Patton was not only an excellent ski instructor, he was also an accomplished racer, frequently seen on the circuit. (Courtesy of Bob Patton.)

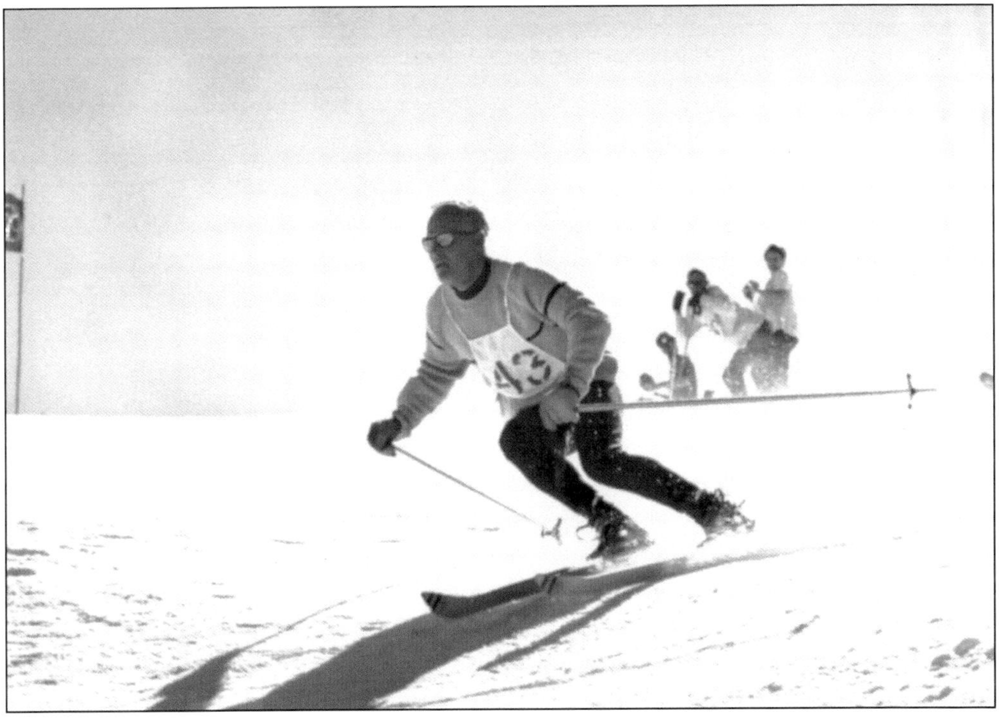

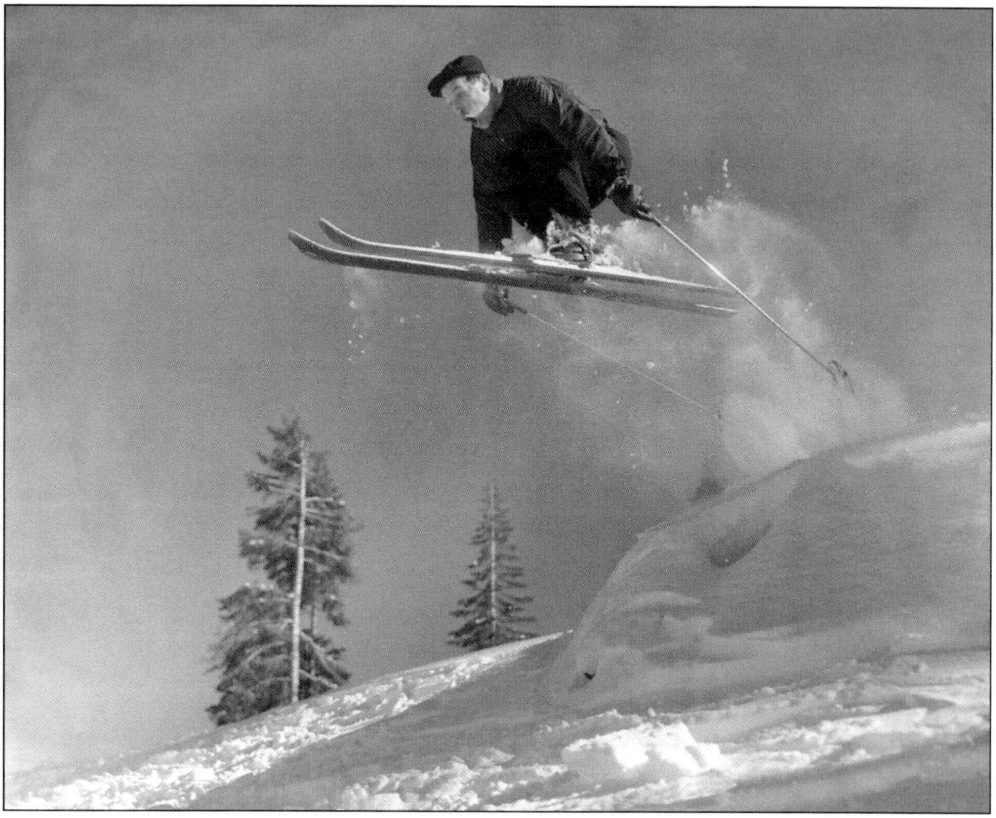

The Modesto Ski Club was founded in 1936. The club built its first cabin in Strawberry, California, several miles from Dodge Ridge ski resort. As the club grew, members purchased a vacant old post office in Pinecrest to build their second lodge. The club was very involved with recreational fun for skiers, racers, ski patrol, ski instructors, and other odd jobs. (Courtesy of Calin Smith.)

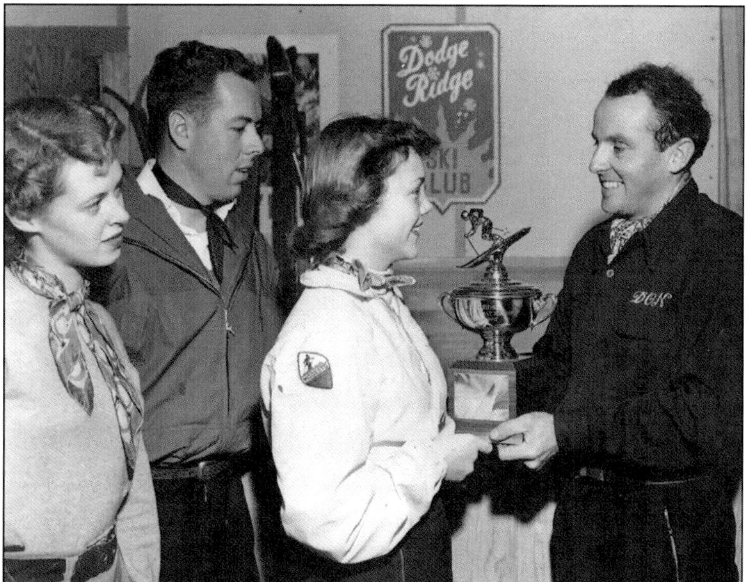

In 1952, Sally Towery and Bob Baker look on as Jeanne Cressey, a member of the Modesto Ski Club, receives a trophy for the Giant Slalom Championship from Don Paulsen at Dodge Ridge. Note the iconic Dodge Ridge Ski Club logo hanging on the wall.

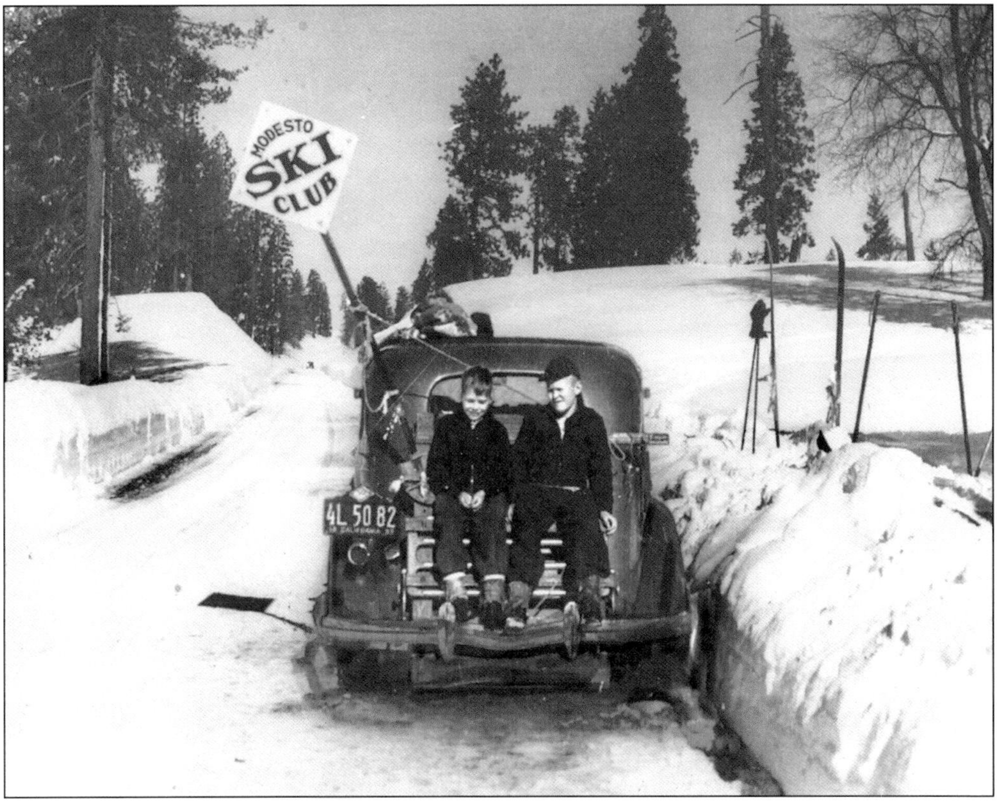

The Modesto Ski Club was extremely popular and very loyal to Dodge Ridge from the beginning. The Baird boys and their family always showed their club pride while at the resort.

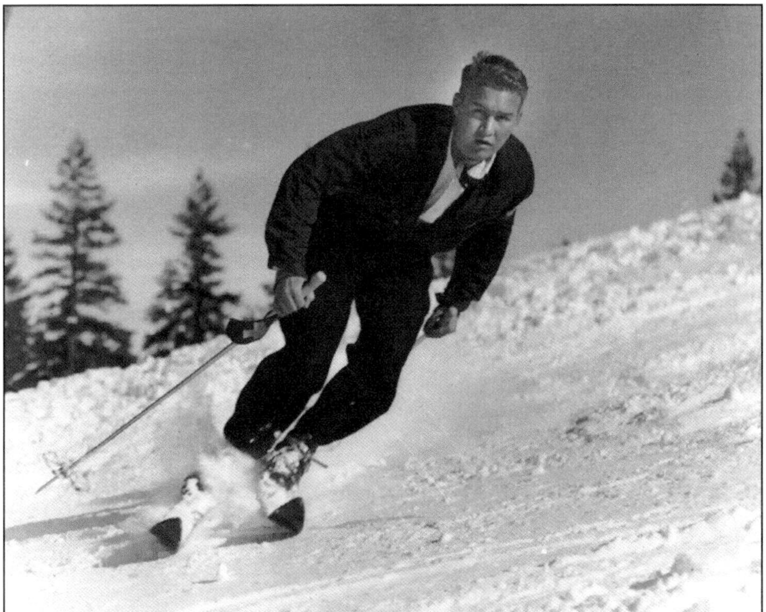

Bob Baird enjoys a day on the slopes. He and his family were regulars at Dodge Ridge. They were spotted skiing and picnicking with other club member families throughout the season for decades.

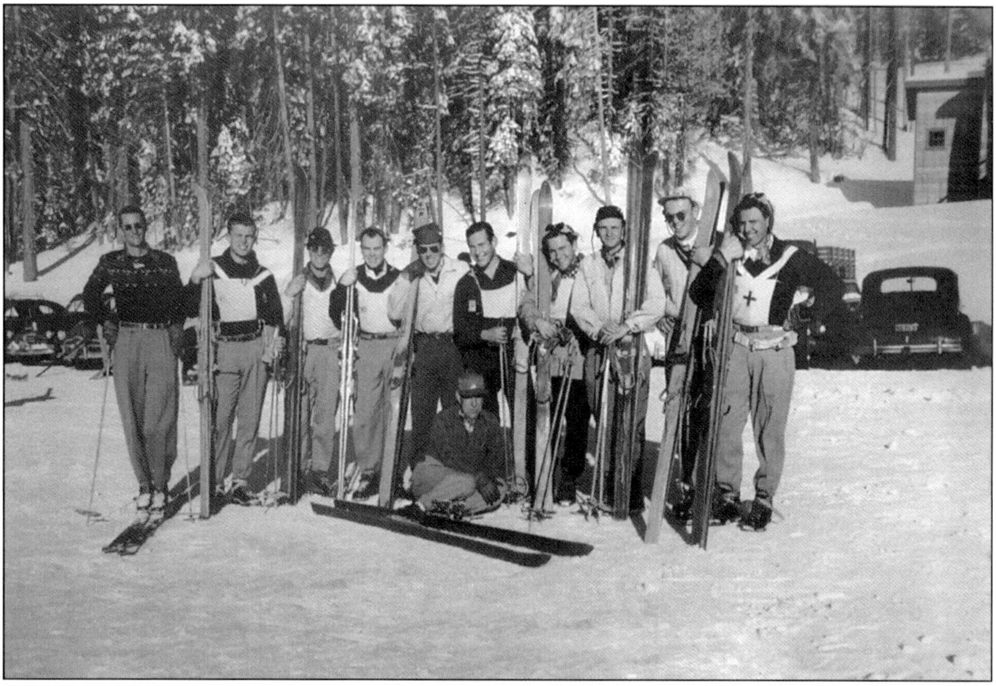

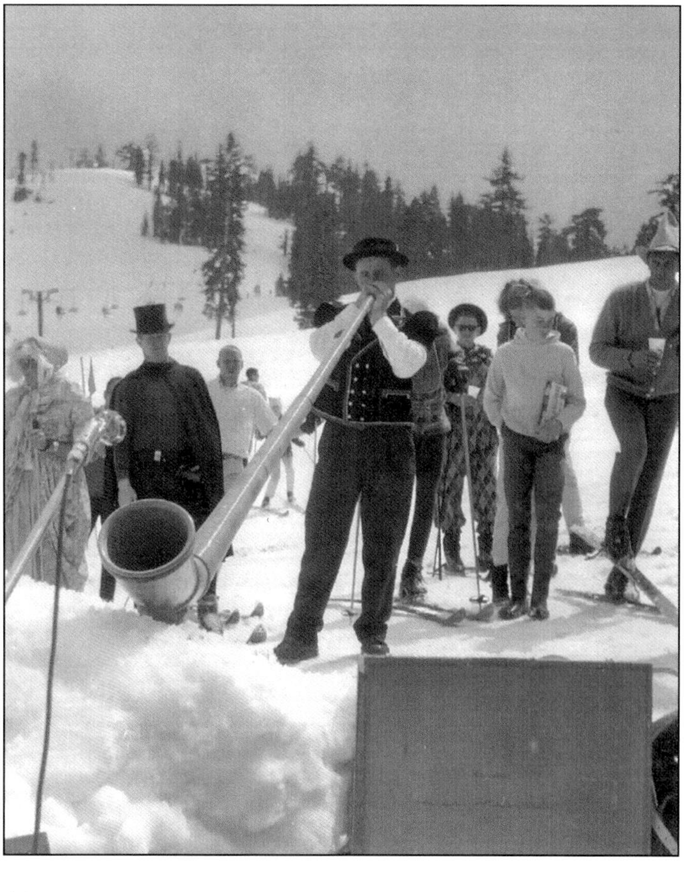

The Modesto Ski Club has been skiing at Dodge Ridge since 1950 when it opened. Many of them served as instructors and volunteers for the ski patrol. Standing from left to right are ski school director Ken Floto, unidentified, ? Horton, Bob ?, ? Baker, Cappy Cook, unidentified, Jim Crow, two unidentified persons, and Pop Horton seated up front.

Each spring, the Modesto Ski Club organized a Carnivale event. The iconic Alpenhorn opened the ceremonies, and then costumed shenanigans ensued throughout the day with races, food, and raucous fun. Participation was open to all individuals, not just club members.

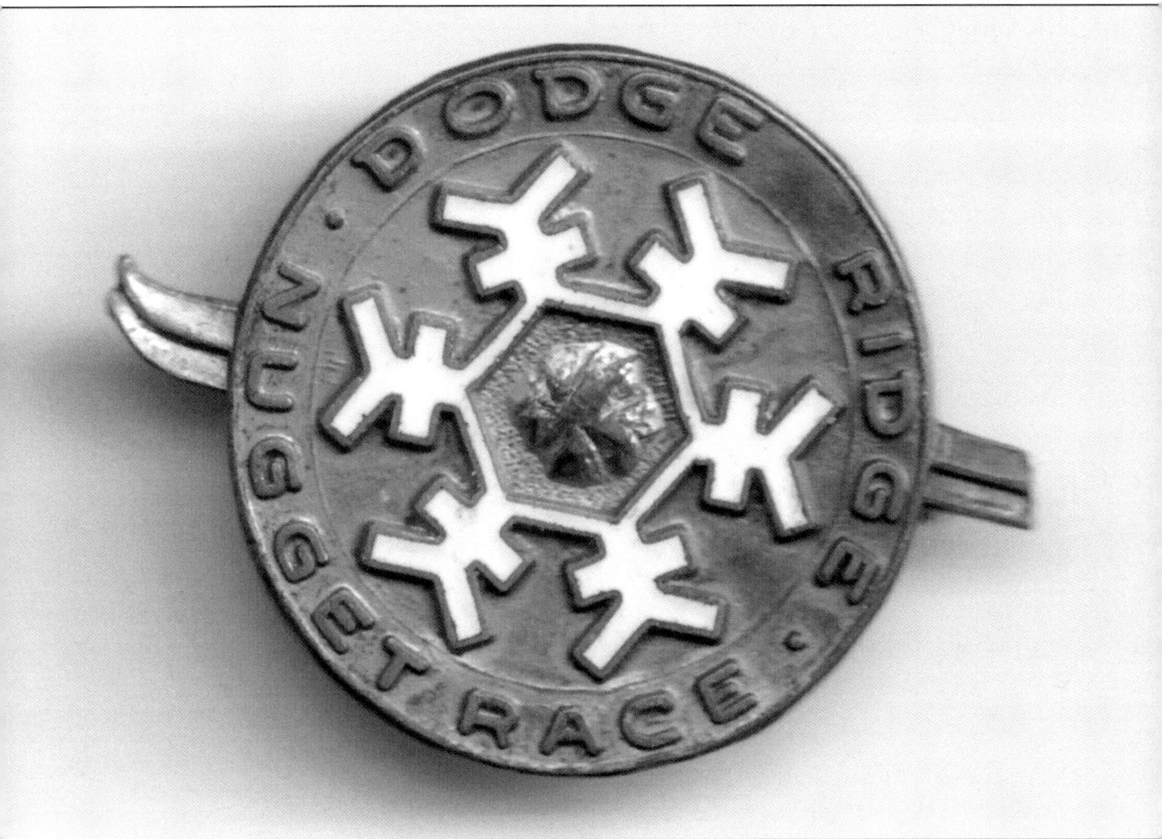

The Gold Nugget Race was held at Chair Five from the 1950s through 1972, and then it switched to Nastar races. The Gold Nugget Race was a weekly event in which participants could win a gold, silver, or bronze medal. Winners could purchase this gold nugget pin depicting skis going through a snowflake. At the end of the season, there was a championship costume race. (Courtesy of Andre Armand.)

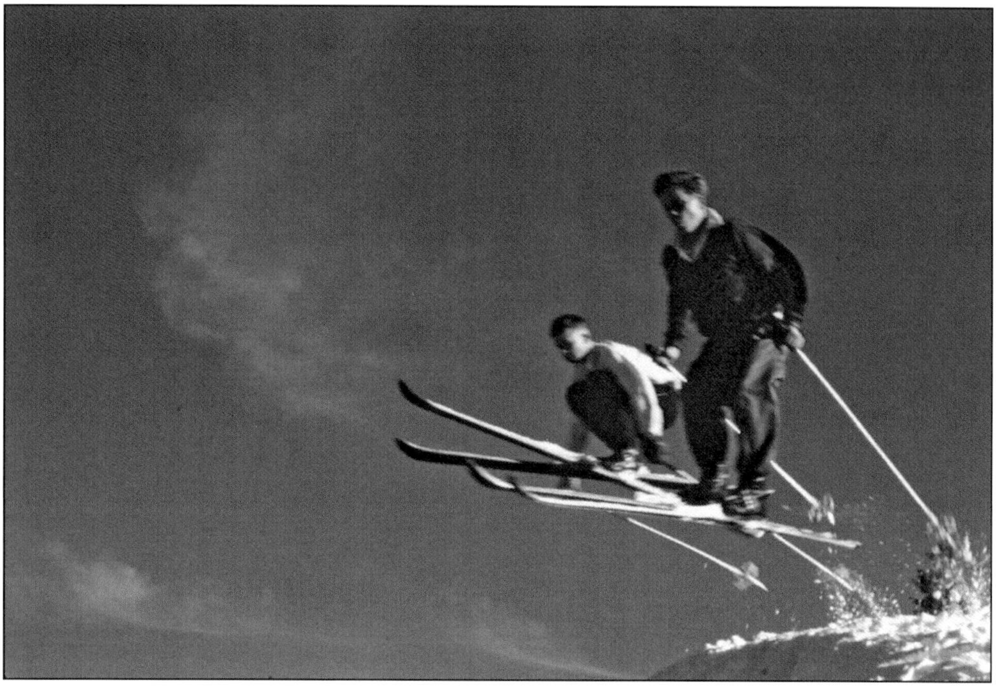

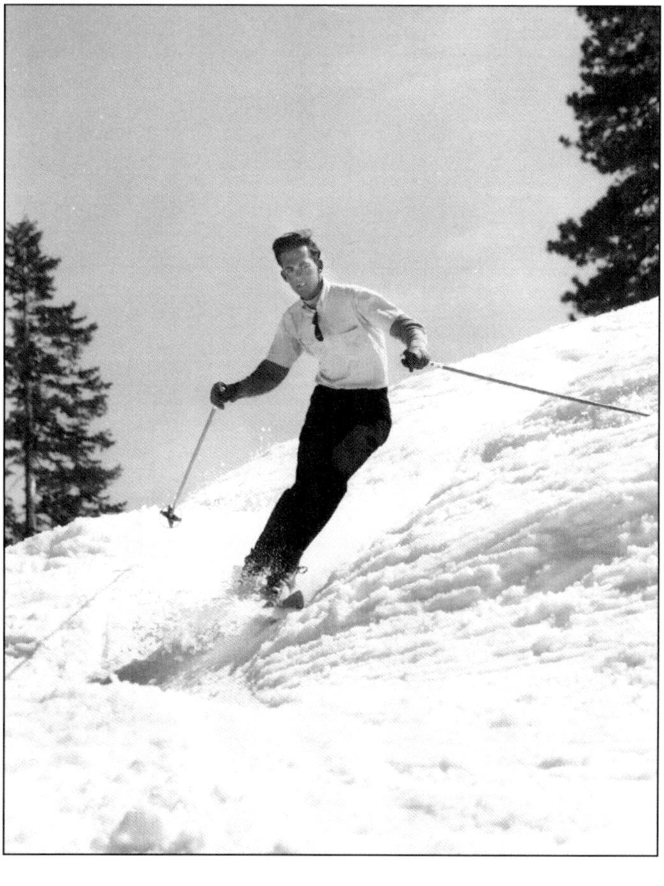

Here are two daredevils from the 1954–1955 season Dodge Ridge Junior Race Team catching air back when street clothing was worn, unlike the padded outfits and helmets required today.

This is Rennie Babbington, a member of the Modesto Ski Club in 1962. Babbington was an educator in Modesto who enjoyed getting away to the mountains as much as possible. He and his family had a cabin in Pinecrest. (Courtesy of Calin Smith.)

This is the ski jumping contest during the Modesto Ski Club Carnivale, held on the left side of Chair One. There used to be a very large rock in the middle of the run where they placed a piano, and people jumped over the piano and the piano player (the piano is in the lower right-hand corner of this picture). One year, Bob Patton, son of ski school director Ray Patton, did a flip over the head of the startled piano player, who did not miss a note while playing.

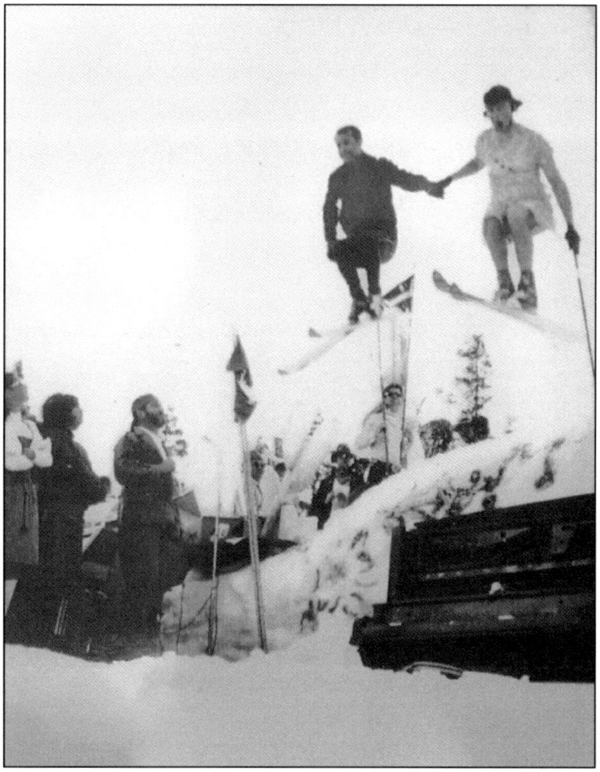

The Paul Masson Winery sponsored a Barrel Stave Slalom Race at Dodge Ridge that required participants to race on skis made from wine barrels. They were shorter and not as sturdy as regular skis. The man in the center without a bib is Early Purdy, with friends Lori Maynard and Sonny Maynard to the right.

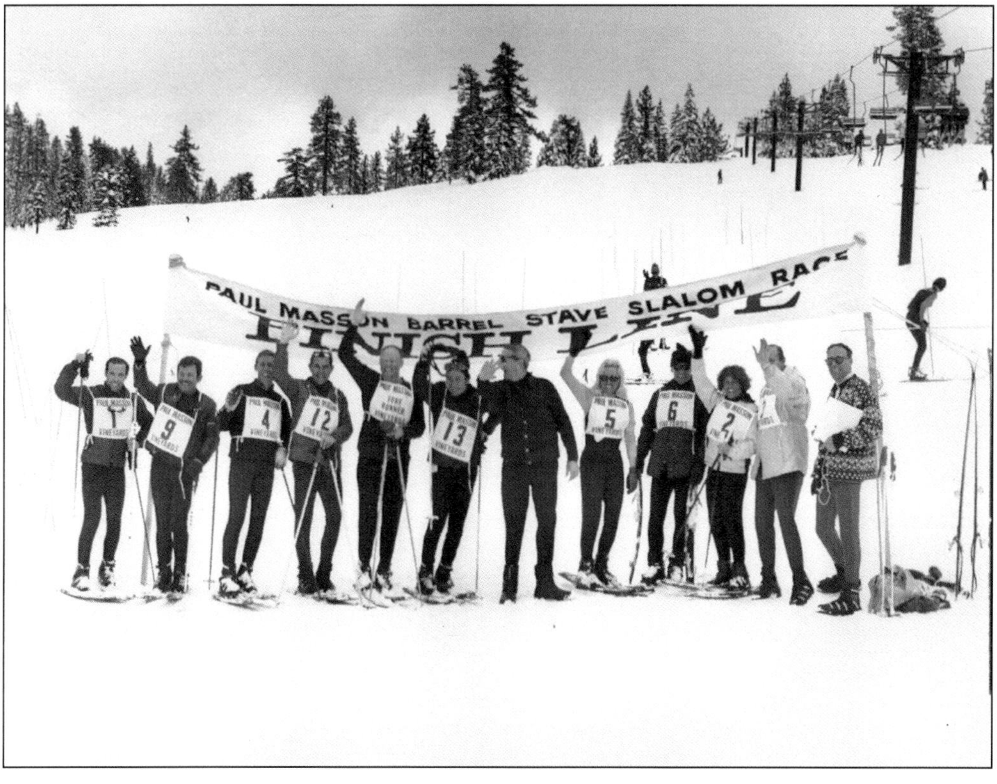

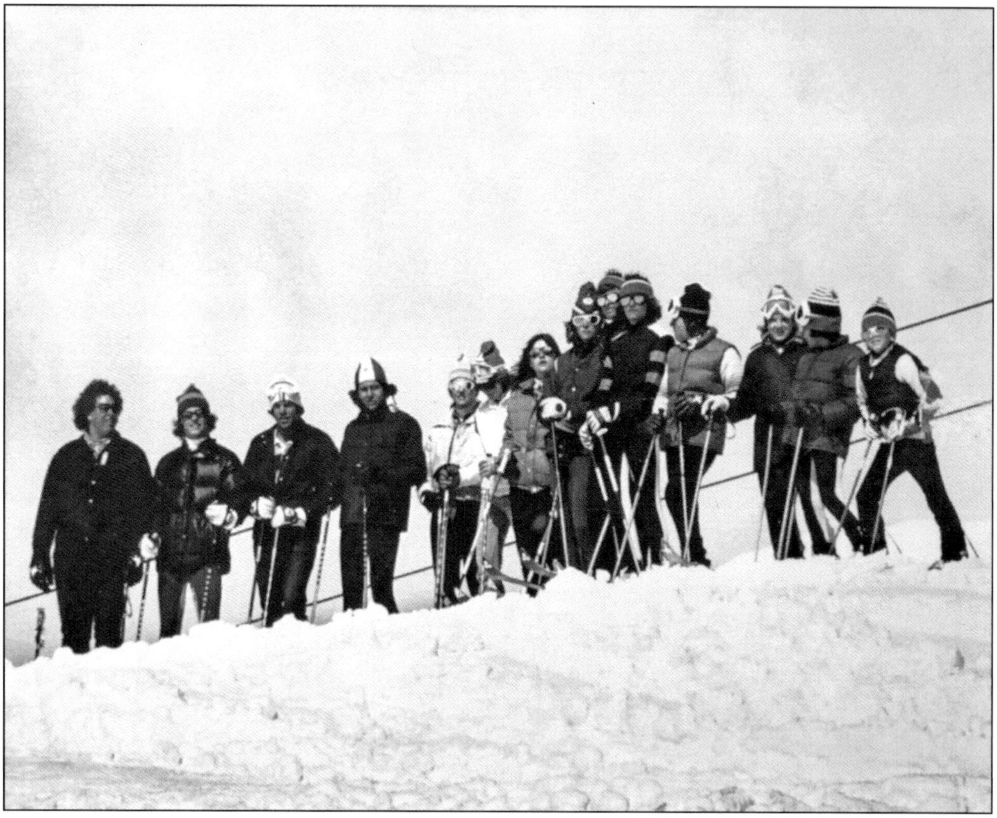

This crew coached the race team in the 1960s. Greg Overacker, on the far left, was head of the Hot Shots Forest Service crew, an elite group of wildland firefighters, and a Nastar racer pacesetter. Third from left is Tim Ryan. Matt Jense is on the far right.

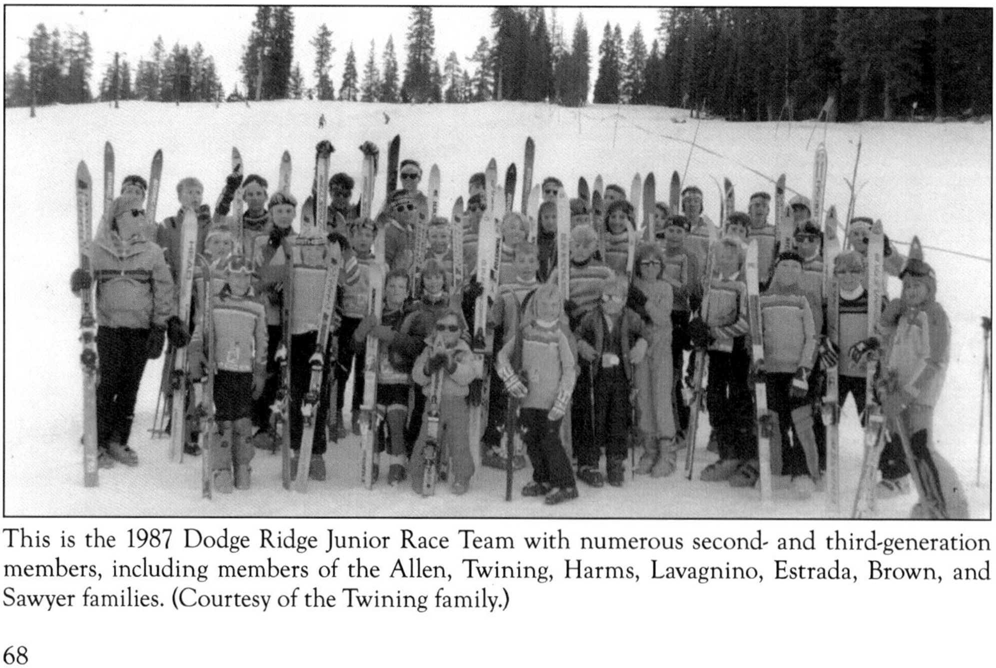

This is the 1987 Dodge Ridge Junior Race Team with numerous second- and third-generation members, including members of the Allen, Twining, Harms, Lavagnino, Estrada, Brown, and Sawyer families. (Courtesy of the Twining family.)

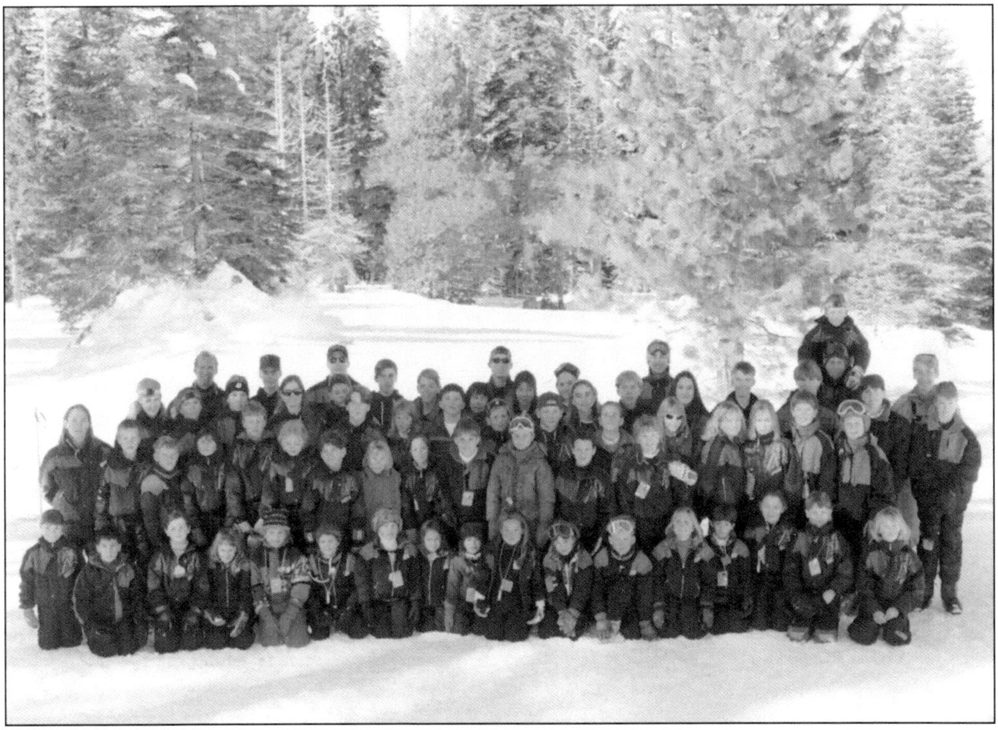

This is the 1994–1995 Dodge Ridge Race Team. Many consider this the heyday of the race team with the best records of success under their leader and longtime skier at Dodge Ridge, Earl Hitch. Some of these racers are now coaches. (Courtesy of the Harms family.)

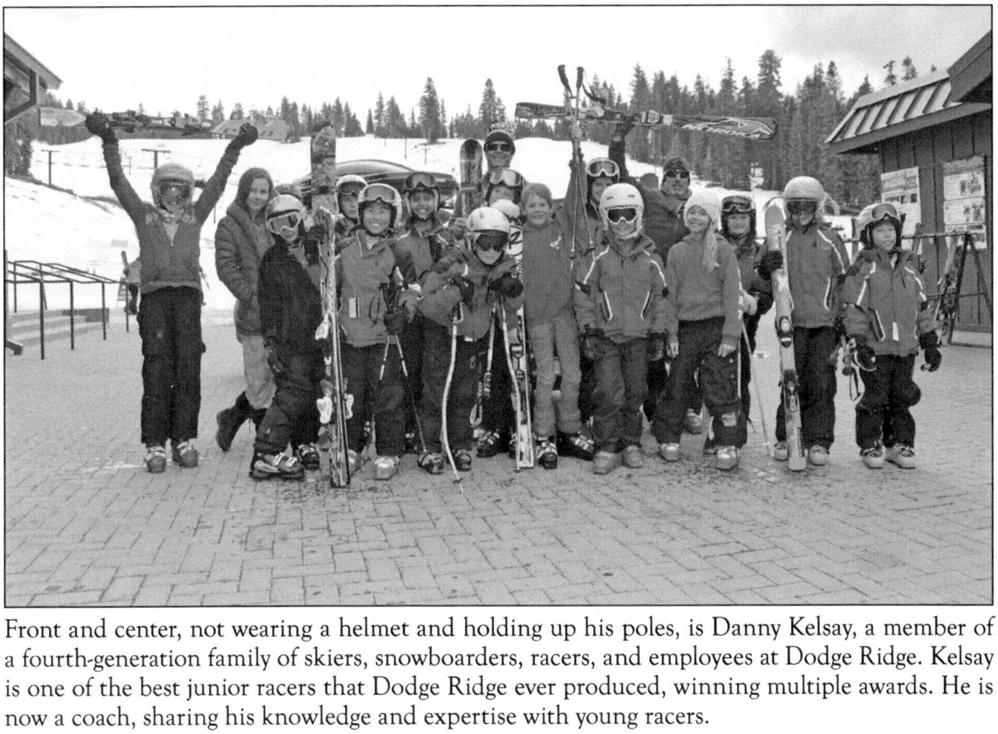

Front and center, not wearing a helmet and holding up his poles, is Danny Kelsay, a member of a fourth-generation family of skiers, snowboarders, racers, and employees at Dodge Ridge. Kelsay is one of the best junior racers that Dodge Ridge ever produced, winning multiple awards. He is now a coach, sharing his knowledge and expertise with young racers.

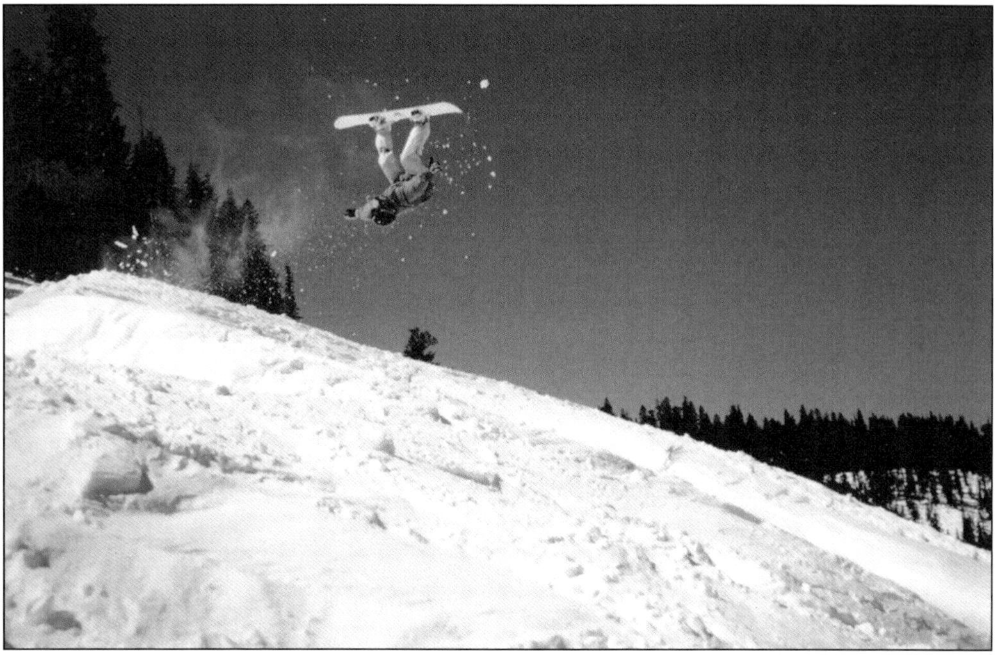

At the age of two, Justin Calbert started skiing at Dodge Ridge. In the third grade, he switched to snowboarding. Calbert is one person who represents what many people want to have happen in the world of snowboarding. He is like the little engine who could with willpower, aptitude, and devotion. He wrote Frank Helm a letter pitching why Dodge Ridge should embrace snowboarding, and Helm agreed. (Courtesy of Justin Calbert.)

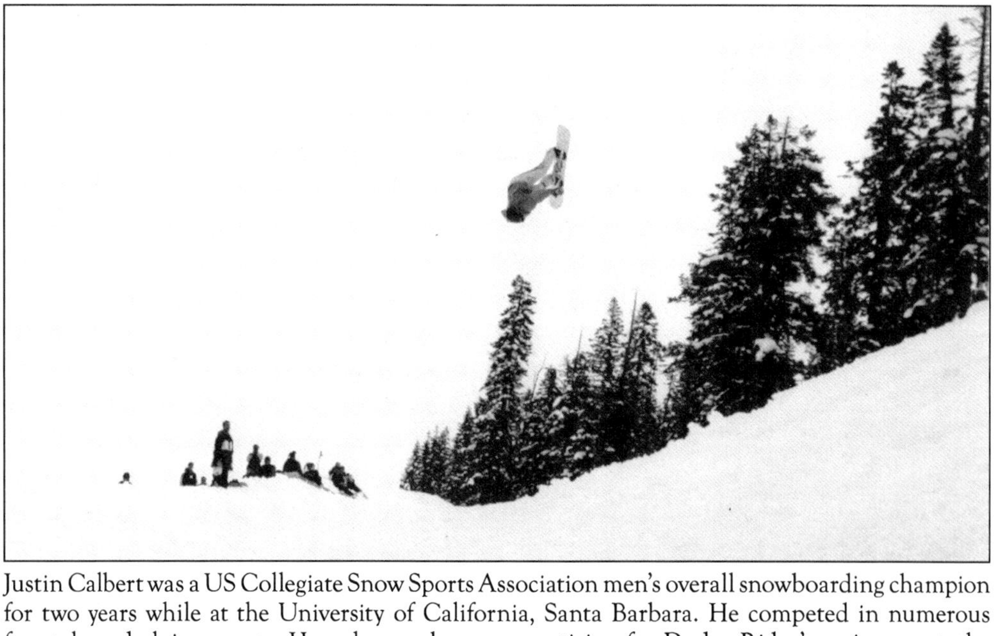

Justin Calbert was a US Collegiate Snow Sports Association men's overall snowboarding champion for two years while at the University of California, Santa Barbara. He competed in numerous freestyle and alpine events. Here, he can be seen practicing for Dodge Ridge's major event, the Superfly Slopestyle. He worked for the US Olympic Team. He was a sponsored rider, competitor, coach, event organizer and staff member, judge, and marketing publicity representative. (Courtesy of Justin Calbert.)

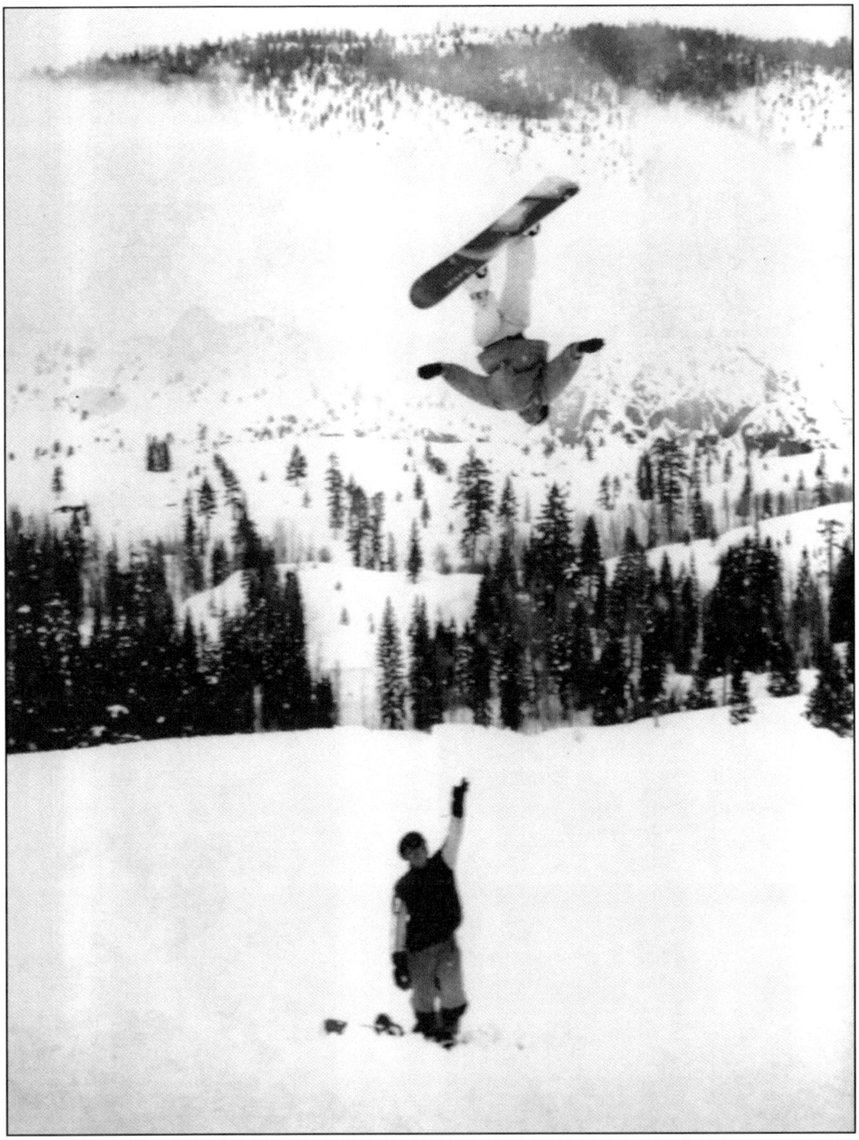

Justin Calbert flies upside down on his board as local Chad Van Ness checks out the big jump. Calbert had jumped the Face Rock at Dodge Ridge countless times, but on January 28, 2021, he hit a rock, sending him over the edge and immersing him head-first in eight feet of powder. Sixteen-year-old Ben Ronnenberg, off-duty firefighter Jerad Heinrich, and his brother-in-law Brock De Jong were first on the scene. After almost 20 minutes, Justin's lifeless body was pulled out. The Dodge Ridge Ski Patrol team, including director Carl Richter and patrollers Russell Phillips, Matt Michaels, Trevor Sandberg, and Chris Vasquez, arrived and cleared Calbert's airway, performed CPR, and transported him to the First Aid Room. Dr. Cody Andersen, a coworker of Justin's wife, Casey, witnessed the fall and rushed to help. He saw Justin's lifeless body being brought down on the ski patrol sled and went into the ski patrol office, telling them that he was an ER doctor and could help. Due to bad road conditions, Dr. Andersen stayed with Justin until he was safely aboard the medical helicopter bound for the Doctor's Medical Hospital in Modesto. Everyone's efforts contributed to a good outcome, but Calbert does not remember two days of his life. (Courtesy of Justin Calbert.)

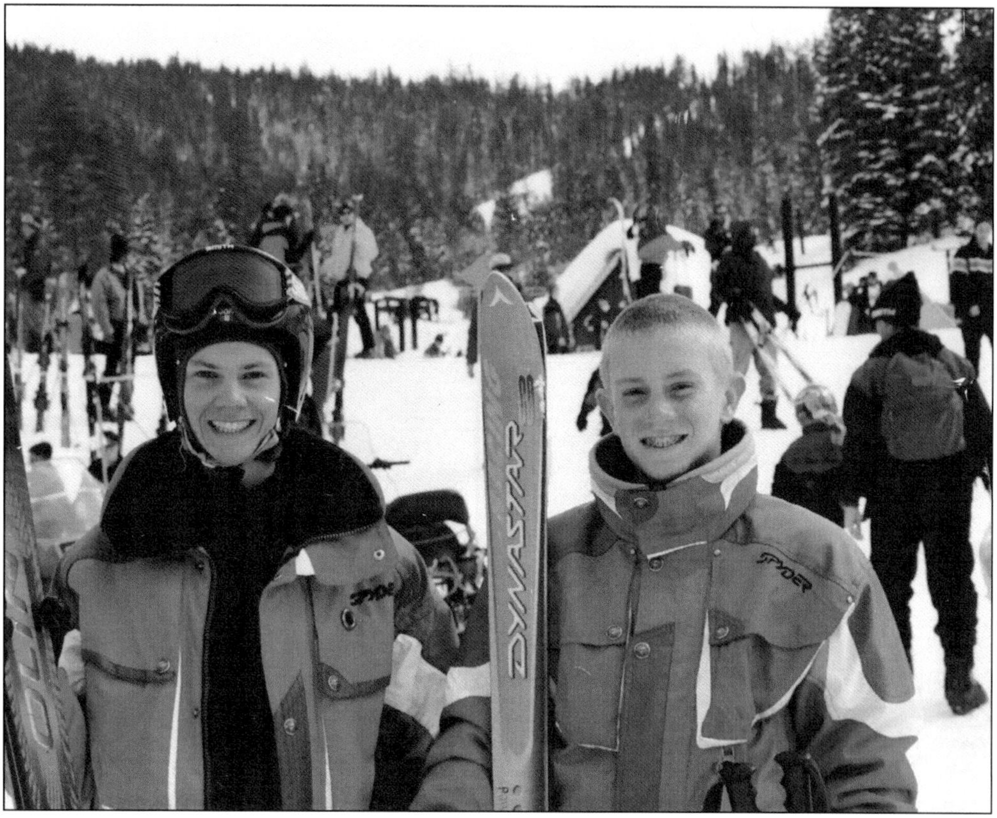

Shown here are brothers Patrick Rapp, 14, and Bobby Rapp, 12, who were both active on the race team. Patrick qualified for the Junior Olympics. For his whole life, Bobby wanted to be a police officer, a firefighter, or a soldier like his grandfather. As a soldier, Bobby earned Military Achievement Medals, the Iraq Campaign Medal, the Afghanistan Service Medal, the Meritorious Service Medal, the War on Terrorism Service Medal, a Purple Heart, and a Bronze Star. (Courtesy of Jennifer Rapp.)

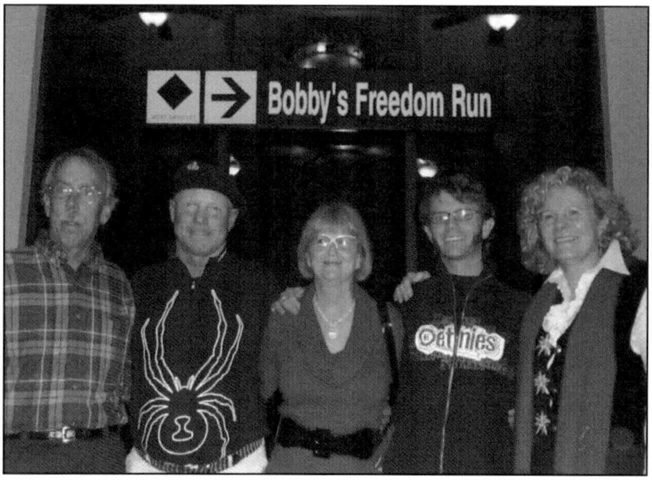

Deployed soldiers are required to write a letter making their final wishes known. Bobby's letter mentioned that it would be fun to name a ski run after him. In 2008, when news broke that Bobby had been killed in action in Afghanistan, Frank Helm, unaware of the letter, sent condolences and a desire to name a run after Bobby. From left to right celebrating the naming of the run are Frank Helm, Ted Rapp, Jennifer Rapp, Patrick Rapp, and Sally Helm.

Ryan Lavagnino grew up skiing at Dodge Ridge and won numerous races. Lavagnino, along with Brittney Mahanna and Carin Twining, also multigenerational skiers, qualified for the National Junior Olympics in slalom, giant slalom, and super giant slalom. His parents, Steve and Susie Lavagnino, are also longtime fixtures on the slopes at Dodge Ridge. (Courtesy of the Lavagnino family.)

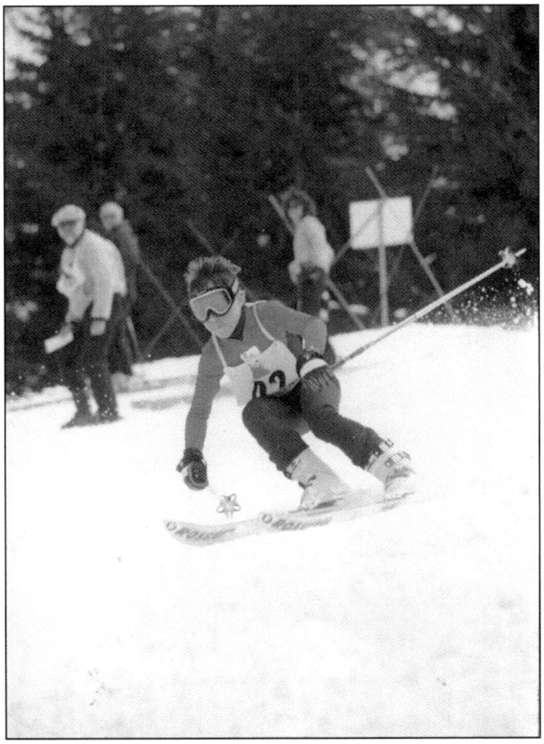

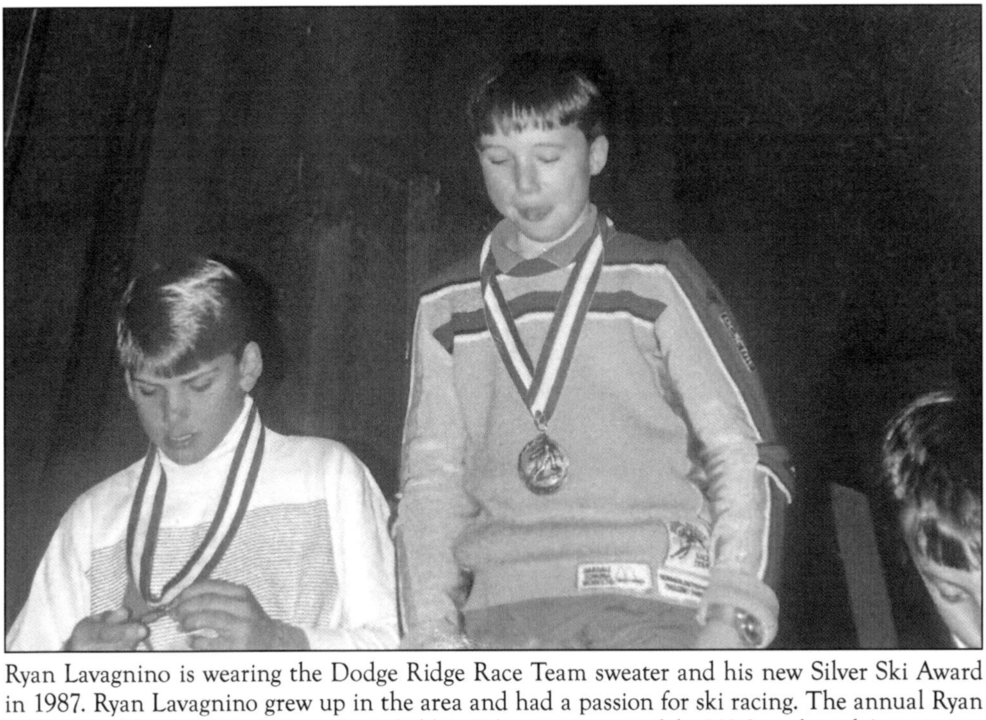

Ryan Lavagnino is wearing the Dodge Ridge Race Team sweater and his new Silver Ski Award in 1987. Ryan Lavagnino grew up in the area and had a passion for ski racing. The annual Ryan Lavagnino Classic Giant Slalom Race, held in February as part of the US Snowboard Association (USSA) Far West Central Series, was created in his memory. There is also a run named Ry's Run. (Courtesy of the Lavagnino family.)

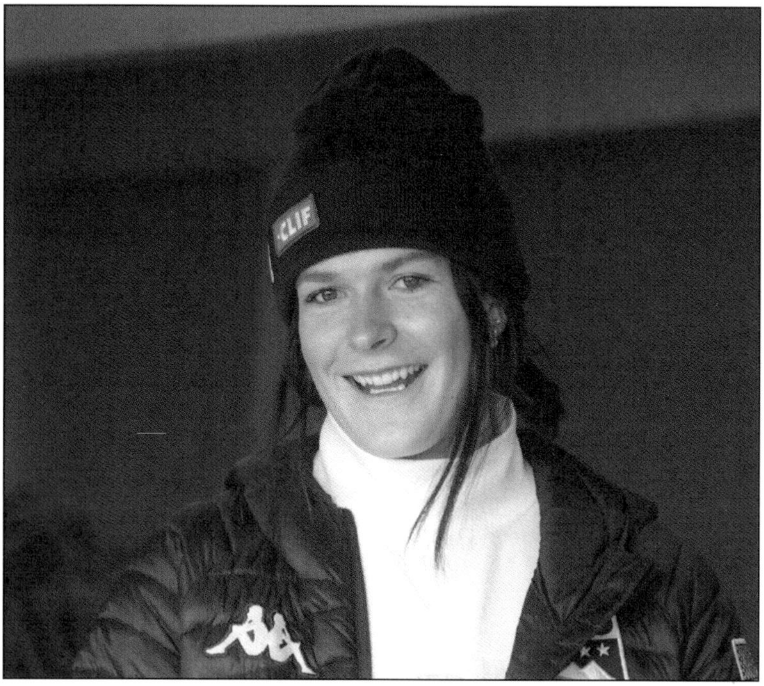

Keely Cashman started skiing as soon as she could walk and entered her first race at the age of five. Racing has always been her passion. She is a World Cup alpine ski racer and an Olympian. She met her goal of representing the United States skiing in the 2022 Winter Olympics in Beijing, where she finished 27th in the super-G and 17th in downhill as the top American finisher in this category.

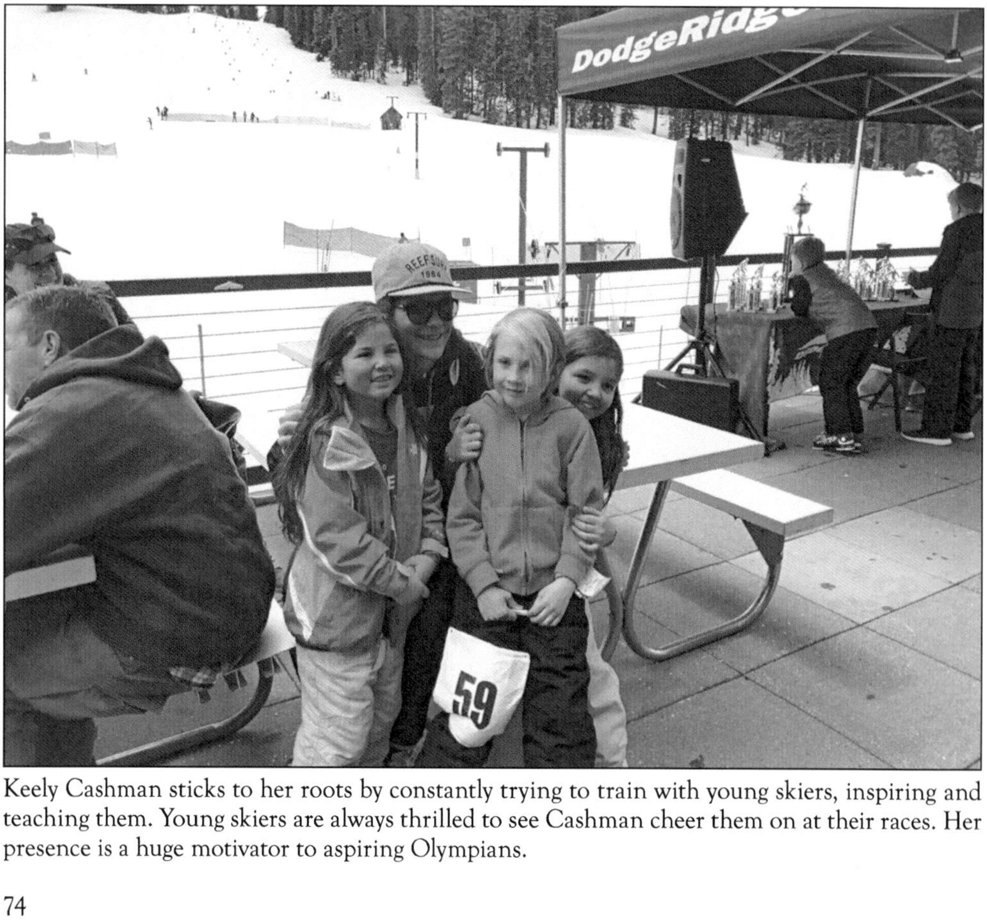

Keely Cashman sticks to her roots by constantly trying to train with young skiers, inspiring and teaching them. Young skiers are always thrilled to see Cashman cheer them on at their races. Her presence is a huge motivator to aspiring Olympians.

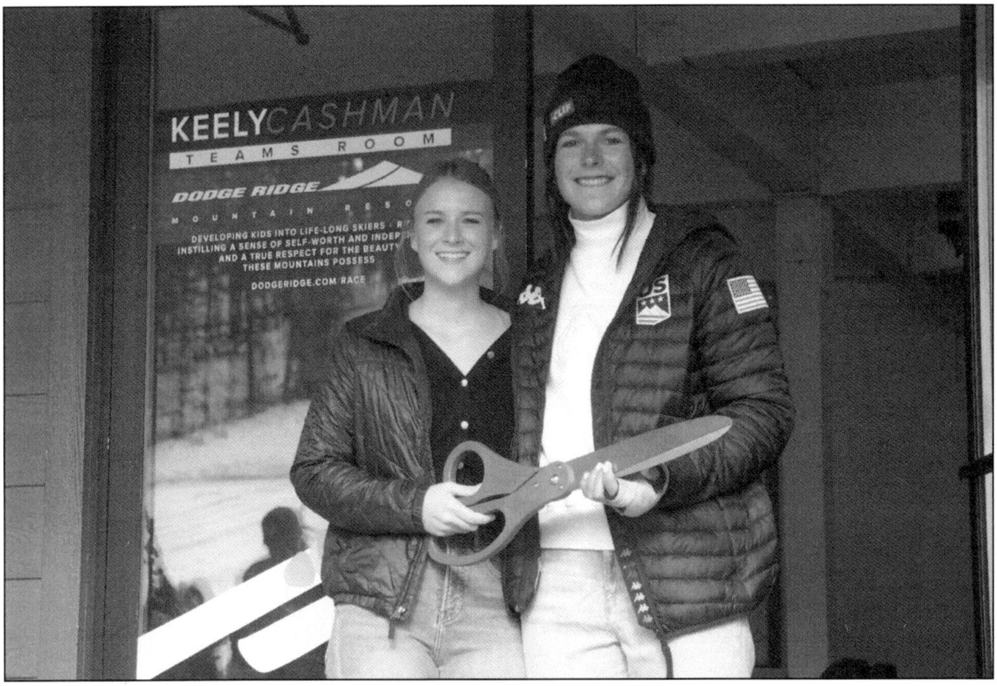

Dodge Ridge is committed to developing children into lifelong skiers within a positive environment. Dodge Ridge honored Cashman's accomplishments by naming the race team center the Keely Cashman Teams Room. On November 26, 2022, a formal dedication ceremony was held. Cashman and her cousin and current race team manager, Libby Rimmer, shared ribbon-cutting duties.

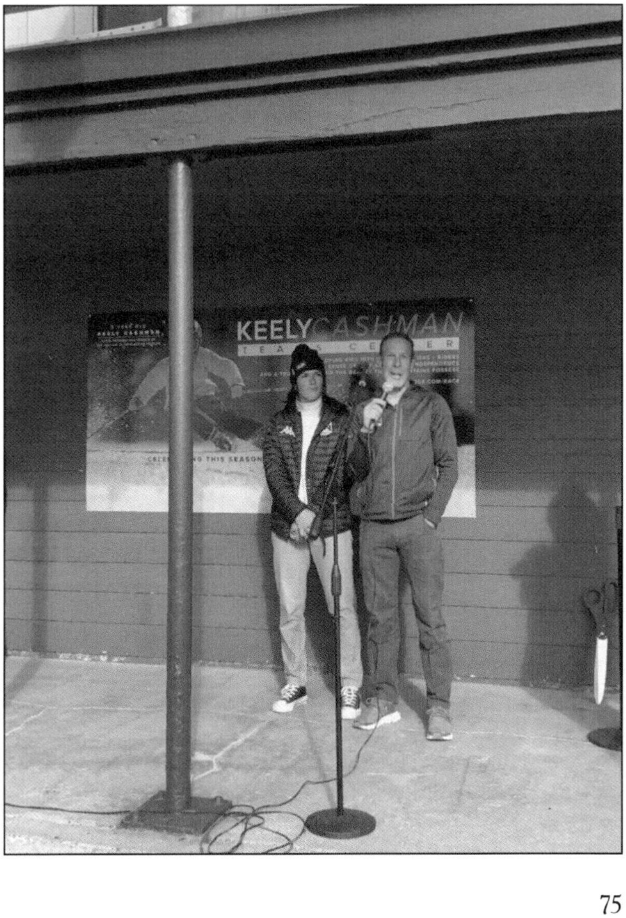

John Cashman, Keely's father, is one of her coaches. He has extensive experience as a former ski racer, Squaw Valley Ski Team coach, and on the US Ski and Alpine staff as the U16 National Training Group (NTG) head coach for the USSA. In addition to being a world-class ski coach, John is known in Pinecrest for his award-winning chili recipe.

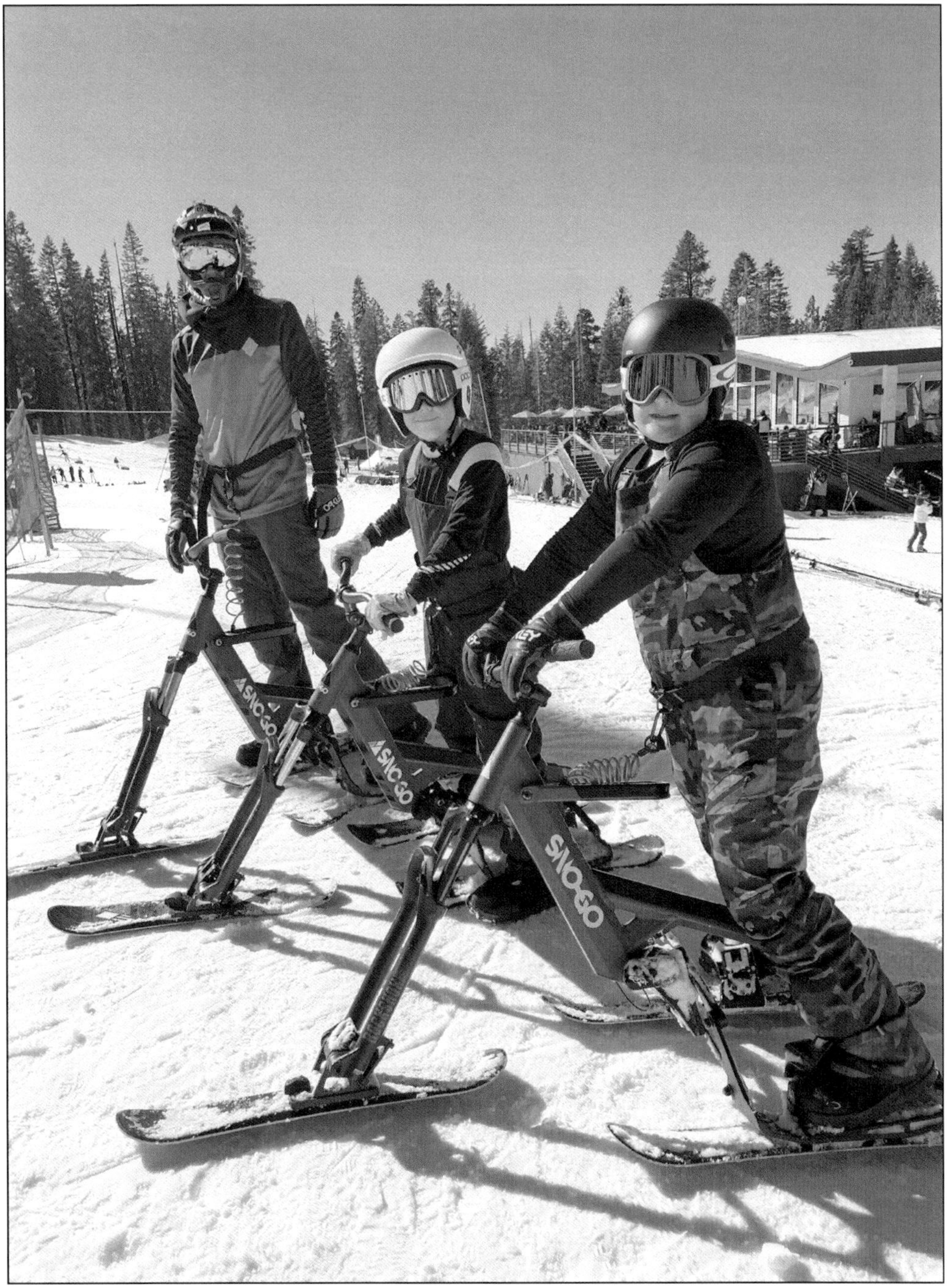

Sno-Go is a bike with skis instead of wheels. The technology helps people with injuries or physical limitations ski with better support and balance than regular skis. They are considered foot passengers, so they are restricted to certain areas. Dodge Ridge was an early adapter to allow this device, and it has opened up a whole new world for some guests, as well as a renewed confidence in others who thought they had to give up skiing due to injury.

Three

Dodge Ridge Family, Friends, Connections, and Multigenerations

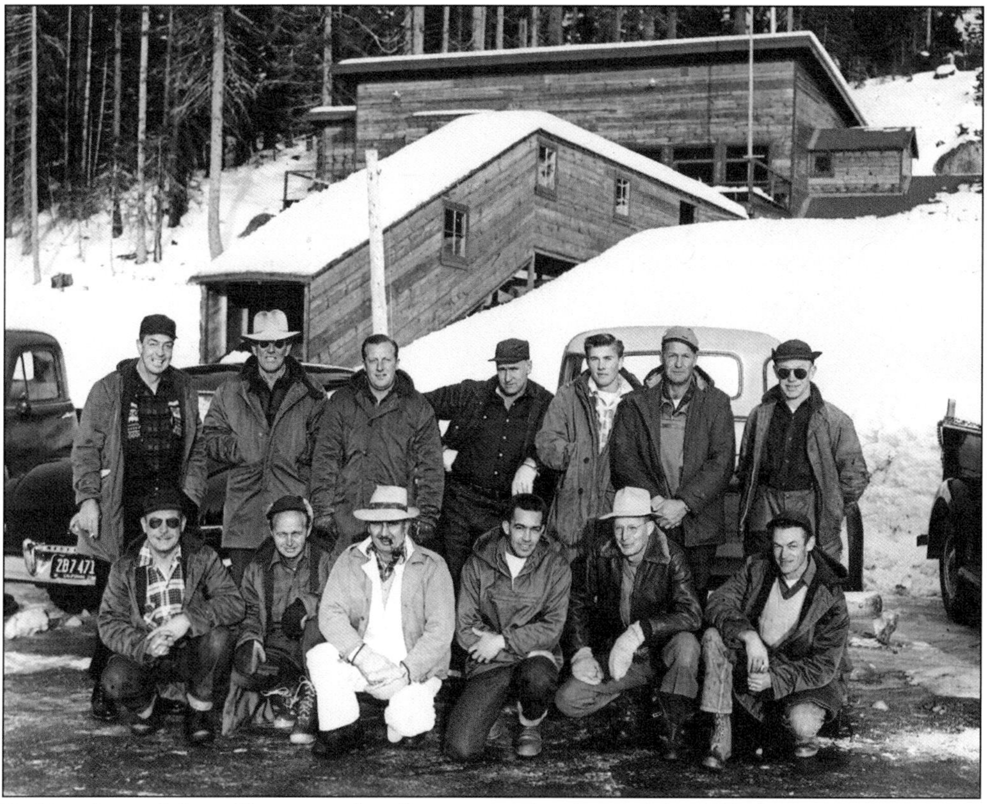

Earl Purdy, top left, and his original staff are pictured in front of the old lodge. Most of these men were friends, loggers, and farmers who knew how to get the land ready, built, and maintained for skiers who wanted a proper ski resort not far from home. (Photograph by John L. Corbett, courtesy of Calin Smith.)

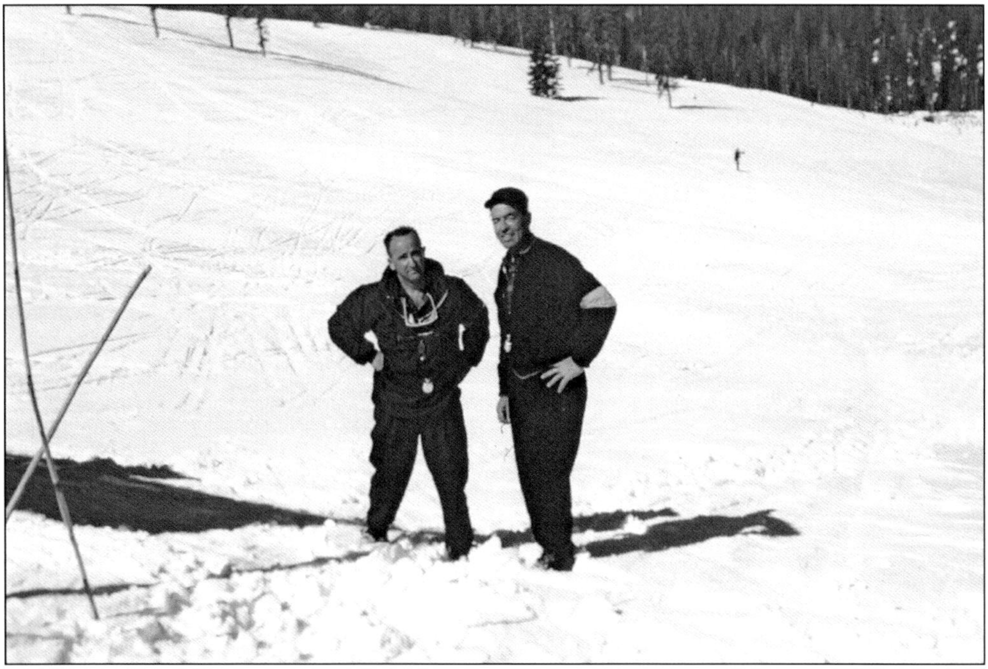

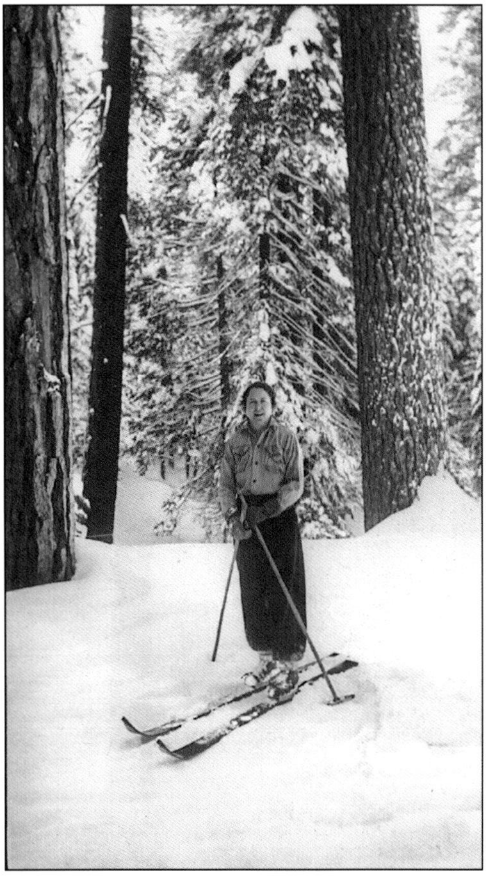

On the left is Dr. Norman Morrison of San Mateo, standing next to his friend and owner of Dodge Ridge, Earl Purdy on the right, as they inspect the resort. Dr. Morrison is one of the investors in the closed corporation Earl Purdy created to raise the funds needed to create the resort.

Ardys Baird was part of a family that were members of the Modesto Ski Club. They were very dedicated to skiing at Dodge Ridge from the beginning. Note her bear-trap bindings and lace-up boots with straps that did not provide much support around one's ankles nor properly release someone if they fell, as well as the extra-long bamboo poles that could poke someone in the eye if they fell.

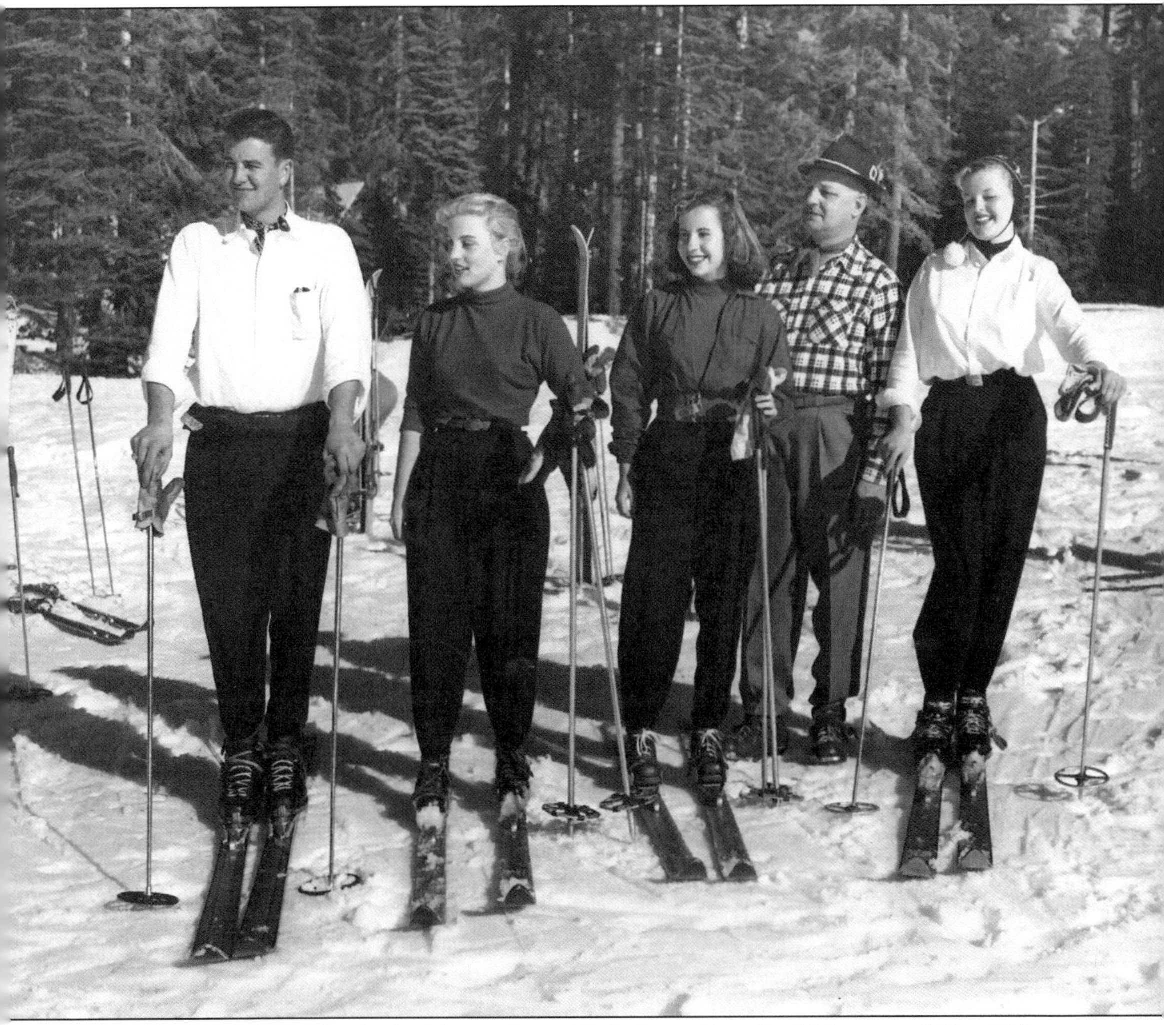

In 1954, from left to right, Dick Volonte, Penny Tuck, Janice Roe, Dr. Volonte, and Cara Volonte pose for a group photograph. The three on the left were part of the ski race team and well-versed in classic ripping. The equipment required much more body movement from one's legs and arms, but the excitement and the reward were still exhilarating, and that has not changed.

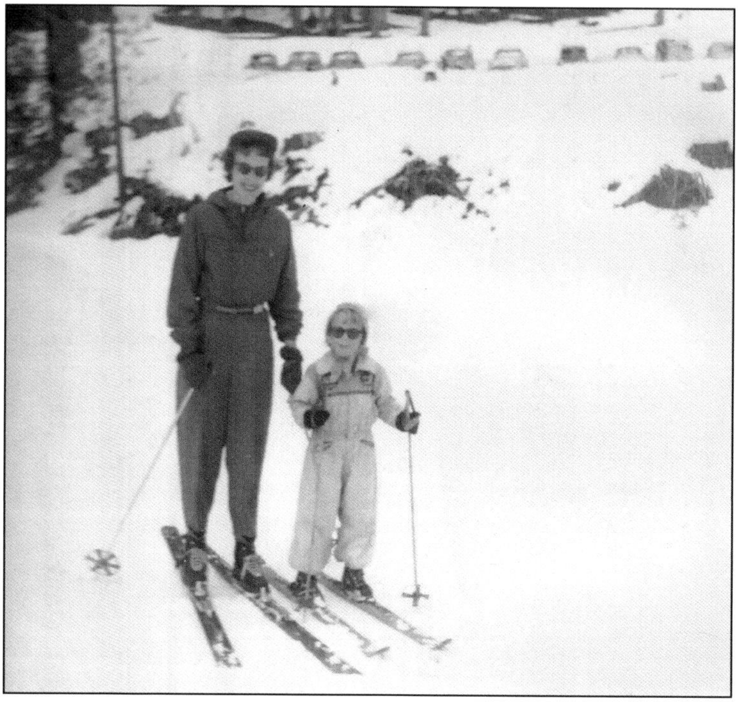

This is Jean Lindstrom and her daughter Sally Lindstrom (Harms) in 1956. Jean Lindstrom really did not like skiing, but her daughter Sally took to skiing immediately. Sally's children and grandchildren were active race team participants.

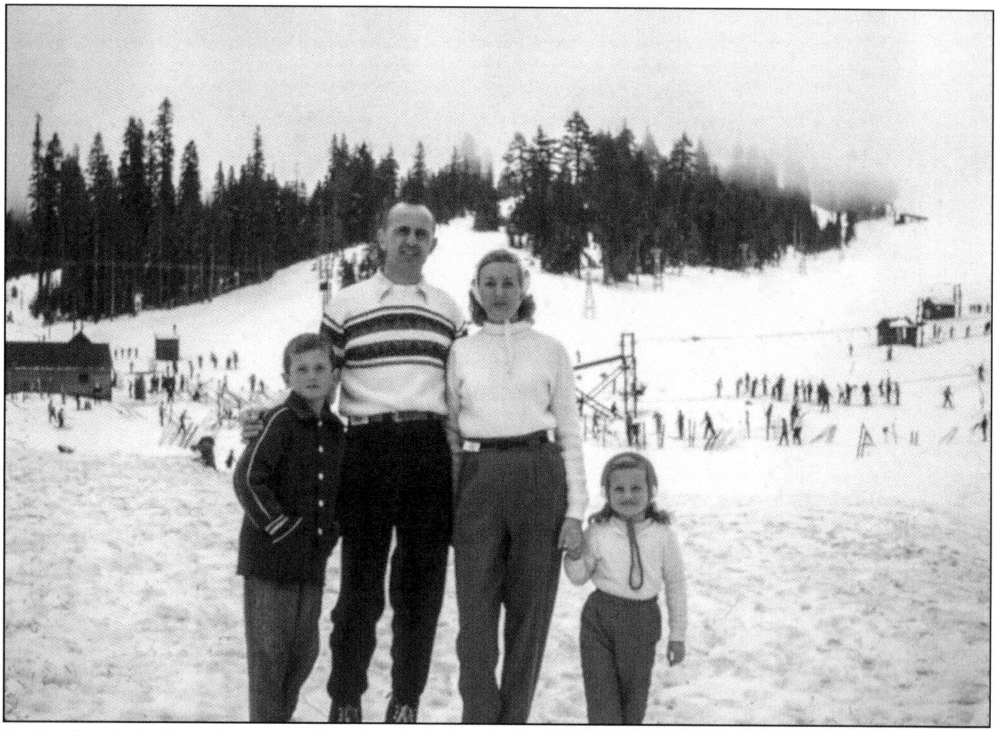

In Dodge Ridge's early years, families like the Smiths regularly went skiing there. From left to right are David, Irving, Joanne, and Diane Smith. They and their friends frequently enjoyed the mountain's offerings. The children learned to ski and enjoyed making snowmen and having snowball fights.

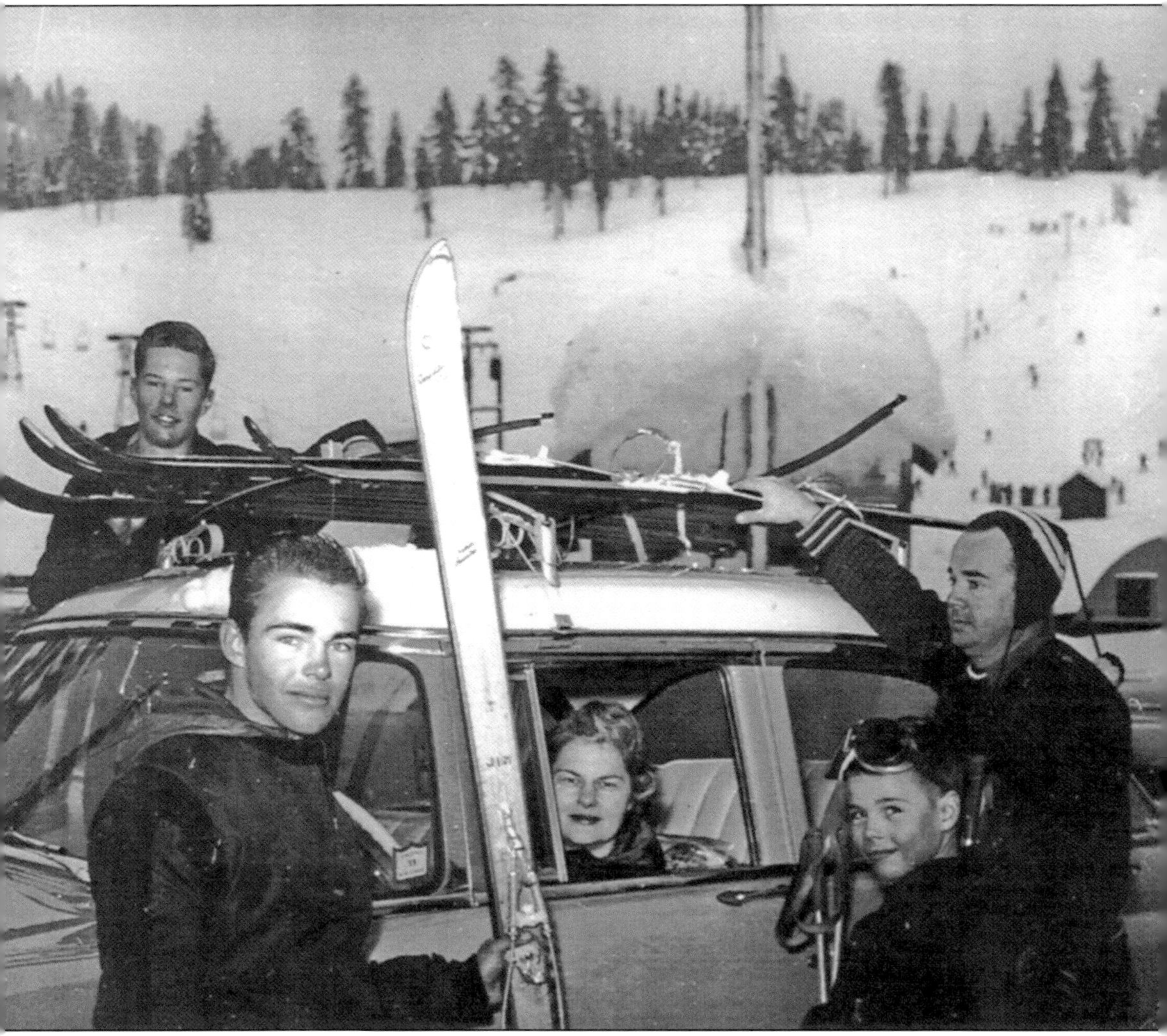

The Foley family had a cabin on Dodge Ridge Road. Ud Foley was a senior mechanic for United Airlines in San Francisco. He raced with the Twining family, who lived in Strawberry. His boys, seen here from left to right, Mike (the oldest), Jim, and Steve, learned to ski and race at Dodge in the 1950s. The kids were the ski racers with the Twining kids.

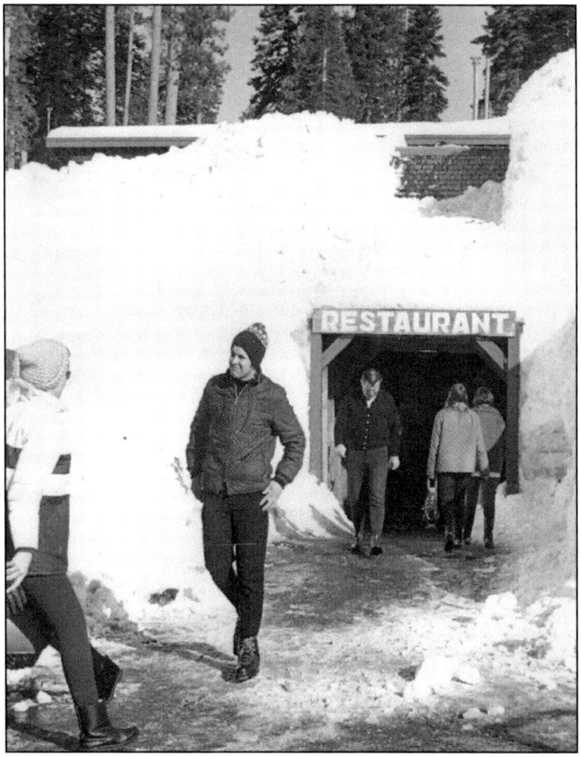

Motherlode Lodge Restaurant, on what is now the upper parking lot, had a tunnel and stairs leading to the restaurant. This photograph shows an extreme snowfall, creating an igloo effect. The building also housed some offices and employee lockers. It was a bit of a hike from the base of the ski area, so after it burned down, the lodge was relocated to the base of the ski area.

Earl Purdy sits at the main desk in the old lodge where the upper parking lot is today. The microphone on the desk was in constant use throughout the day, with announcements or admonishments such as "David, get off the cat," only it sounded like "David, David, David, get off the cat, cat, cat" as it spewed from the speakers on the lifts and echoed through the park.

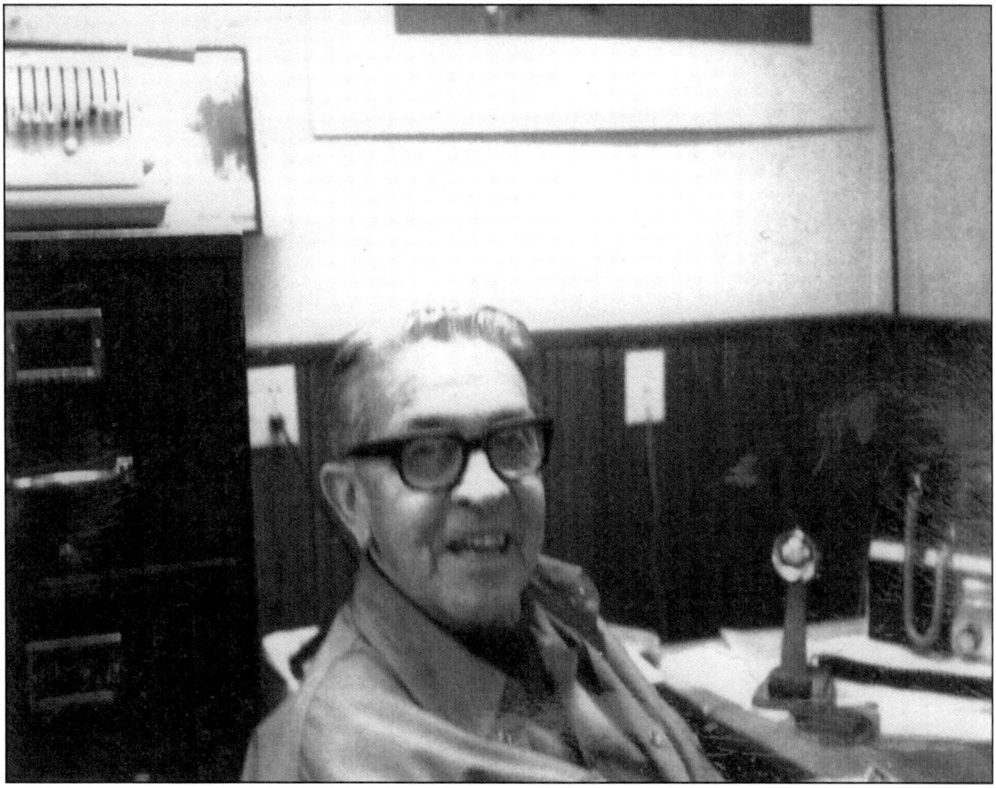

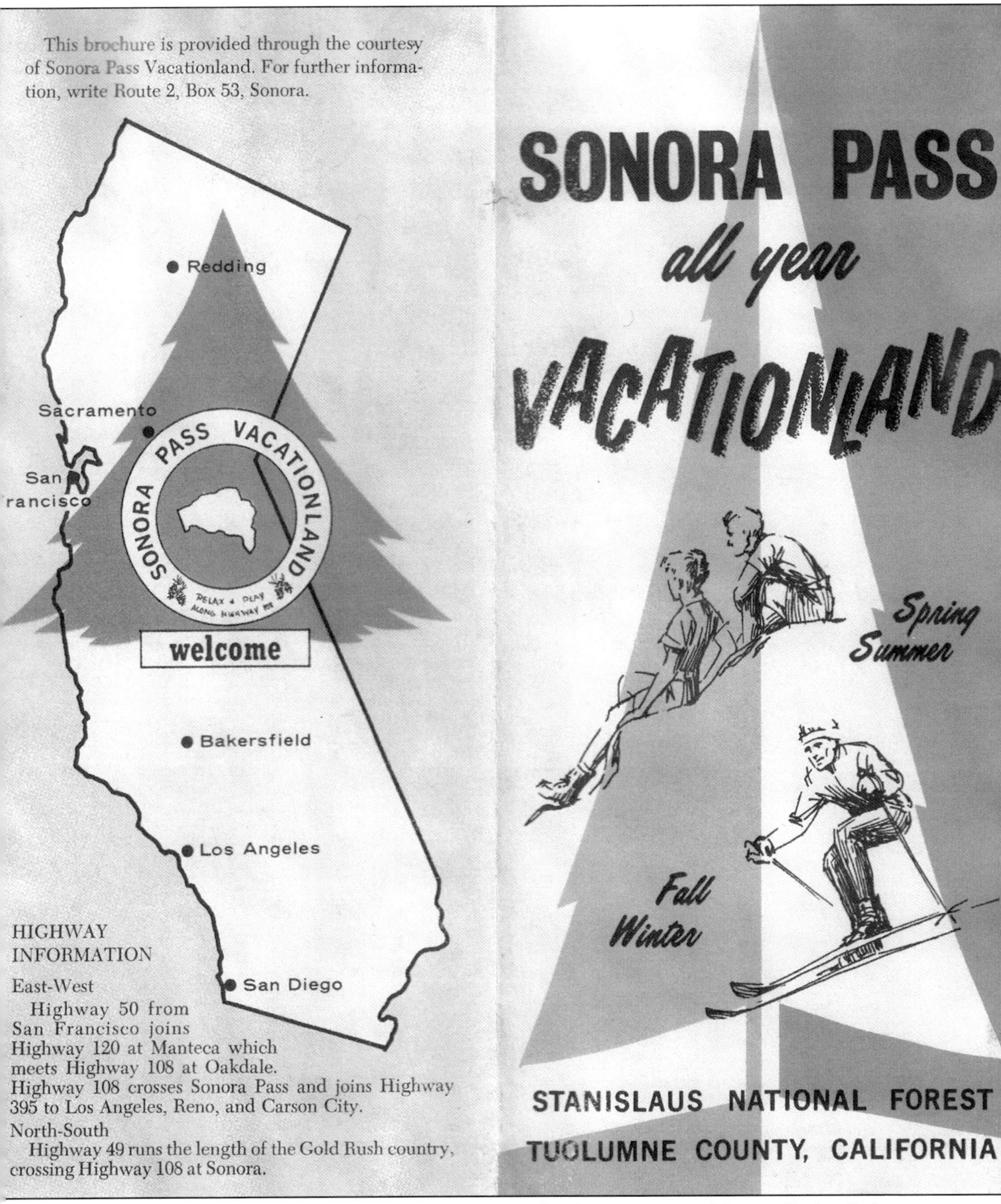

In 1950, Earl Purdy joined the Sonora Pass Vacationland organization. He saw Dodge Ridge as a vital player in the recreational tourism growth plus employment opportunities for Tuolumne County. His efforts enhanced and helped grow many businesses, such as restaurants, hotels, and shops.

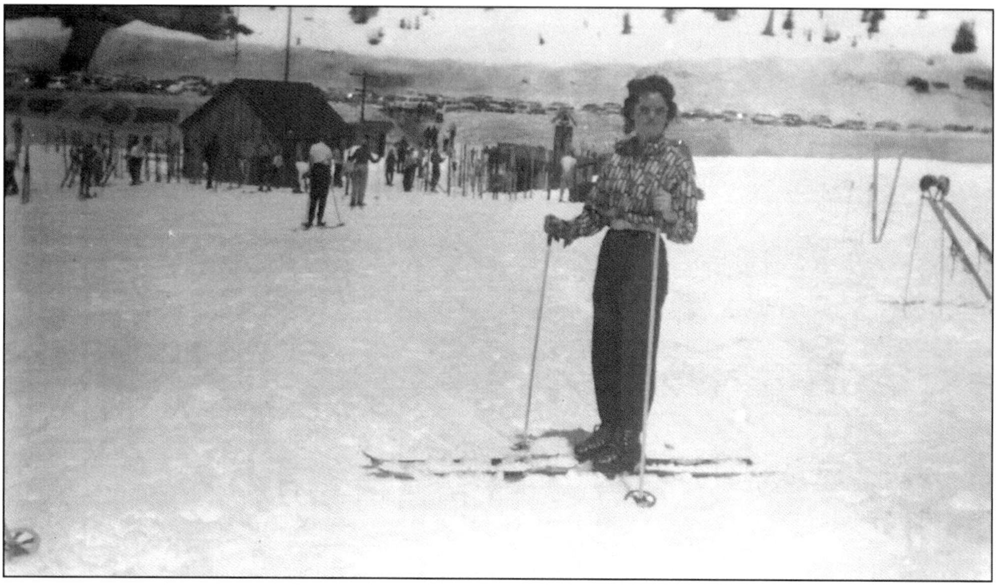

In 1951, Ruth Twining and her husband, Wilbur, moved to Pinecrest and built the Pinecrest Chalet, which welcomed guests such as youth groups, Boy Scouts, and church groups for many years. Ruth is the mother of Richard, Sally, and Chucker, who all grew up in Pinecrest, attended Pinecrest school, and learned to ski at Dodge Ridge. Their children and grandchildren are the third and fourth generations of skiers and racers. (Courtesy of the Twining family.)

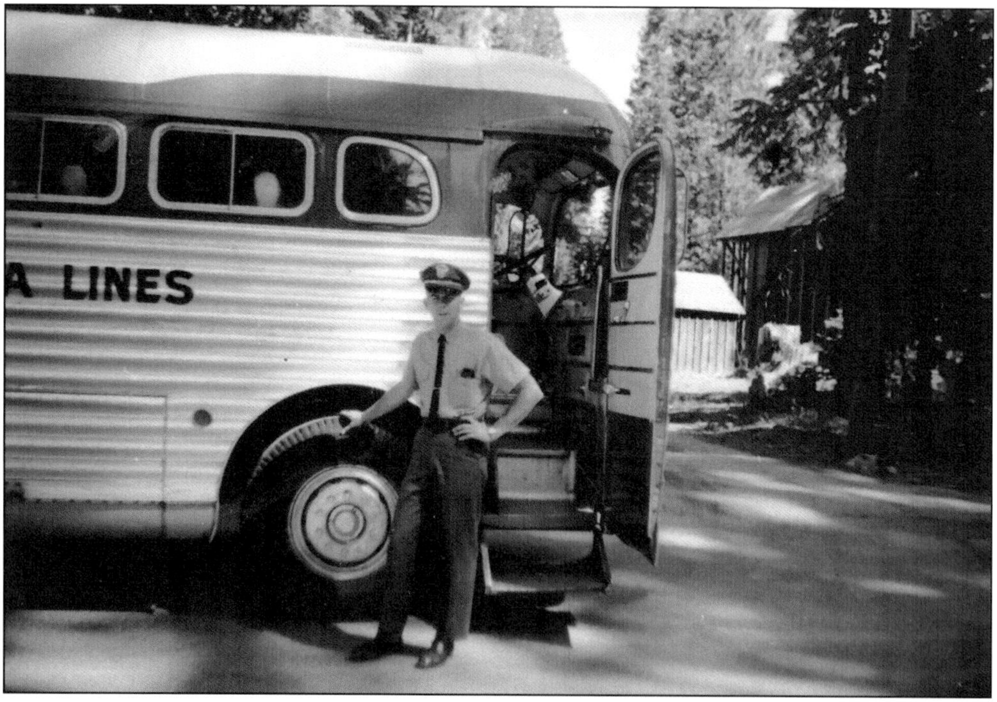

Richard Twining grew up in Pinecrest. He was responsible for shuttling skiers from the Bay Area to Dodge Ridge—a great service for both skiers and the resort. He was the owner of Scenic Hyway Tours in San Francisco and was very proud of his work. He was also one of the seven founders of the Pacific Bus Museum and its first president. (Courtesy of the Twining family.)

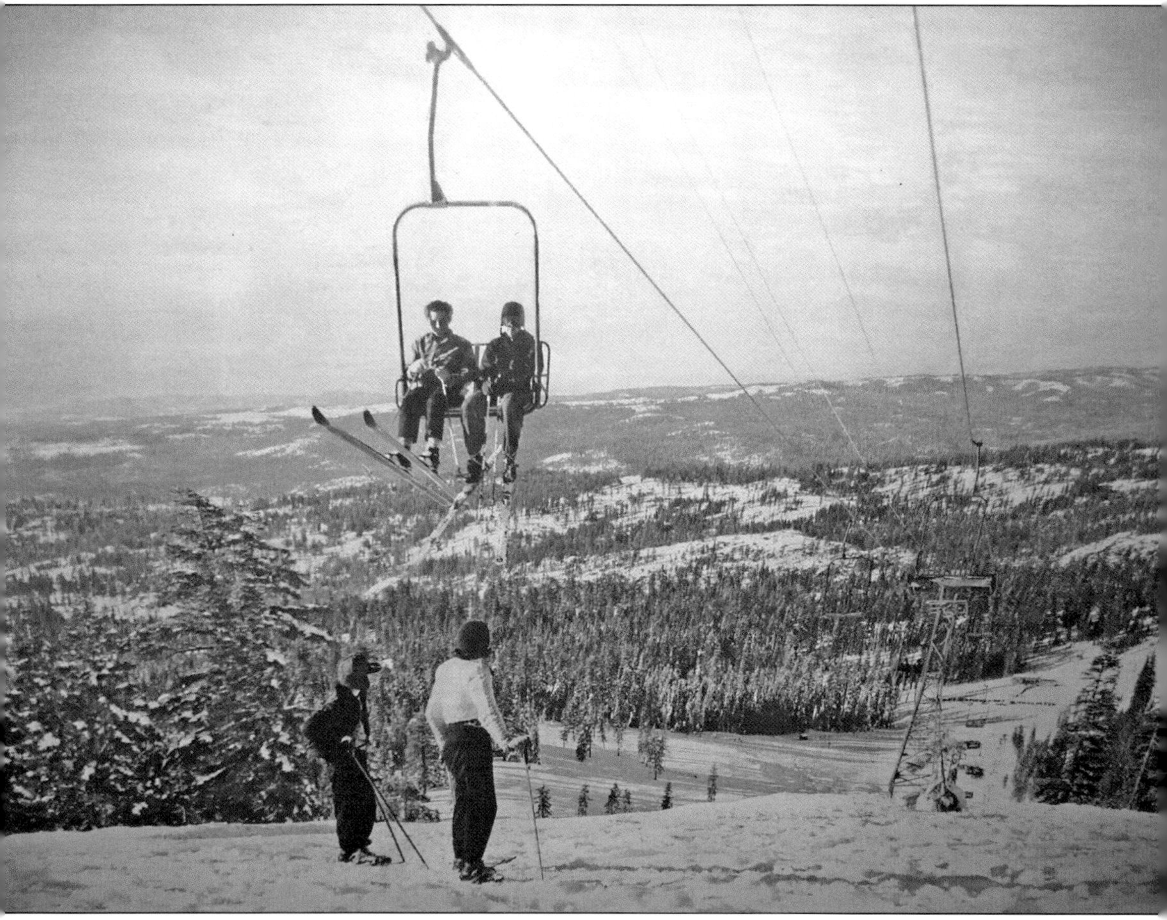

In this 1958 image are Richard Twining and his father, Wilbur Twining, riding the Heron Chair Three while Chucker Twining and his mother, Ruth Twining, wait for them to join in skiing down the run. The Twining family have been a part of Dodge Ridge since the early years as skiers, employees, and racers and are still at it.

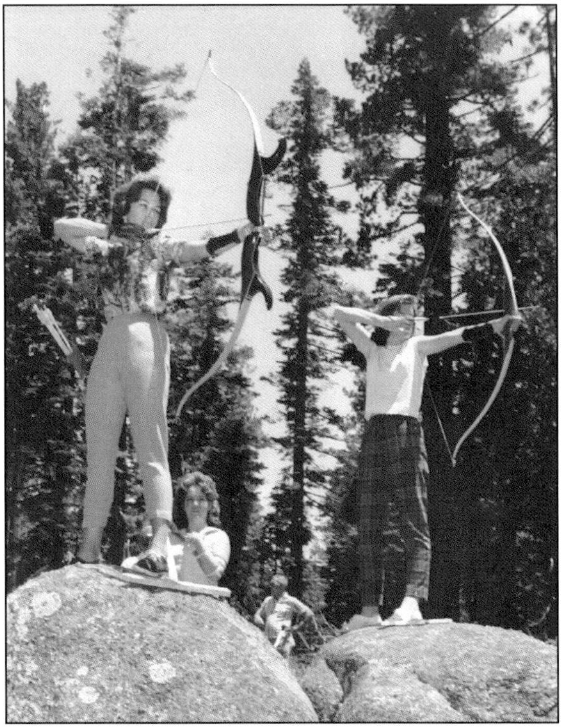

The Sierra Bowmen of Sonora, in conjunction with Sonora Pass Vacationland, Inc., sponsored approximately 700 bow hunters and field archers for the California State Championship Tournament held at Dodge Ridge. Competitors included numerous past champions for both women and men. The photograph below includes the Mountain House in the background. Originally owned by Stanford University, it is now owned by a private club that allows members to stay there when they come up to ski. There is no other lodging available at the resort.

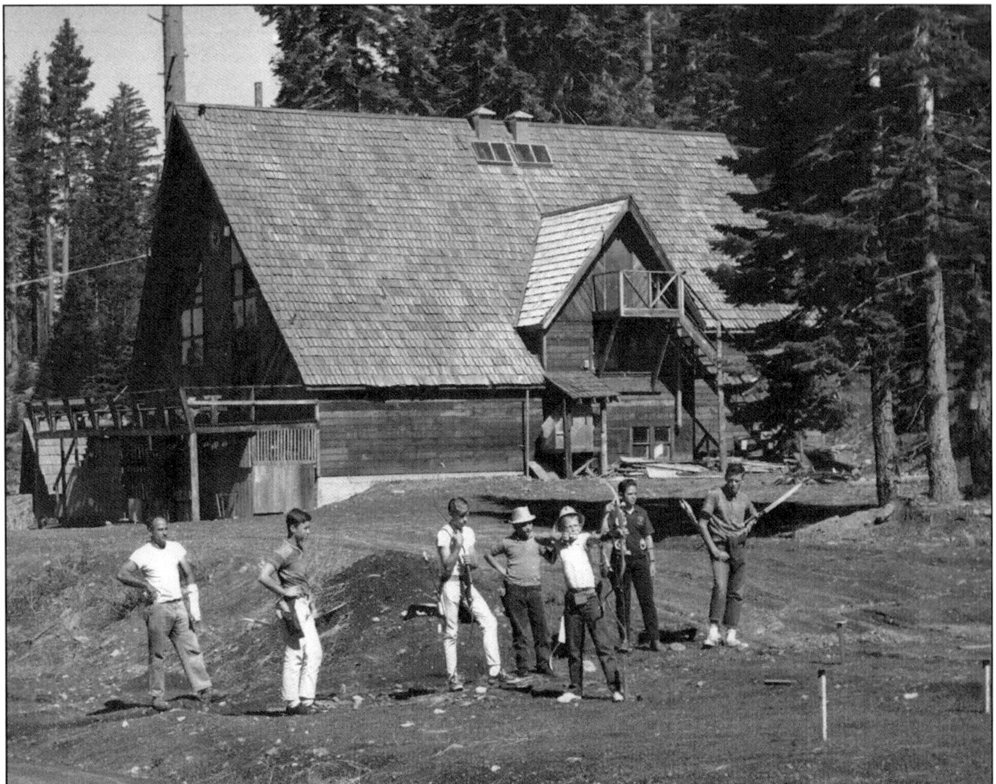

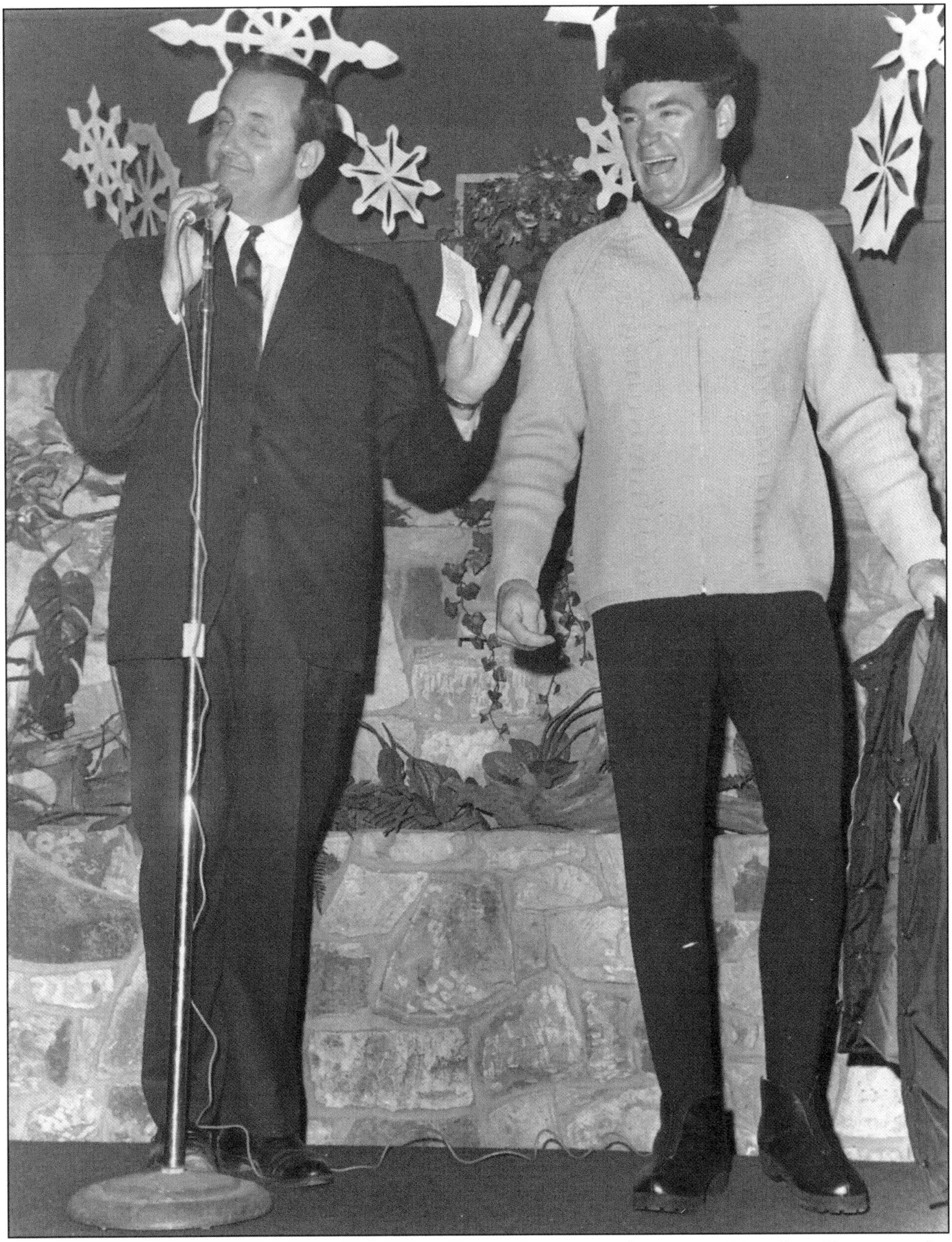

Dave McElhatton, on the left, was a beloved evening news anchor at KPIX in San Francisco for decades. He and his family had a cabin in Strawberry and were regulars at Dodge Ridge. He loved being the master of ceremonies for the Dodge Ridge Social Club, helping to raise funds for the Dodge Ridge Junior Race Team. He was in the first class of inductees into the Bay Area Hall of Fame.

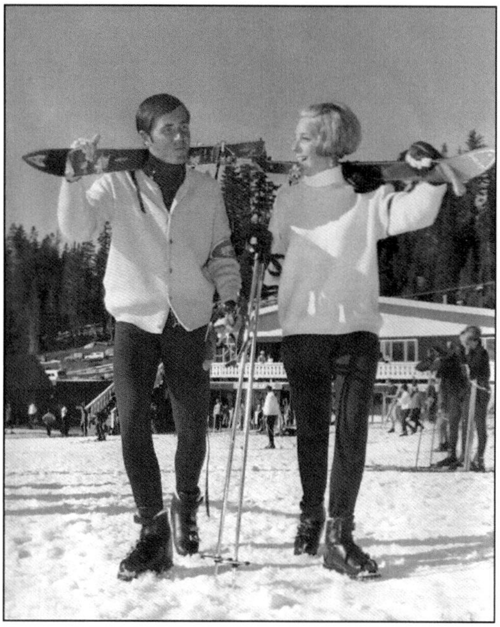

In 1968, the Harms and the Lindstrom families each went skiing on New Year's Eve day. Don Harms was on ski patrol waiting at Chair Five when he spotted Sally Lindstrom at the front of the line. He quickly yelled, "Single!" and hopped into the chair next to Sally. Their children and grandchildren still ski the mountain. One grandchild is a well-known racer, Danny Kelsay. (Courtesy of the Harms family.)

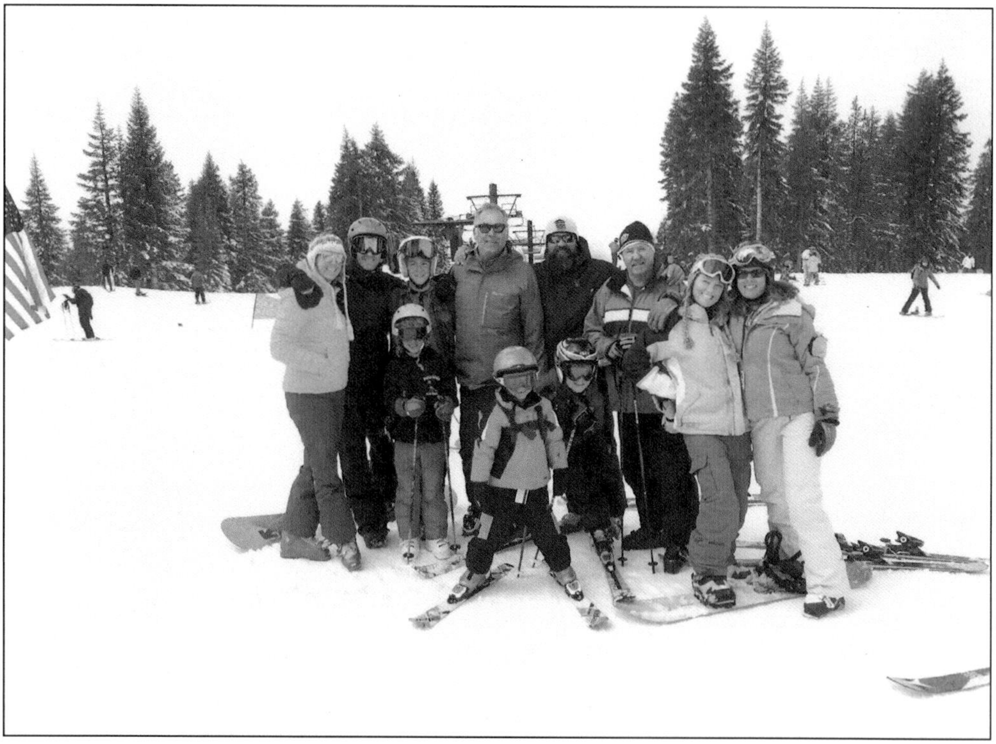

Four generations of the Harms-Lindstrom family have played a role at Dodge Ridge. From left to right, the adults are Melissa and Ryan Vallelunga, Danny Kelsay, Jeff Lindstrom, Adam Harms, Don Harms, Felicia Harms, and Jacki Lindstrom, and the kids in front are Jacee Vallelunga, Casey Vallelunga, and Beni Harms—all avid skiers and regulars at Dodge Ridge. Some have worked there, and some still work there, which is typical of Dodge Ridge families. (Courtesy of the Harms family.)

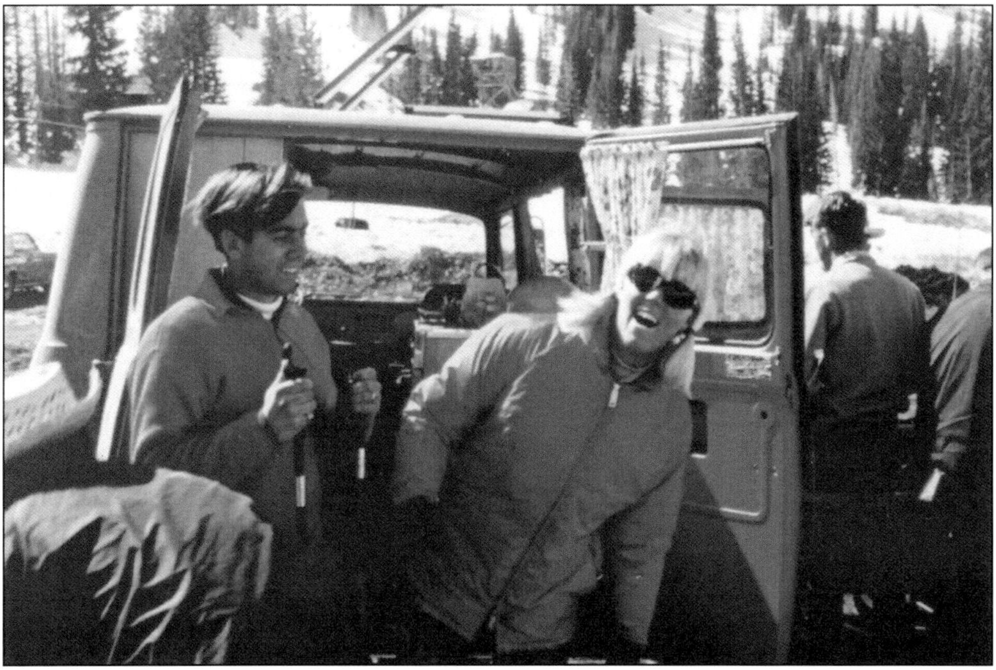

Rick Saletta and Sally Twining are seen here in 1966. They were both frequently at Dodge Ridge and traveled regularly to other resorts. Sally caught the eye of a representative for Bonne Bell, who signed her as a Bonne Bell girl, which resulted in her life-size picture being featured at ski resorts—one of the more unique industry jobs for a young girl. (Courtesy of Tom McCollum.)

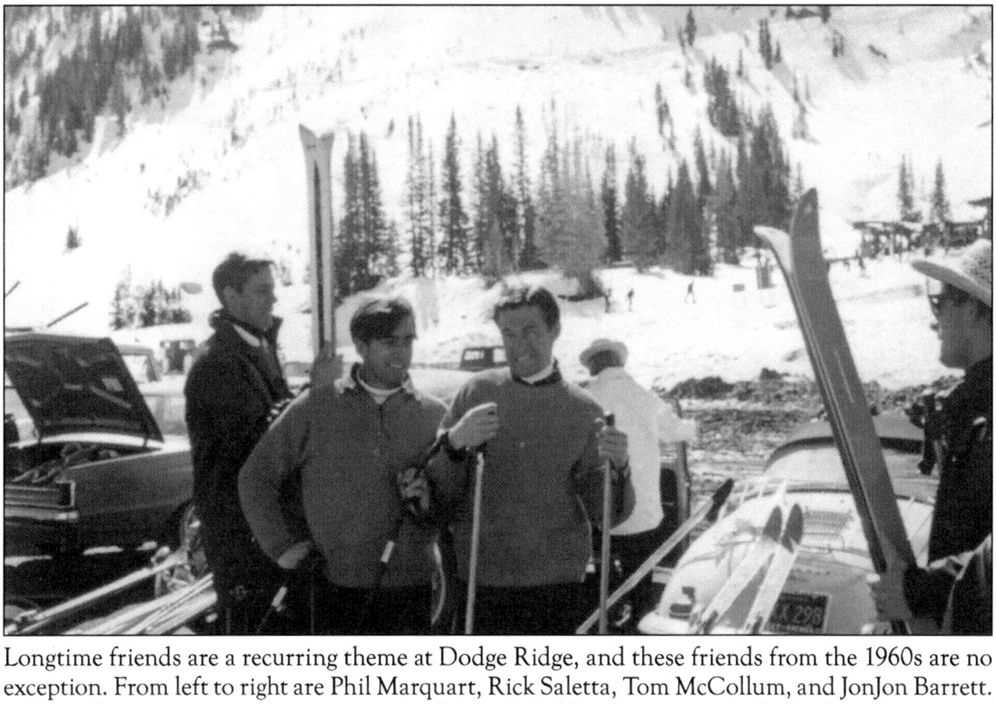

Longtime friends are a recurring theme at Dodge Ridge, and these friends from the 1960s are no exception. From left to right are Phil Marquart, Rick Saletta, Tom McCollum, and JonJon Barrett. Some still participate in the reunion of old friends held every year at Dodge Ridge. (Courtesy of Tom McCollum.)

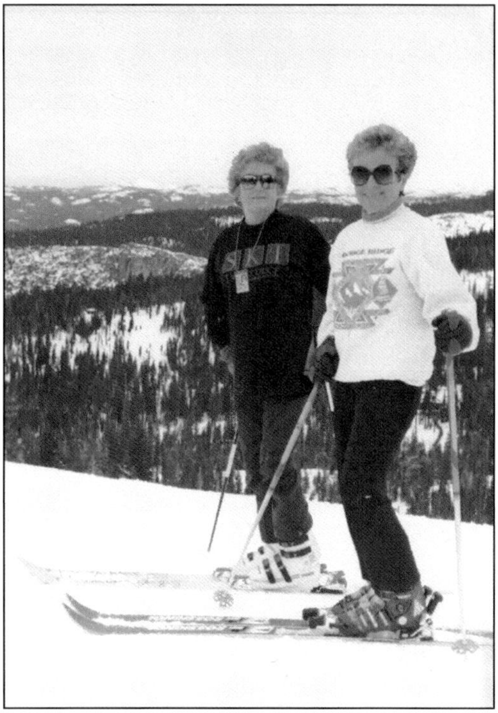

Longtime friends and original Dodge Ridge skiers Leslie Rolfe (left) and Carol Cochran (right) were avid skiers and worked at the resort part-time. They were often in the parking lot, acquainting guests with the resort. The most common question upon arrival was "Where is the bathroom?" They knew where all the bottles were buried near Chair Five back in the day. Cochran still has the sweatshirt she is wearing here. (Courtesy of Carol Cochran.)

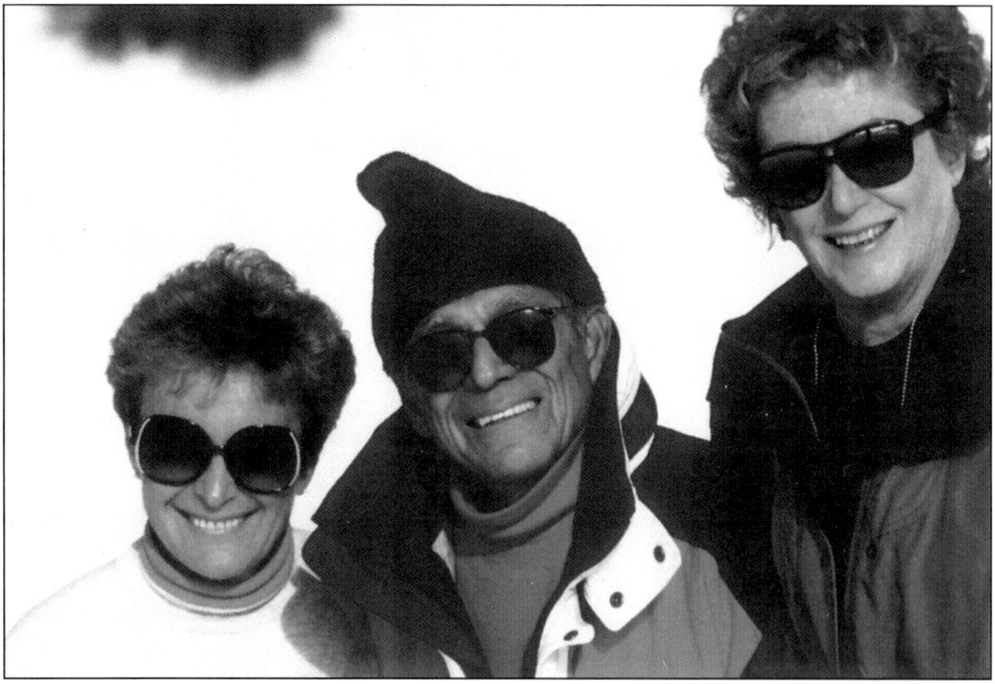

These three have been skiing together for decades, since Chair Five was as far as one could go. From left to right are Carol McDonald Cochran, Frank Borrego, and Leslie Rolfe. Rolfe is a well-known artist who also worked in the sports shop at Dodge Ridge. Cochran has been skiing at Dodge Ridge since shortly after it opened. Borrego taught business and English at Sonora High School. (Courtesy of Carol Cochran.)

Dinner Meeting at Sneed's Strawberry Inn 7 P.M. Dec. 15

Dodge Ridge SKI CLUB

SITZMARKS

Free feed. Donations will be for Jr. Race Team.

DECEMBER 1962

ATTENTION ALL D.R.S.C. MEMBERS: SHAPE UP FOR HANGOVER RACE ON NEW YEAR'S DAY!!

Race chairman, Hank Overacker, suggests all interested members get together and set up a fairly open slalom on the gentle slopes between the old and new platter pull lifts, and start practicing. All age groups are urged to participate. Meanwhile, Hank will continue training for New Year's eve. He says there is more to this elbow bending business than meets the eye! It's not easy to stay up half the night, smoke up a storm, try to keep up with THOSE drinking skiers, then face a brisk beautiful day and set up the course for the famous HANGOVER RACE. This takes DRIVE. O.K. Hank, back to your stool for more training.

OCTOBER DINNER MEETING SMASHING SUCCESS

Following a LONG social hour at Long Barn Lodge, dinner, prepared by Chauncey Rometti, was termed completely GREAT. Chauncey's ravioli and chicken were a gourmet's delight.

President Richard Holman opened the meeting with this most apropos remark, "Well, my stretch pants don't fit very well this year". (You aren't alone, my friend.) Club officers were introduced. They include Rod Brezina, vice-president, Frank Borrego, secretary-treasurer, Hank Overacker, Race chairman, and editor of Sitzmarks, Carmen King.

Pat Rayner was given honorary membership for her work in printing this publication. It was nice seeing all our skiing buddies again. Everyone agreed, all we need is snow.

FASHION SHOW SCHEDULED FOR JANUARY 12TH

Come one, come all to the D.R.S.C. fashion show to be held January 12th, at the Elk's Hall in Sonora. Cocktails at 6:30. Dinner at 7:45. Admission: $2.85.

A complete selection of ski wear, featuring such names as Bogner, Meggi, Poreth and Magneheim, and many

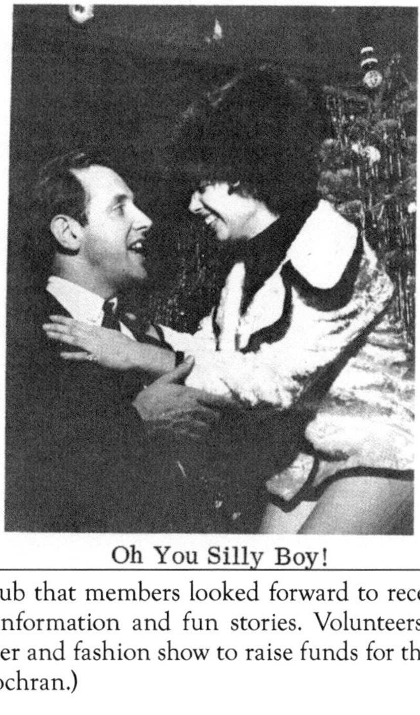

Oh You Silly Boy!

Sitzmarks was a newsletter written by the ski club that members looked forward to receiving in their mailboxes. It contained member event information and fun stories. Volunteers rotated positions every year and held their annual dinner and fashion show to raise funds for the Dodge Ridge Junior Race Team. (Courtesy of Carol Cochran.)

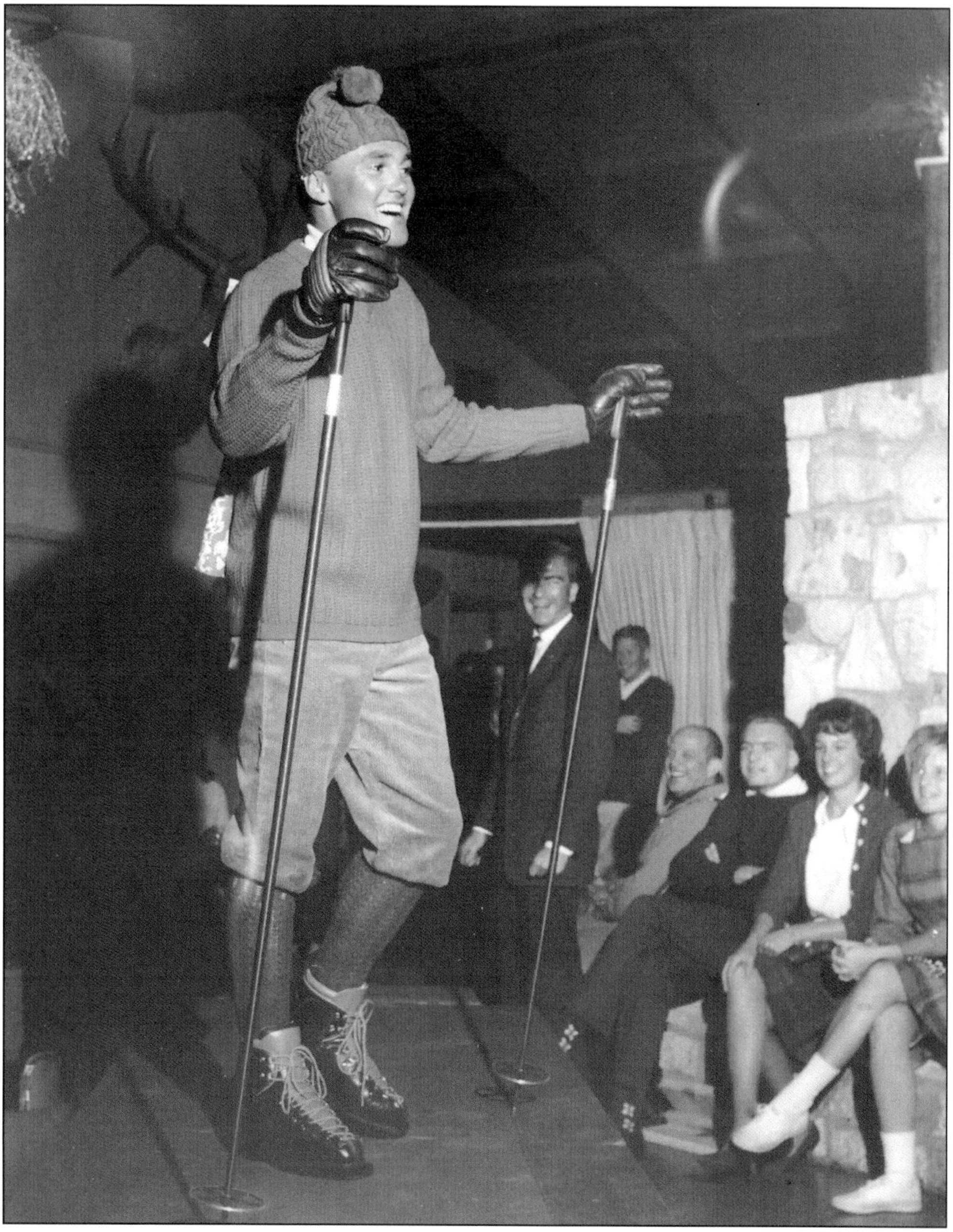

Daryl Hamerton models the latest ski fashions at the Dodge Ridge Ski Club annual fashion show fund-raiser. (Courtesy of Calin Smith.)

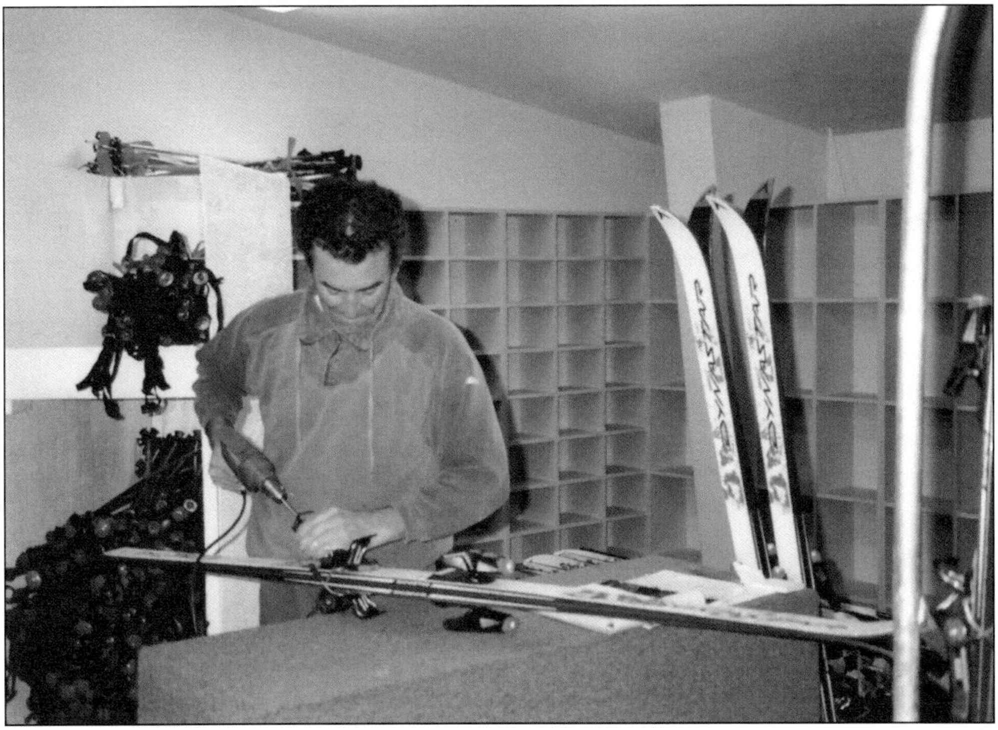

Ernie Rinna, a longtime Pinecrest local, played a crucial role in both managing and actively working in the rental department and ski shop. He was essential in getting equipment ready and in the hands of guests and keeping the equipment maintained throughout the season.

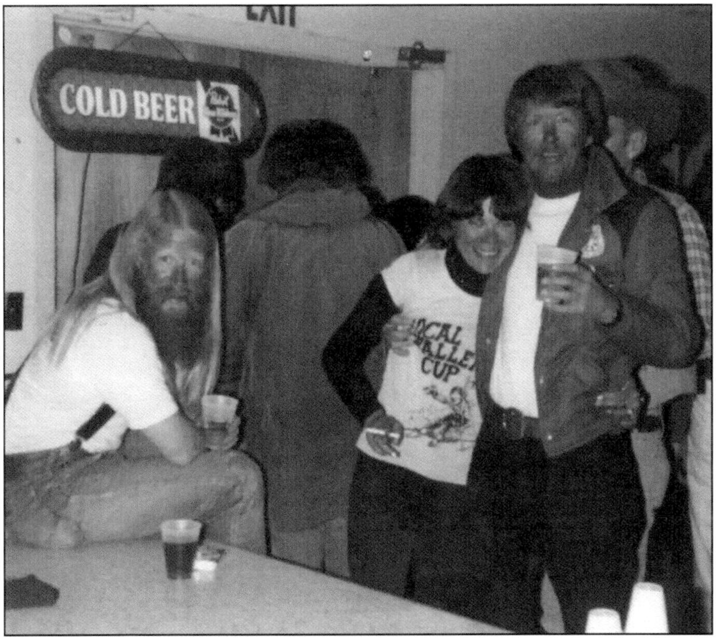

Hanging out in 1978 from left to right are locals Jeff Epps, known to his friends as "Effy Jepps," and Sally and Rich Davis, owners of the sports shop at Pinecrest Lake. Their son Mike now manages the store. Epps was a fixture on the slopes. It is another generational family story of friends who grew up together, skied together, and lived in the area their entire lives. (Courtesy of Mike Davis.)

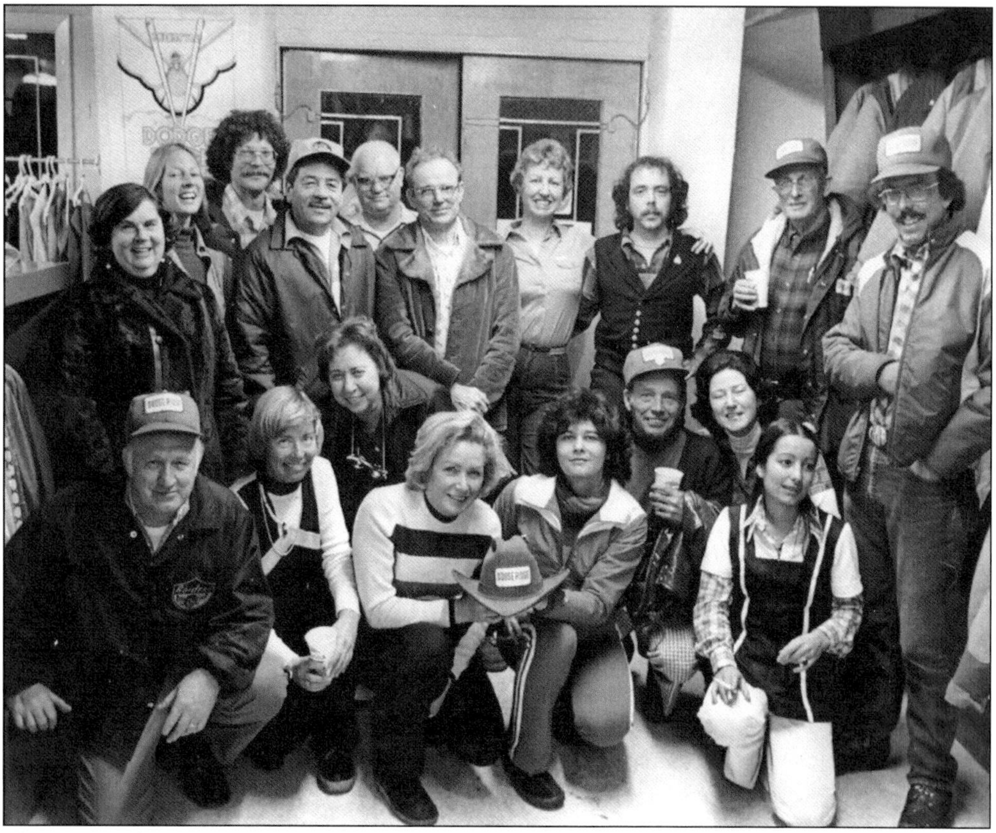

This is the blending of the Earl Purdy era with the coming Helm era, with staff from the loft operations, maintenance, and cafeteria. Frank Helm, standing in front at far right, spent a year learning every aspect of the resort. Judy Helm is second from the left in the first row. Carl Williams is on the right behind Helm. Without Williams, there would be no road into the resort.

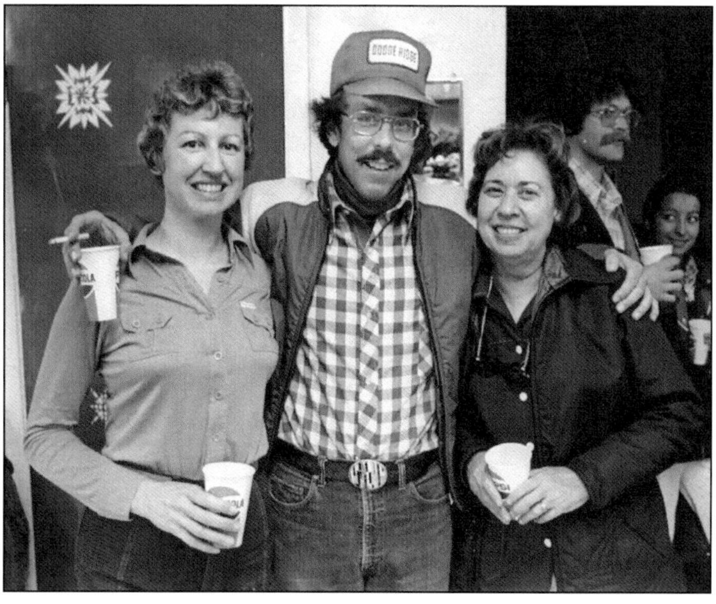

While learning the ropes, it was clear that the kitchen crew was a key part of the team at Dodge Ridge. From left to right are Maxine Waldo, Frank Helm, and Gwen Street, who managed the café crew. Street had absolutely no patience with anyone who sat on the tables that were meant for eating.

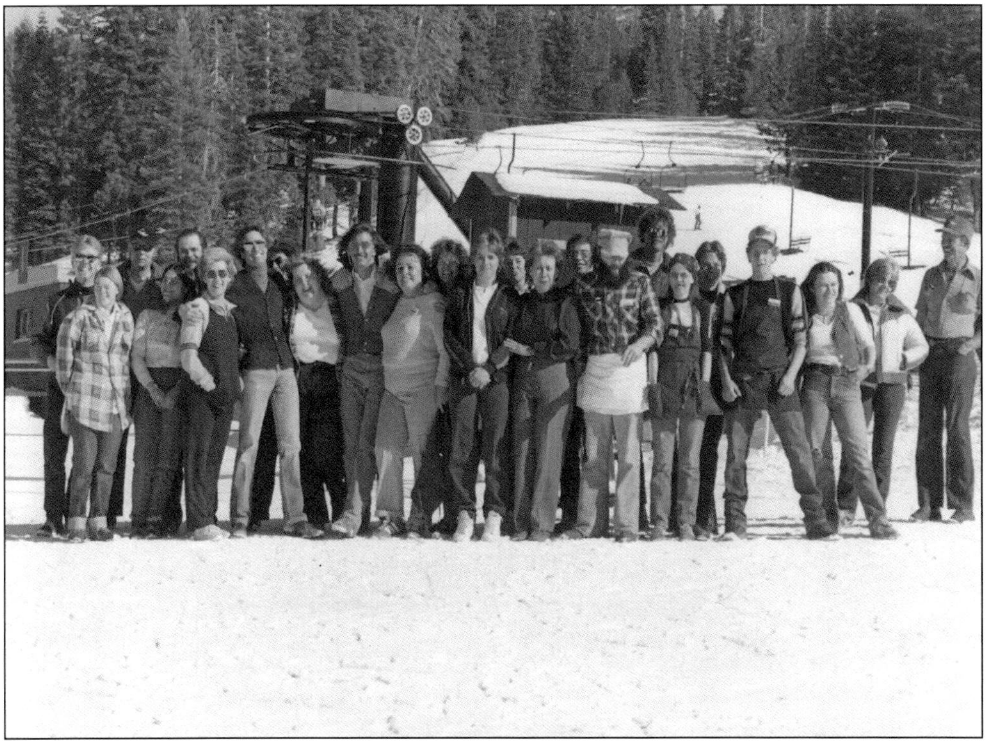

Shown here are the cafeteria crew from the mid-1970s. They had to be prepared to turn on a dime and cook for the masses when it snowed and figure out how to deal with slower and unpredictable days. They could jump in where needed at any given time. The team was diverse and happy to be working in a fun environment and appreciated by the owners.

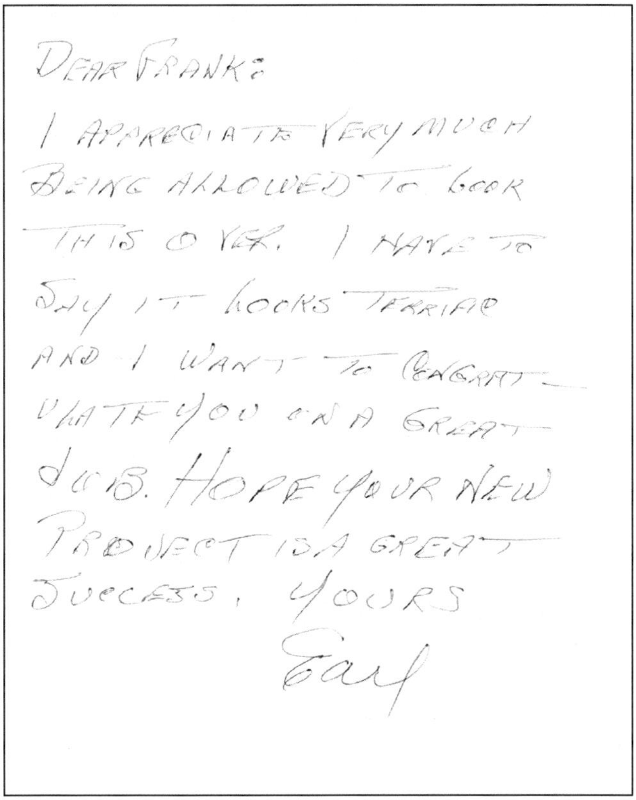

DEAR FRANK:
I APPRECIATE VERY MUCH
BEING ALLOWED TO LOOK
THIS OVER. I HAVE TO
SAY IT LOOKS TERRIFIC
AND I WANT TO CONGRAT-
ULATE YOU ON A GREAT
JOB. HOPE YOUR NEW
PROJECT IS A GREAT
SUCCESS. YOURS
Earl

Frank Helm made an official offer to purchase Dodge Ridge. Earl Purdy responded with this handwritten note confirming his acceptance and congratulations. It reads, "Dear Frank, I appreciate very much being allowed to look this over. I have to say it looks terrific and I want to congratulate you on a great job. Hope your new project is a great success. Yours, Earl."

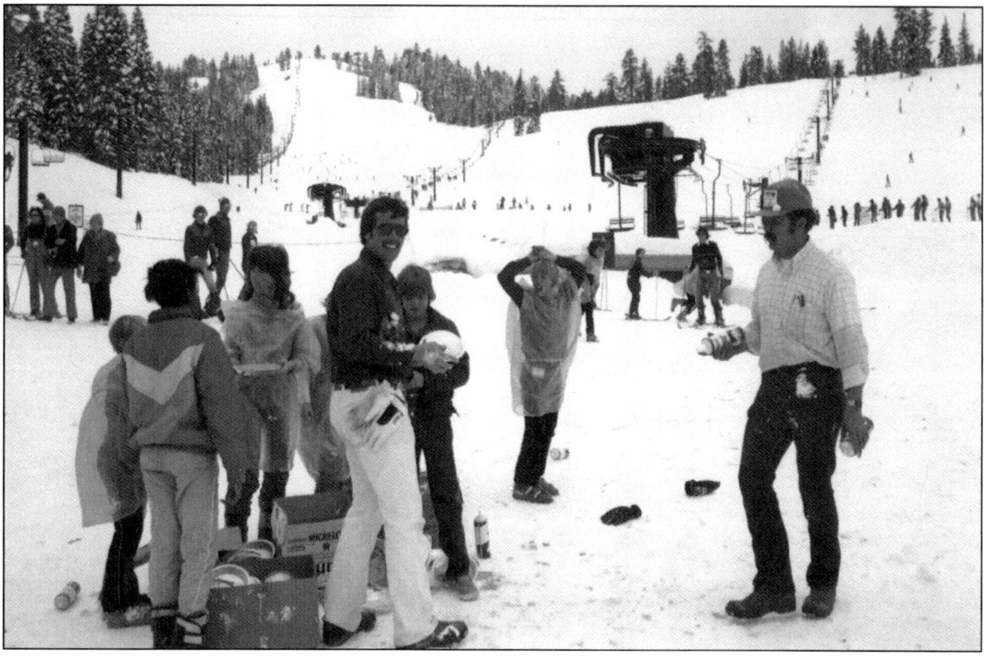

Rick Flint, facing the camera with a pie in his hands, was the general manager and head of spring shenanigans from 1981 to 1987. He was known for his strong business skills and for promoting camaraderie amongst the employees through fun activities, such as his progressive dinners and pie-throwing fun in the snow, shown here.

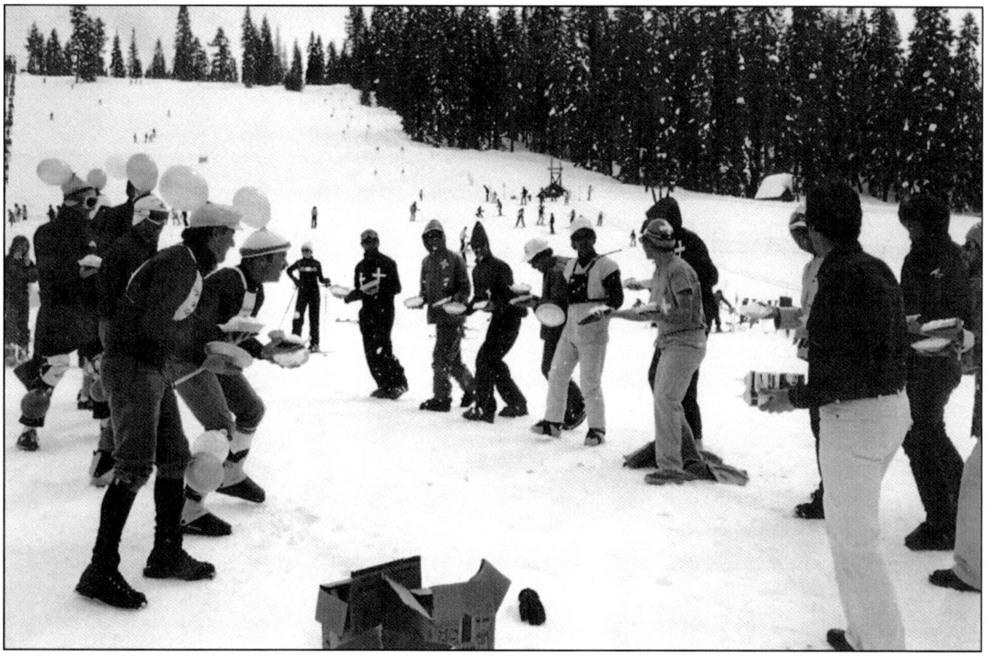

Part of the fun of the spring events was not only the camaraderie but also the chance to compete against fellow employees. Ski patrol versus ski instructor whip-cream pie toss was a fun way to show who was better in a competition—or who wore it better. Guests loved participating and seeing the employees join in on the fun.

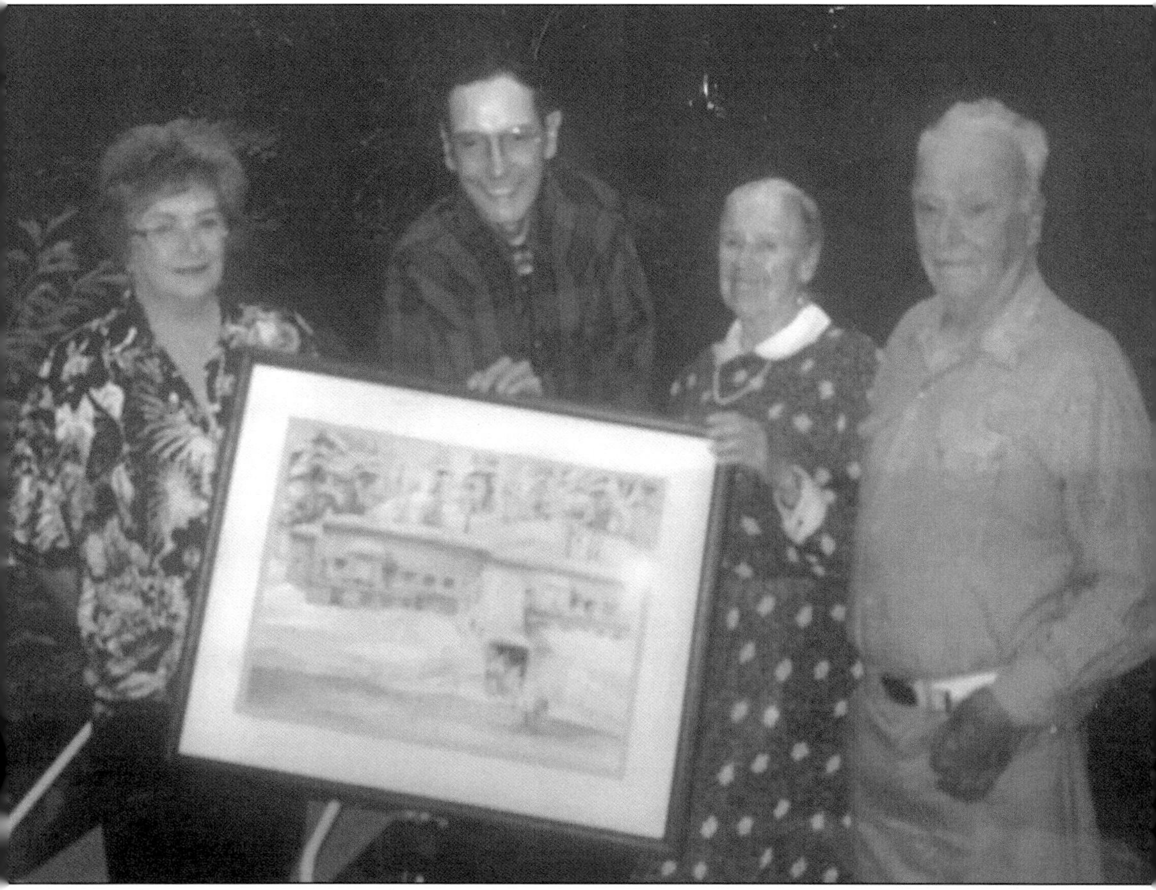

From left to right are renowned artist Leslie Rolf, George Purdy, and Edith and Gordon Morrison in the mid-1990s at the Helm family home. They are holding Leslie's gift, which is a watercolor painting of the original lodge. The Morrisons were investors with Early Purdy. George was Earl's son. Leslie, an excellent skier, worked part-time at Dodge Ridge. (Courtesy of the Helm family.)

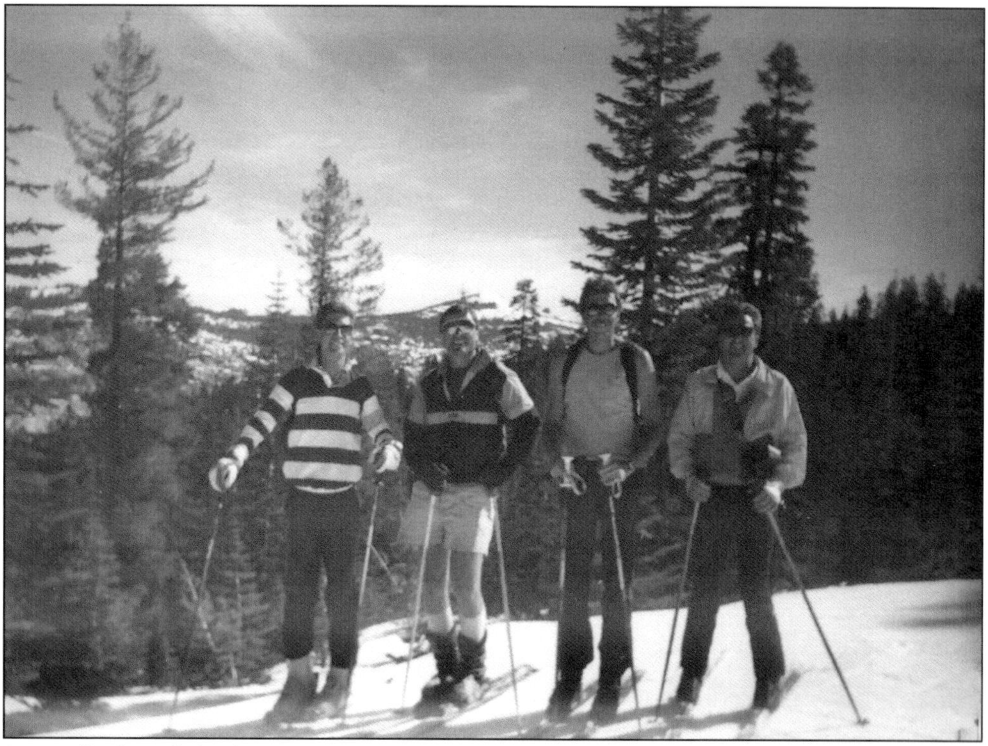

Dave Alley literally built the expansion portion of the resort. He had a concrete background, so he did the foundation for the Waystation and part of the old lodge. He felled trees and worked with Preston Hough doing snow surveys and laying out the runs for Chairs Seven and Eight. He skied the dickens out of them prior to opening and knows every square inch. Pictured from left to right are Paul Mundy, Preston Hough, Dave Alley, and Dave Blank.

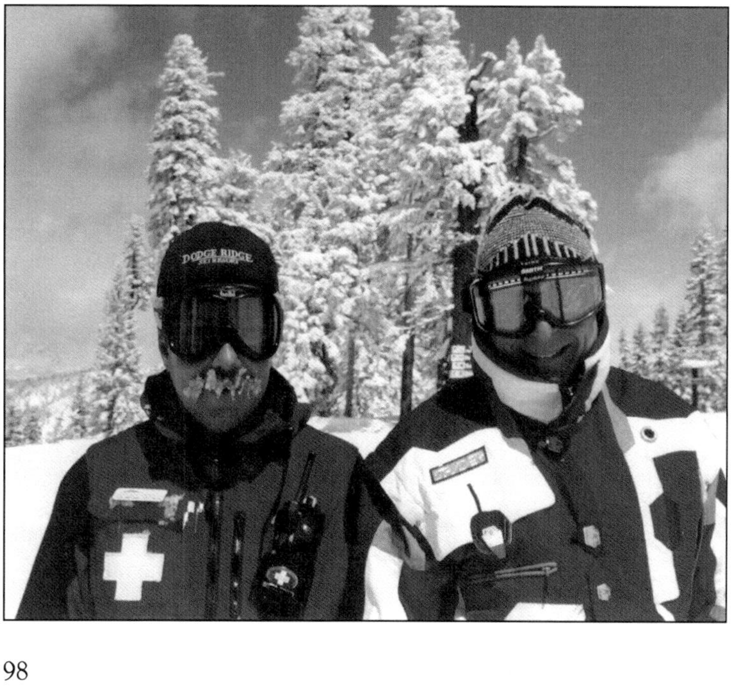

Dave Alley (left) quickly rose through the ranks at Dodge Ridge. He knows how to ski the mountain on any given day. Buz Carrade (right) and Frank Helm grew up together. The master expansion plan that significantly increased the size of the resort would not have been possible without input from Alley and Carrade.

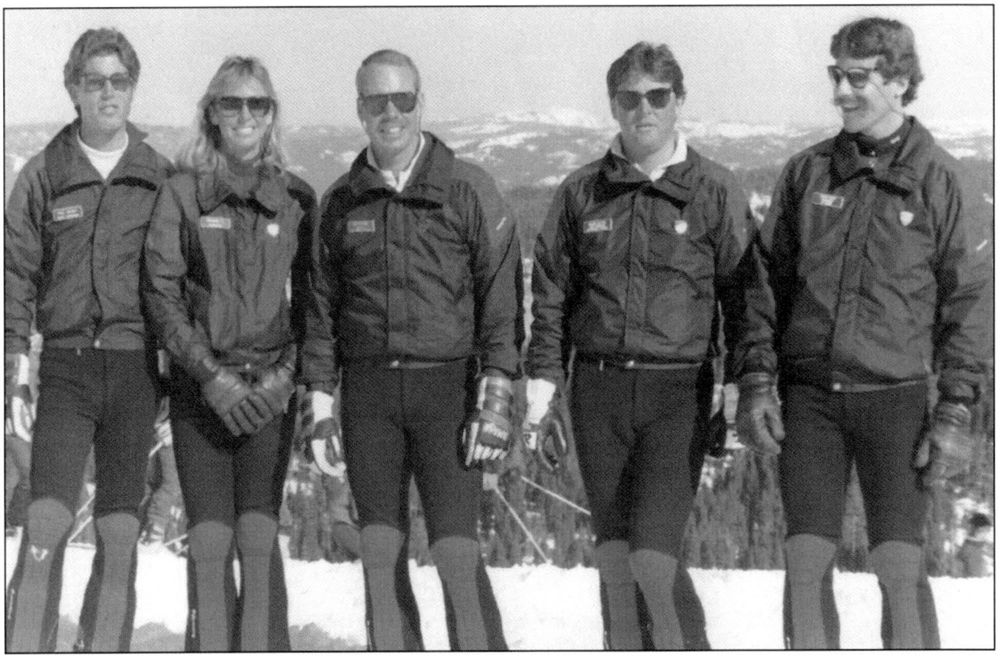

From left to right in this 1981 image are Paul Mundy, children's ski school supervisor; Rhonda Sancibrian, adult ski school supervisor; Jon Mahanna, ski school supervisor; Devon Salter, assistant ski school director; and Brian Rush, adult ski school supervisor, all sporting the latest Descente ski pants at the top of Chair Three. (Courtesy of the Mundy family archives.)

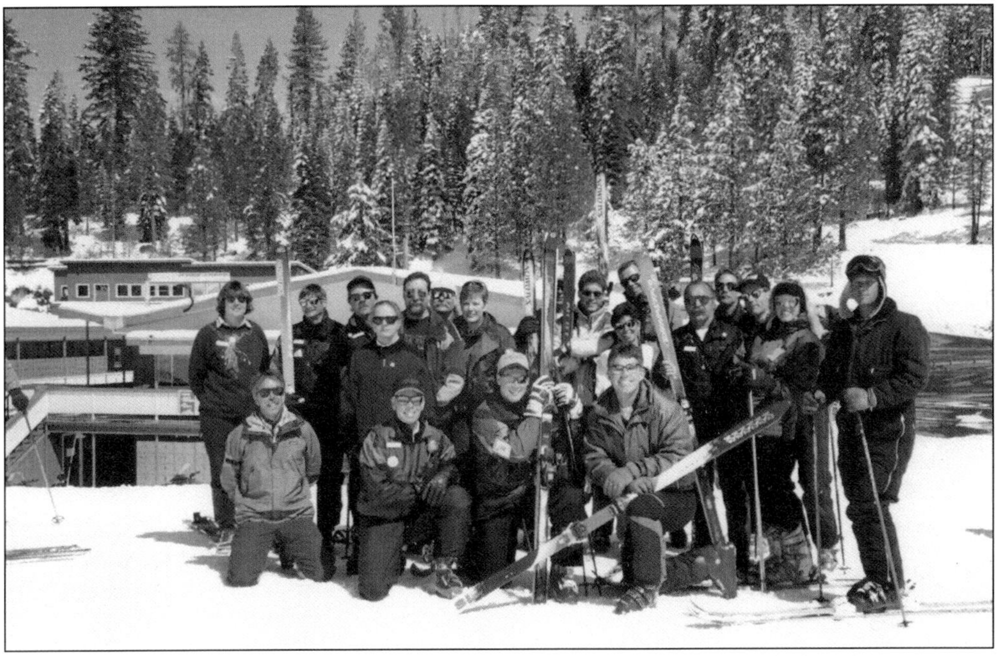

Staff photographs were popular. This one shows the management team, including ski instructors, the ski patrol, lift operations, maintenance, and sales staff—the core of what makes Dodge Ridge run behind the scenes. They are the heart of soul of the operation and lend their knowledge and expertise to every one of their staff.

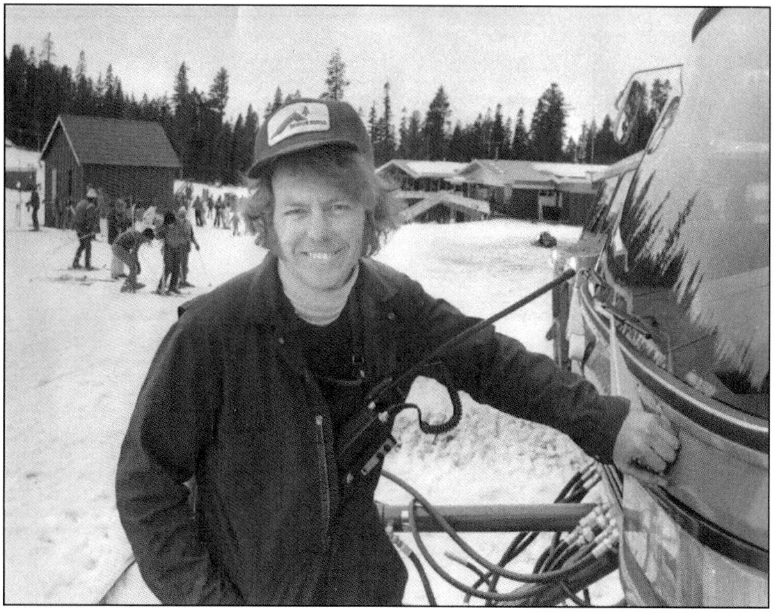

This is Steve Locke, who worked in lift engineering in the 1980s. He was the lead engineer who built the new Yon Chair Three, the first new lift under Frank Helm after he took over Dodge Ridge.

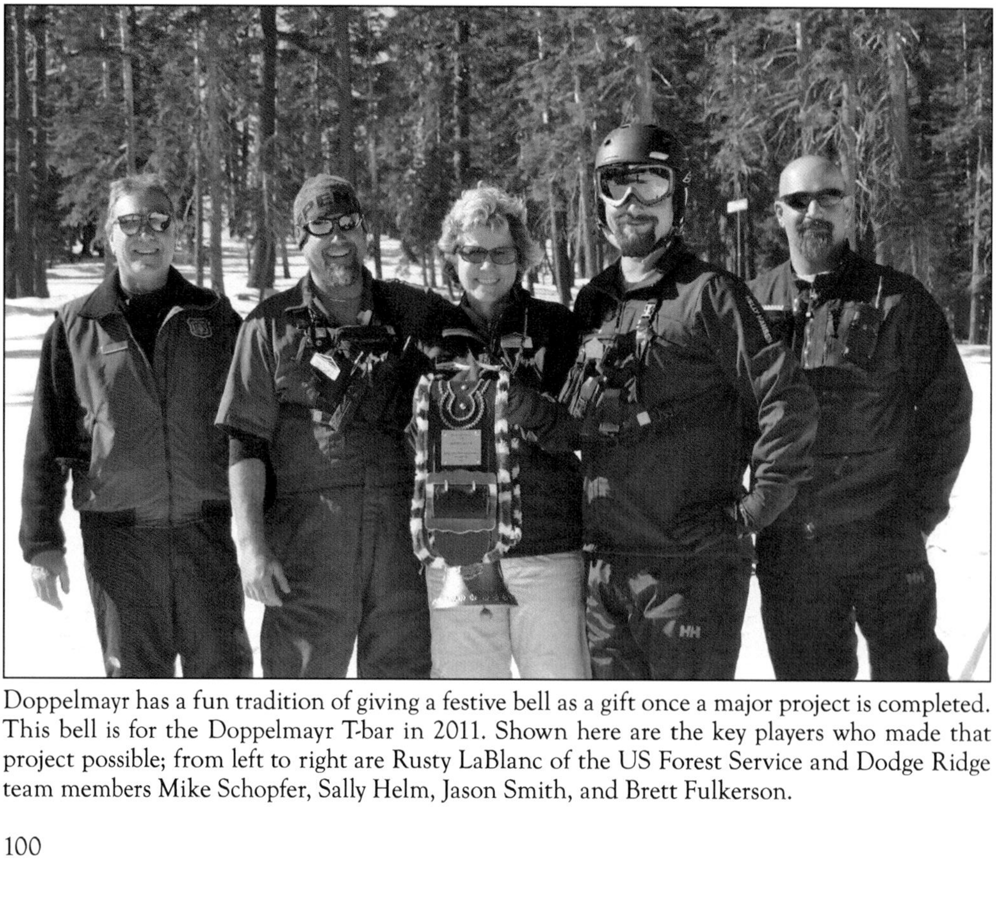

Doppelmayr has a fun tradition of giving a festive bell as a gift once a major project is completed. This bell is for the Doppelmayr T-bar in 2011. Shown here are the key players who made that project possible; from left to right are Rusty LaBlanc of the US Forest Service and Dodge Ridge team members Mike Schopfer, Sally Helm, Jason Smith, and Brett Fulkerson.

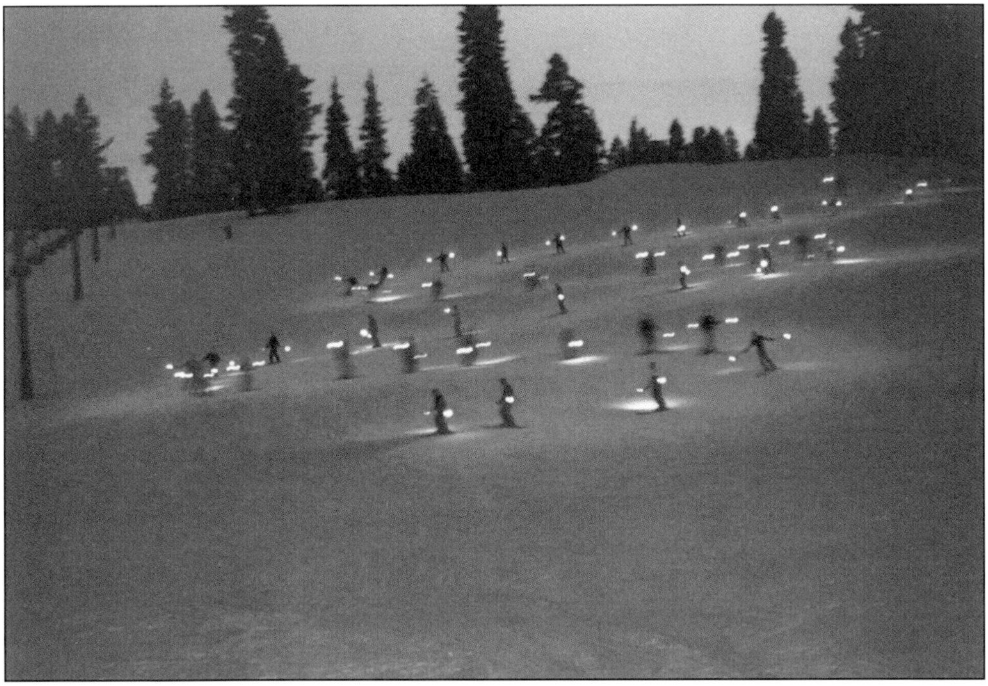

A torchlight parade with employees carrying flares kicks off the start of the New Year's Eve celebration. Once the torches were snuffed in the snow, guests were treated to a fireworks display. There was also a torchlight parade during the family-fun carnival, usually held the third week of January.

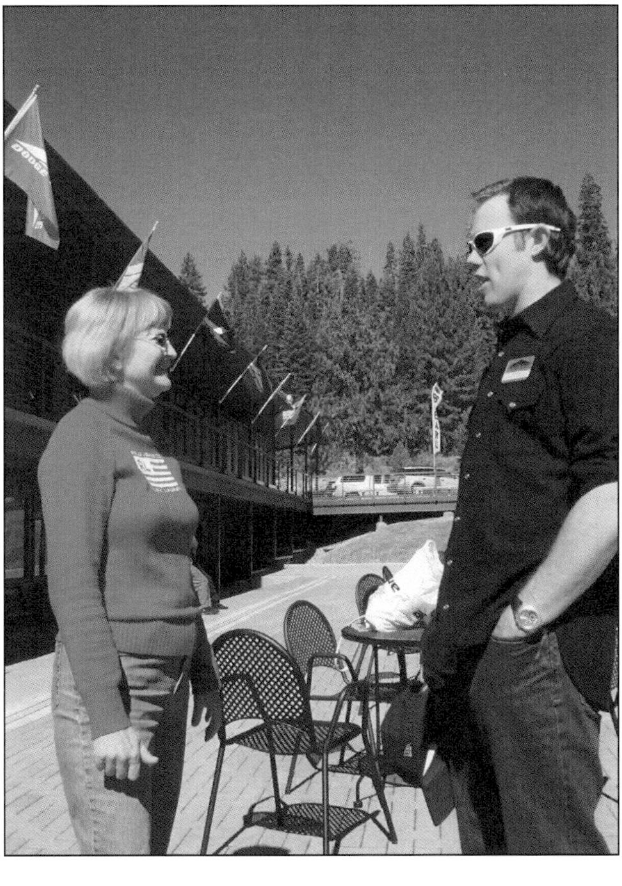

Jennifer Rapp worked at Dodge Ridge in the front office as a ski hostess and in the ticket office at the top of the parking lot. Jennifer Rapp fulfilled her son Bobby Rapp's "If I don't return" wish of donating money to the Dodge Ridge Race Team so that someone in need could receive funds to participate on the race team. Shown here, Jennifer and snow sports director Corby Fisher chat about Bobby Rapp's posthumous gift to the Dodge Ridge Ski Team.

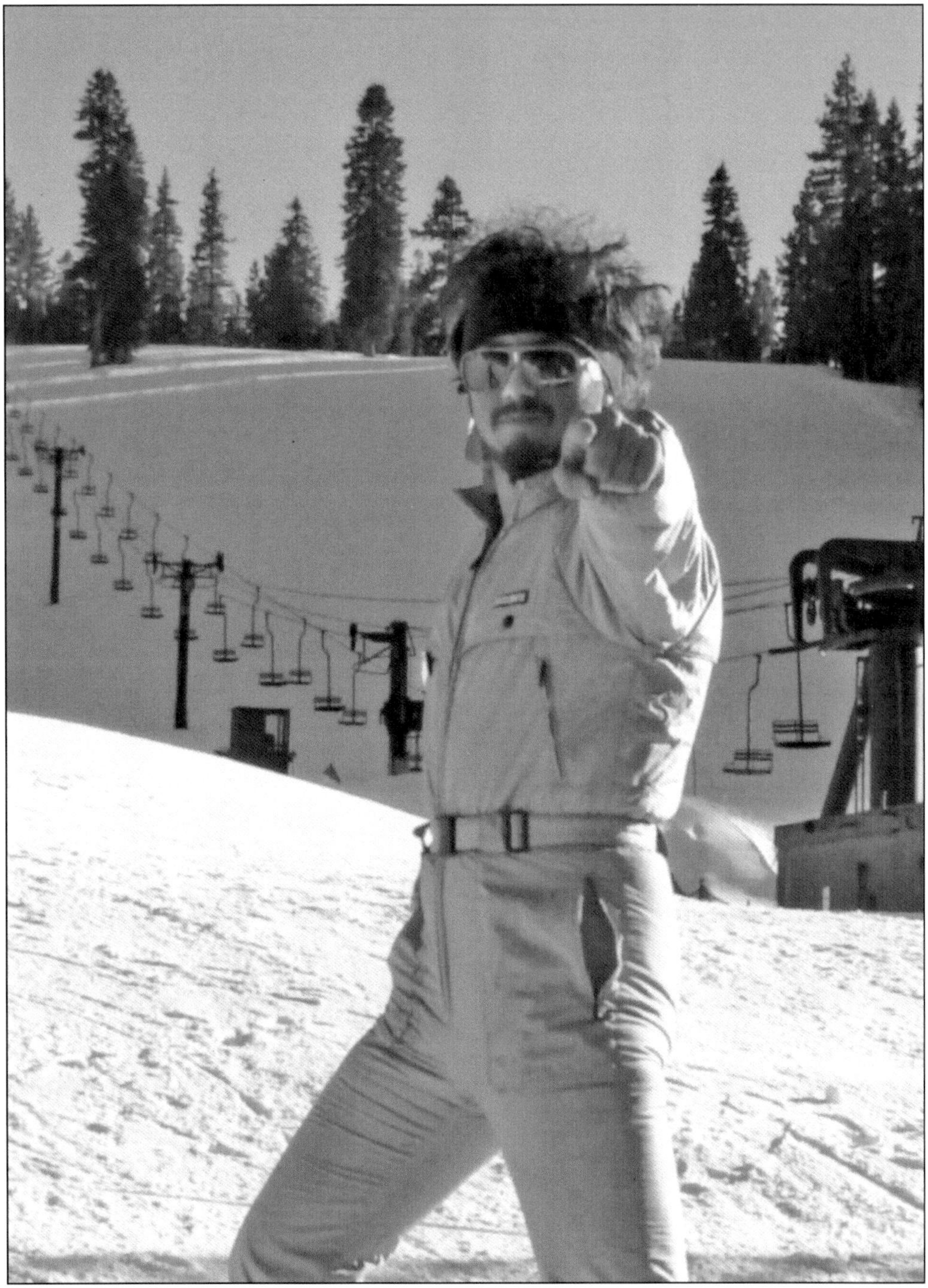

One of the most asked questions at Dodge Ridge is "Where is Bobby Mackey?" Mackey is a longtime employee, and as the retail and rentals manager, he is the go-to guy for anything in the store, equipment ordering, rentals and their maintenance, and general knowledge of the resort. Here, he is sporting the new zinc face protection products. He even will live model in the store window from time to time. This is his employee identification picture.

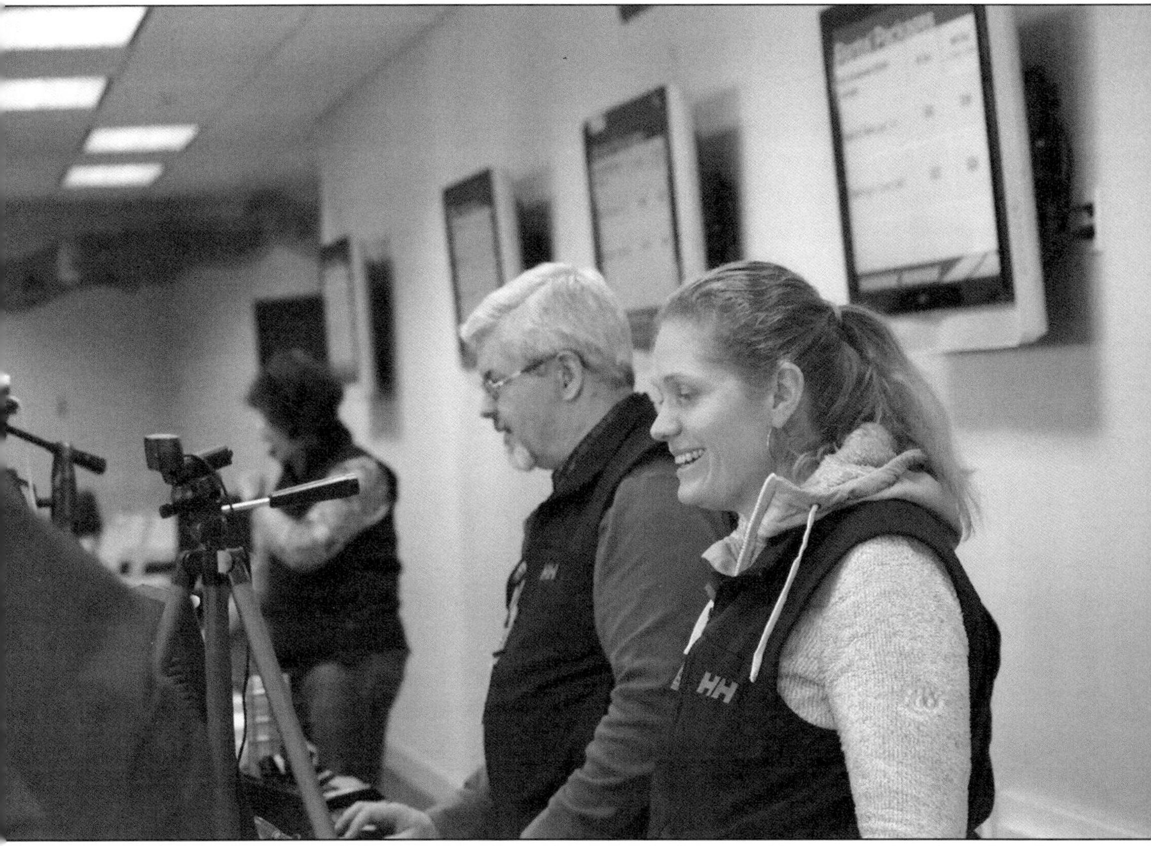

Katie Fromm, daughter of Frank and Sally Helm, attended the Pinecrest school, so her physical education classes were on the slopes every Friday. Dodge Ridge was her playground, and she was on the race team. Her fondest memories are skiing with friends, especially Chair Seven, playing in the trees, making snow forts, and snowball fights. She is now in senior management at Dodge Ridge.

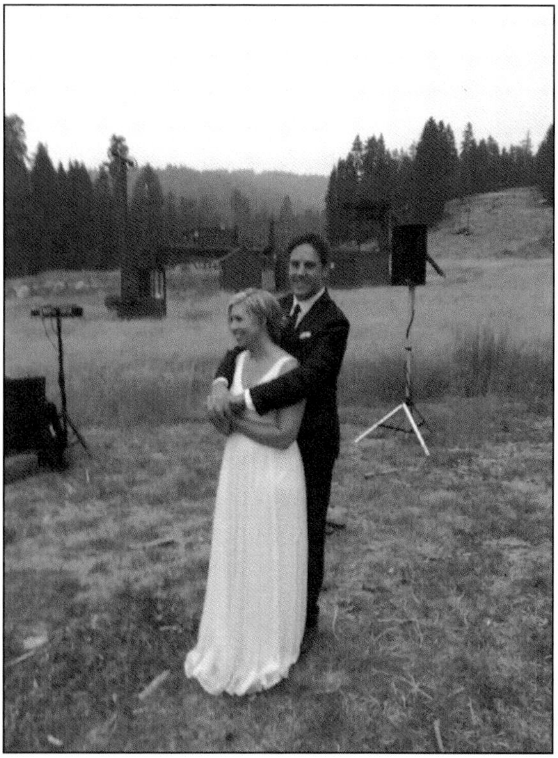

Over the years, there have been multiple generations who not only skied at Dodge Ridge but also worked there, met their spouses there, and made lifelong friends. Rebecca and Jeff Hauff are an example of this. Jeff was the marketing manager, and Rebecca was the director of events and bar manager. She planned their wedding on the hill above the Creekside Lodge. (Courtesy of the Hauff family.)

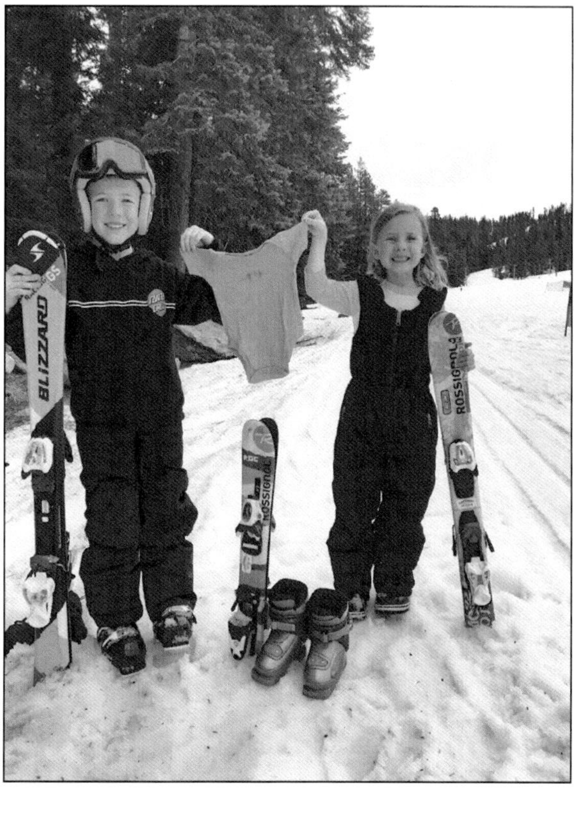

Multigenerational families are popular at Dodge Ridge, not just for guests but also for employees and their families. Logan and Isla Rose Lagarbo are excited to participate in the gender reveal of their new sibling and take the lead on getting their new brother, Emerson Hauff, ready to take on the slopes. It is never too early to get the little ones acclimated to outdoor fun. (Courtesy of the Hauff family.)

Here is a local family that has achieved international fame. Zoe Rimmer is in the backpack held by her mom, Shannon Duston-Rimmer, who is next to her sister Christy Cashman. Christy met her husband, John Cashman (right), at the local Pinecrest school. From left to right in the first row are Bailey Rimmer, Noah Cashman, Libby Rimmer, Keely Cashman (still dreaming of her future in the Olympics), and Jordan Cashman. (Photograph by Rob Bossi.)

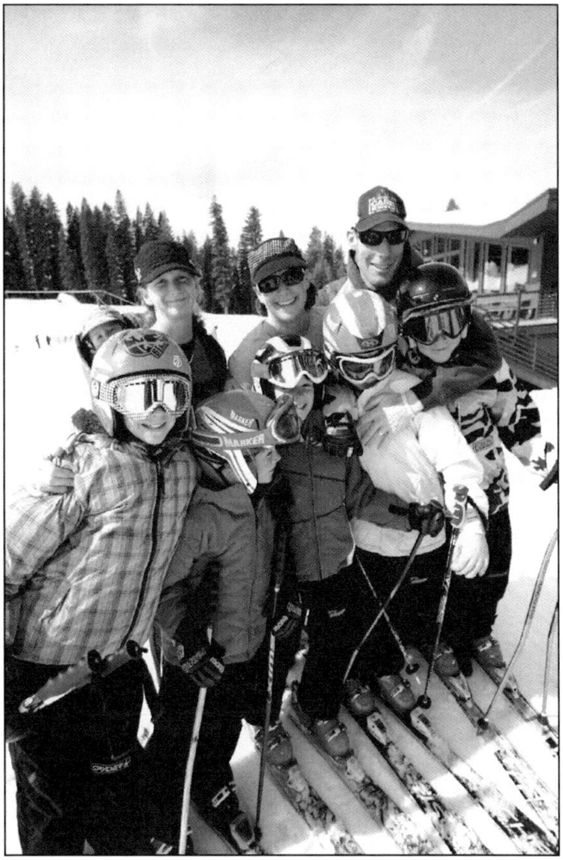

After the excitement of doing well in their races, it is always a good idea to replenish and refuel with a delicious lunch at the Creekside Lodge. From left to right are cousins and siblings Jordan Cashman, Bailey Rimmer, Keely Cashman, Libby Rimmer, and Noah Cashman. (Photograph by Rob Bossi.)

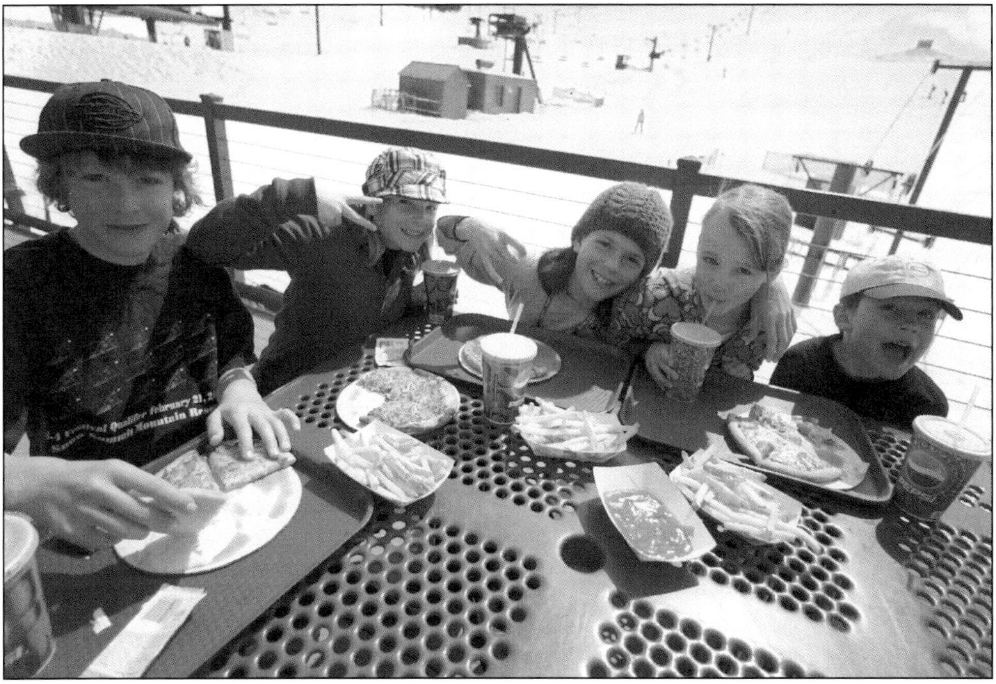

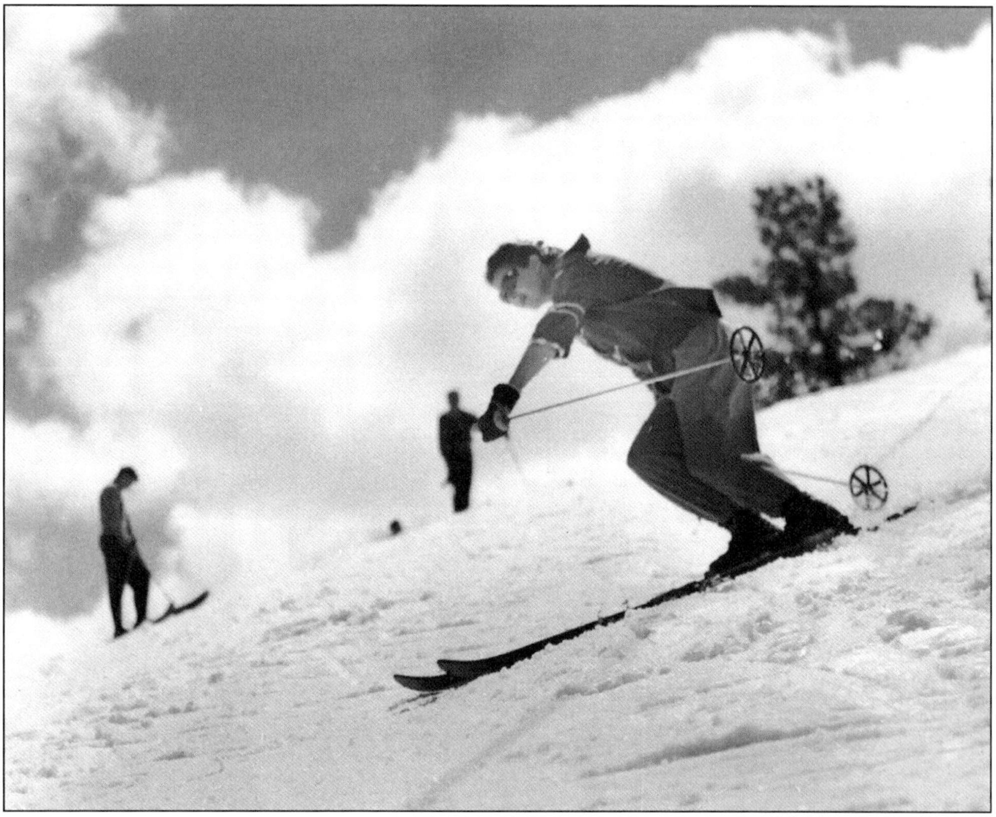

Beverly West Crow was one of the first female ski patrollers at Dodge Ridge. She is from the J.S. West family, who have been serving Tuolumne County with propane, trucking, poultry products, animal feed, and milling for over a century. Her husband is Jim Crow, whose family founded Crows Landing in Stanislaus County. Both volunteered for the National Ski Patrol (NSP) at Dodge Ridge for over 40 years. (Courtesy of Calin Smith.)

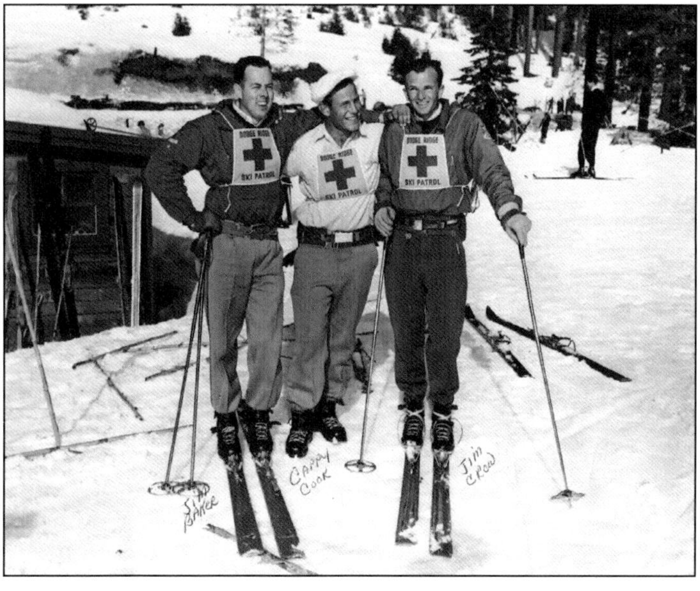

Volunteer ski patrol is a vital part of Dodge Ridge's commitment to safety. These three men, from left to right, are Jim Baker, Cappy Cook, and Jim Crow, who were extremely dedicated to the Dodge Ridge Ski Patrol and the community starting in the 1960s. (Courtesy of Calin Smith.)

This is Al Saletta, a member of the volunteer ski patrol, in 1956. Saletta must have had the fastest feet in the world, because he could ski down 15 feet and make 40 turns. His fashion choices were always a topic of conversation.

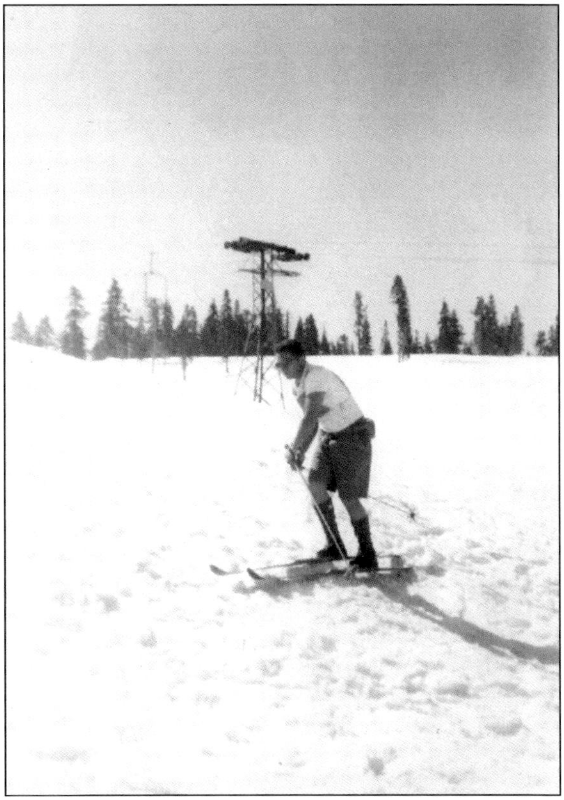

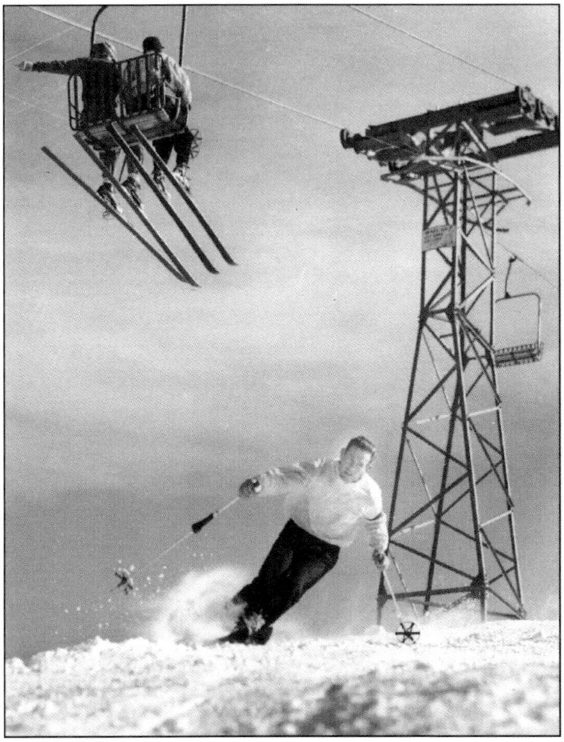

Hart Nathan "Cappy" Cook grew up in Modesto, California, and worked at Dodge Ridge as a professional ski patrol leader and race coach. In the off-season, he was a park ranger at Yosemite National Park. Prior to these roles, Cappy served in the US Army in Garmisch, Germany, from 1954 to 1956 as a noncommissioned officer who oversaw the ski patrol. (Courtesy of Calin Smith.)

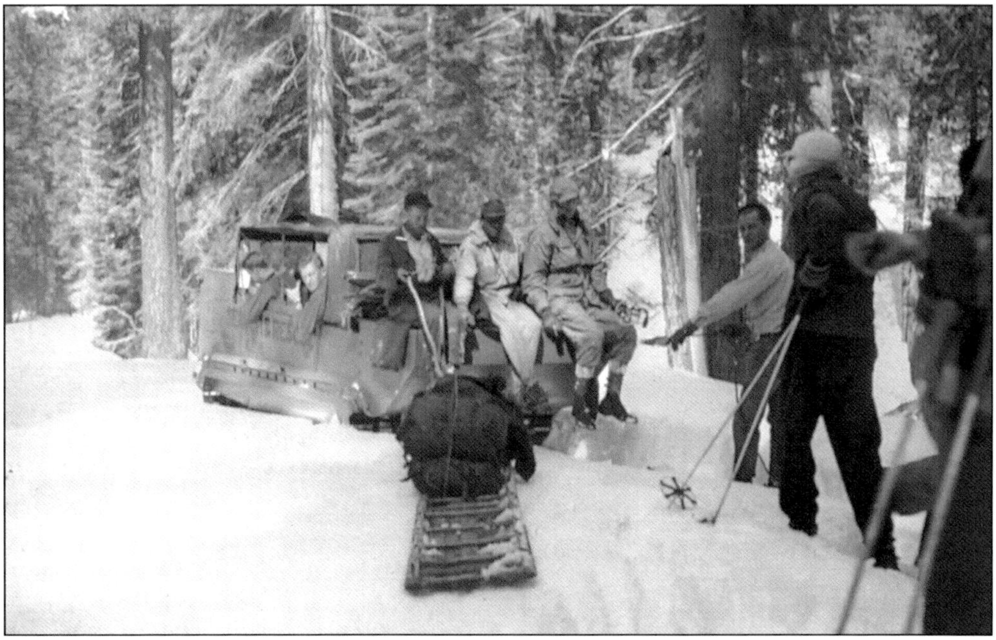

Search-and-rescue equipment and clothing have come a long way since the 1950s. A cat was used to cover the terrain, and patients were hauled down the mountain strapped to a large sled. Today, there are modern snowmobiles with room in the back and more protection to secure an injured skier.

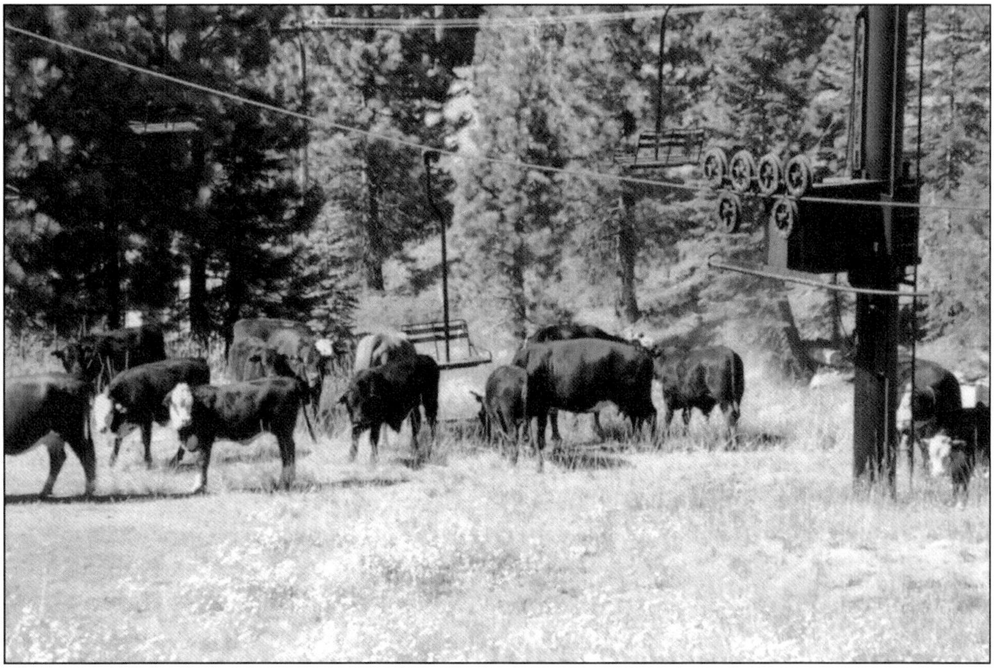

Not all search-and-rescue situations are human-related. Ranchers graze their cattle in the high country during the warmer-weather months, and most of the areas are not fenced in, so wandering happens. Every now and then, some find their way to Dodge Ridge and munch on the delicious grass under the chair lifts until someone notices and contacts the rancher.

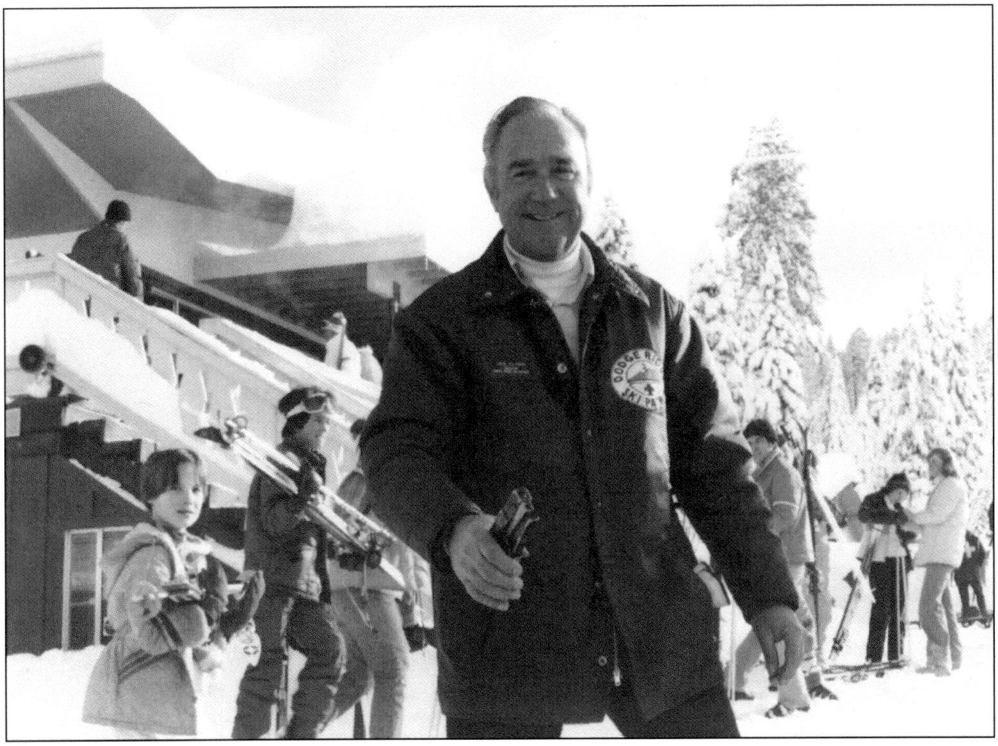

Lee Clark was the director of ski patrol in the 1970s. He was also a police officer in Oakland, California. Kevin Terry took over after Clark retired from Dodge Ridge. The race department used to be through the door on the bottom left under the stairs, where one could sign up for ski school.

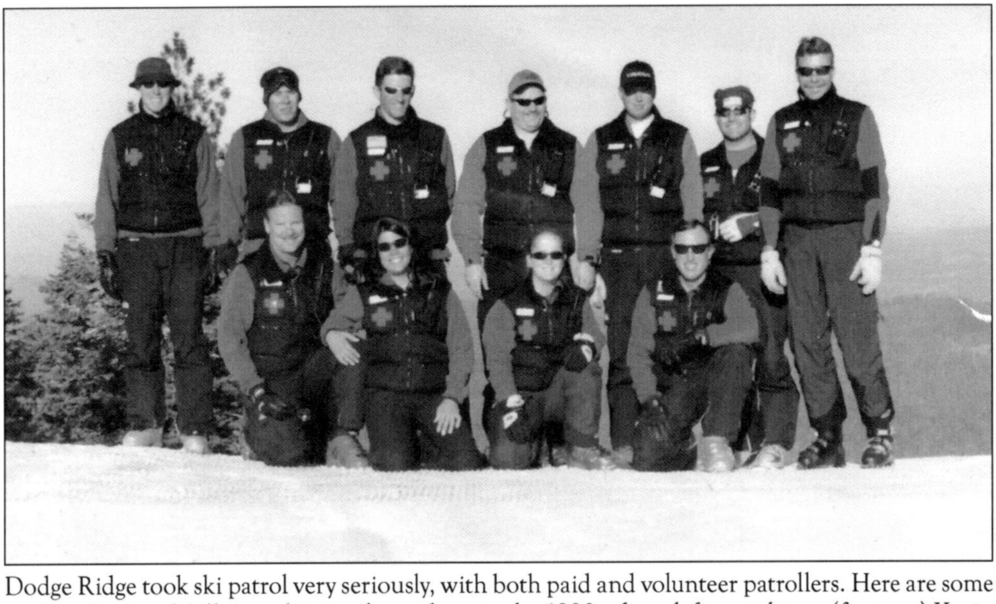

Dodge Ridge took ski patrol very seriously, with both paid and volunteer patrollers. Here are some paid professional full-time ski patrol members in the 1990s; from left to right are (first row) Kevin Terry, Laura Braux, unidentified, and Doug Parker; (second row) Josh Emmonds, Cass Garigus (who joined the Air Force), unidentified, Mike Schmidt, Matt Alley (Dave Alley's son), Steve Darpinian, and Dave Alley.

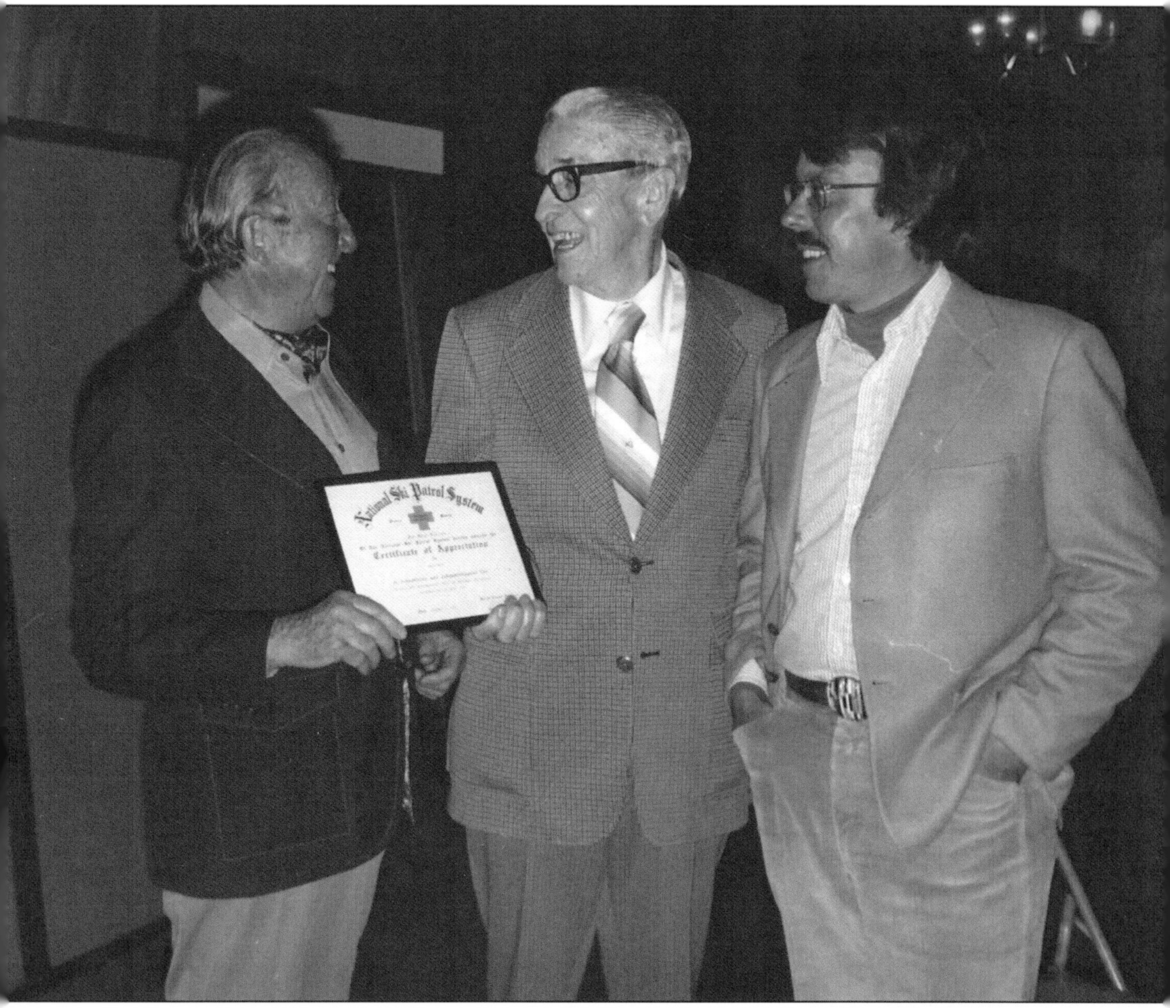

National Ski Patrol team members are fully trained. In 1976, Dr. Fran Conlin, representing the NSP, presents a certificate of appreciation to Earl Purdy (center) and Frank Helm. Numerous employees have received awards from NSP, such as the Bob Mech Award, for enthusiasm, dedication, and outstanding contribution to the Prospector Ski Patrol; the Jim Crow Award, given to a member with over 10 years of service for long-term dedication to the Prospector Ski Patrol or the skiing public at Dodge Ridge; the Bob Ross Award, for friendship and congeniality to Prospector Ski Patrol and Dodge Ridge staff during the year; the Jack Ross Award, for outstanding performance in first aid during the past season; the Jere Woodhead Outstanding Patroller Award, for outstanding leadership and activity throughout the year; the Don Jacop Award, for performance, enthusiasm, leadership, and skill in the Candidate Training Program; the Marla Award; Outstanding Paid Patroller Award; the Mary Ross Award, for outstanding performance in the Dodge Ridge First Aid Room; the LeRoy Giovannoni Award, given by the patrol representative to recognize outstanding contributions to the patrol; Outstanding Mountain Host; and the Angel Pin, for nonmembers of NSP who have provided valuable contributions.

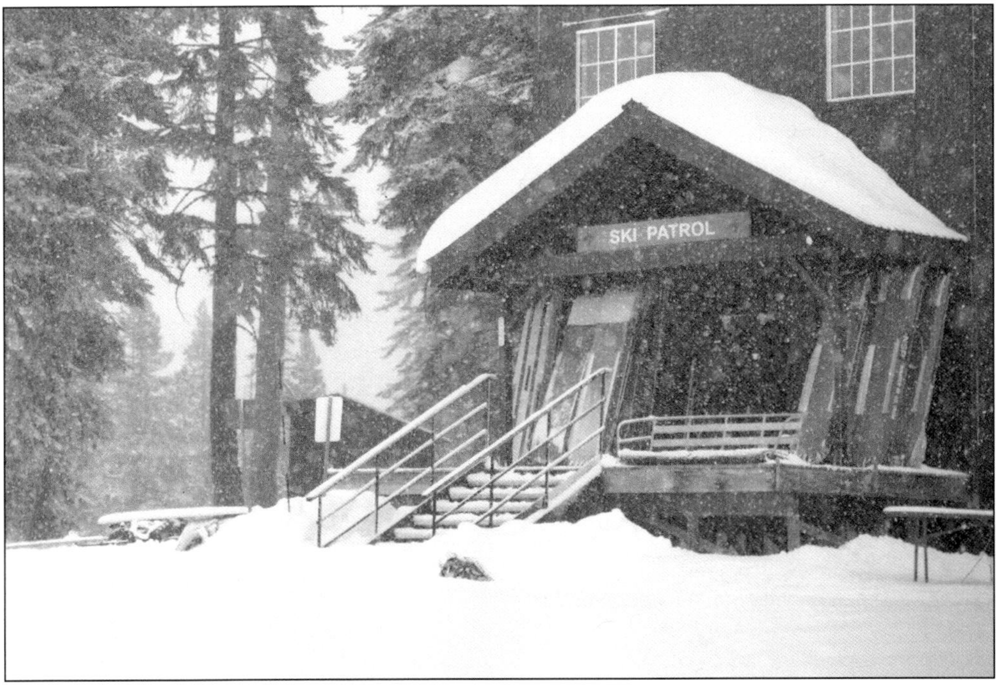

This is the iconic ski patrol building at the top of Chair Seven. It houses the equipment necessary to make sure that guests are safe throughout the resort, rescue equipment is readily available, and staff have a place to hang out protected from the elements.

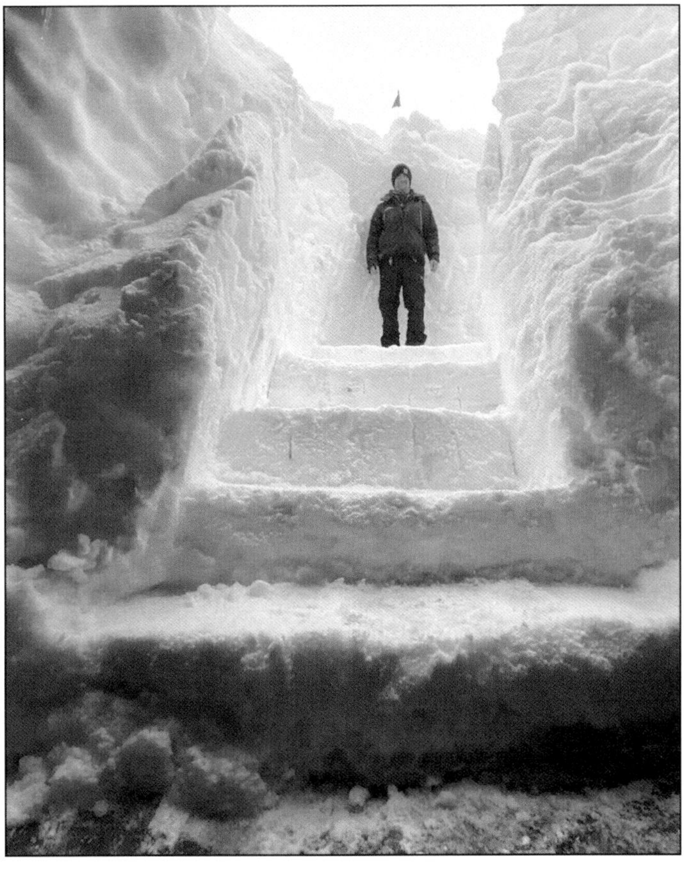

Lift mechanic Chris Nehr stands on the stairs that he and his team had just dug out to reach the motor room of Chair Four during a record-breaking 757 inches of snow fall in the 2022–2023 season. This photograph commemorates a great year and respect for all the hard work the lift mechanics do to create the best possible experience for the guests.

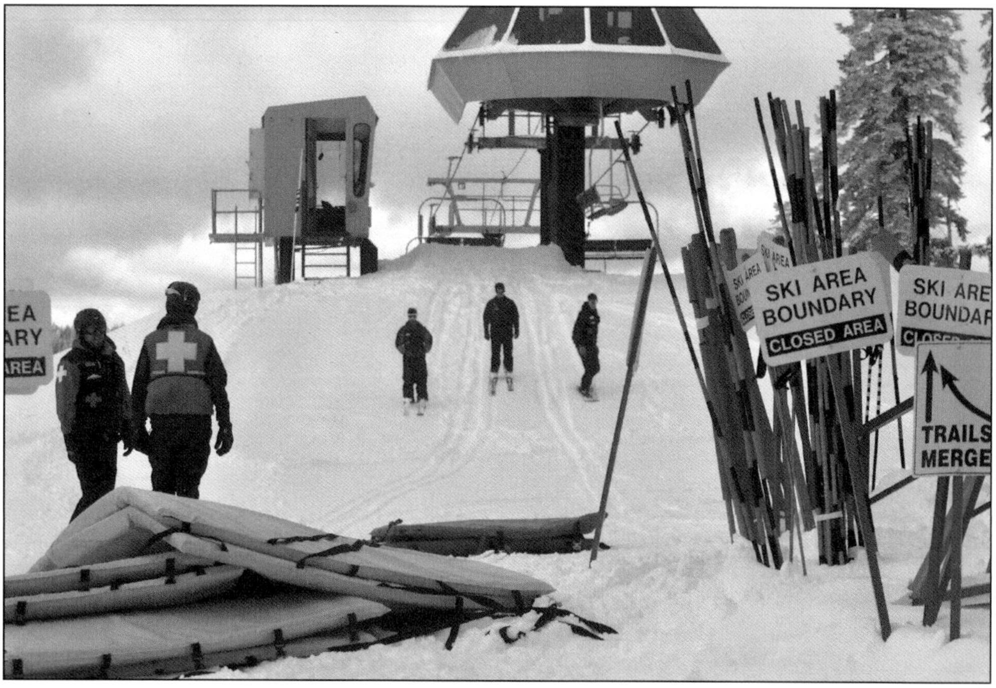

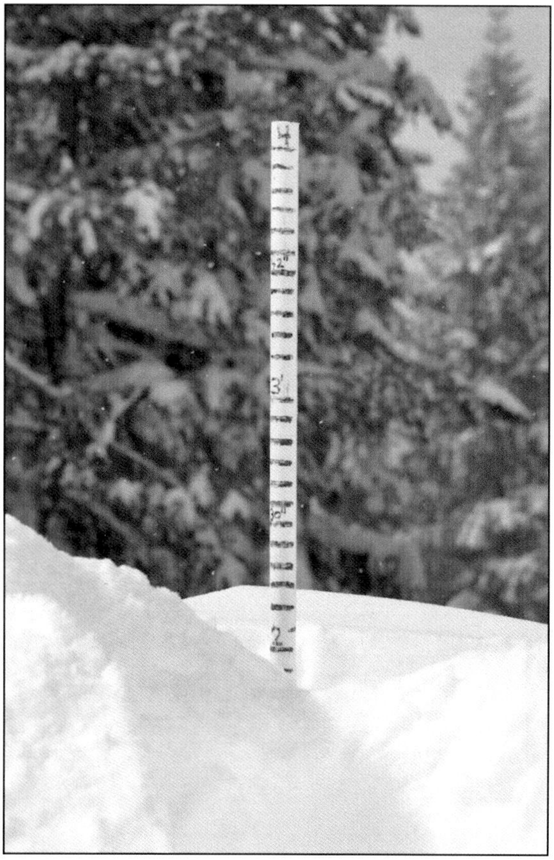

Ski patrol is more than just telling skiers and snowboarders to slow down. Dodge Ridge employs its own professional patrol members who are fully trained and a vital part of keeping everyone safe. They assess the conditions and determine safe boundary lines. They are trained in using explosives for clearing and constantly keep an eye out for guests who may need rescue or assistance from a fall or collision. There are also volunteer ski patrol members who assist Dodge Ridge's patrol team.

This simple yet effective tool is essential for knowing the depth of the snow. It can mean the difference between life and death in certain areas of the resort. It is important for ski patrol to know the conditions so they can be prepared to cordon off areas, close runs, or do whatever is necessary to help guests stay safe.

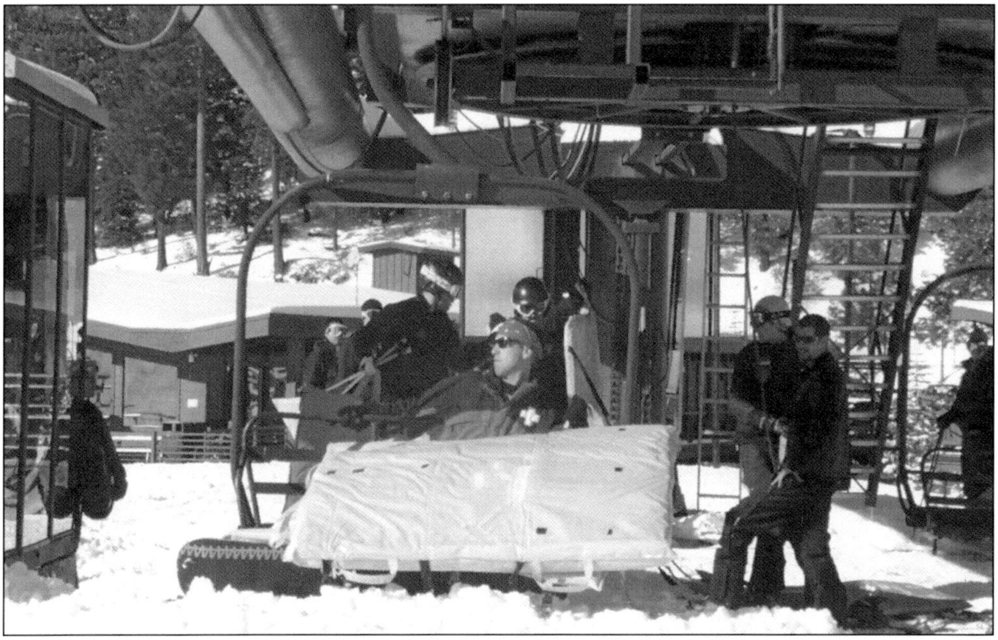

Ski patrol uses padding around the lift towers so skiers do not crash straight into metal. Preparing the resort is a coordinated effort by the entire team to help ensure as safe an environment as possible. In the unlikely event that someone is dangling from a lift, these pads can be stripped off the towers and used as a crash pad.

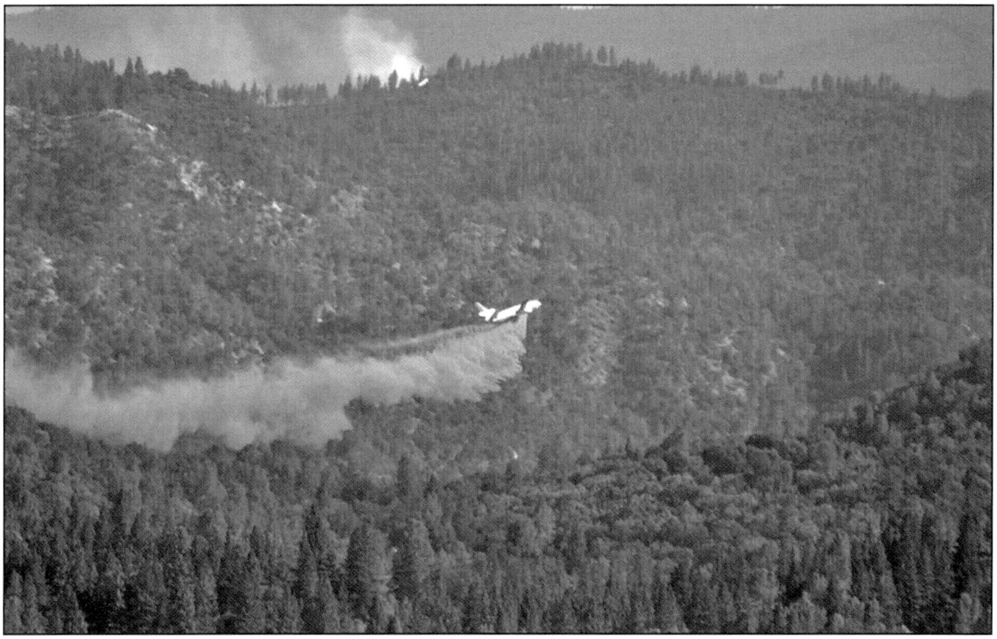

Being part of a forest always poses natural threats of various magnitudes. On August 17, 2013, the Rim Fire broke out in the Jawbone area of the Stanislaus National Forest and quickly spread toward Dodge Ridge Mountain Resort, prompting a full closure for safety. Cal Fire and resort employees cleared trees, creating 44 firebreaks along Dodge Ridge. Planes constantly dropped retardant throughout the forest. Fortunately, their efforts met with success. (Courtesy of Bruce Pedretti.)

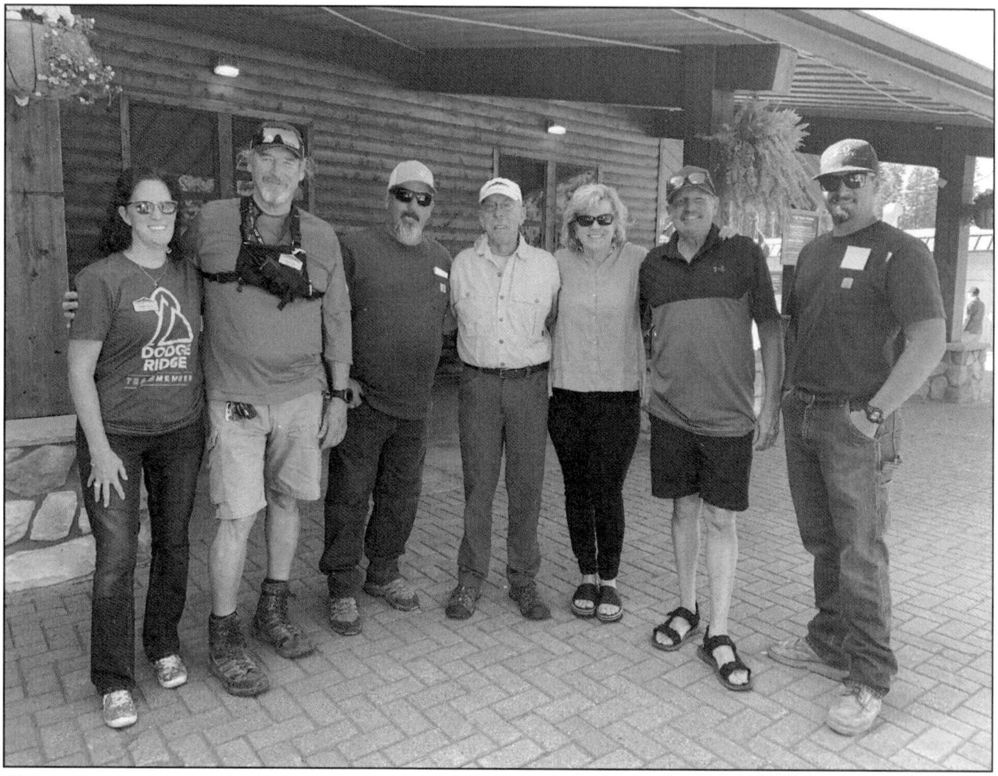

Shown here are some long-term employees who started under the Helms and continued on. From left to right are Kristin Taylor, finance director; Carl Richtor, ski patrol director and National Ski Patrol; Brett Fulkerson, mountain manager; Frank and Sally Helm; Mark Kavanaugh, snow removal manager and snowmaker; and Bradley Fulkerson, lift maintenance technician and equipment operator, who is now in snow removal. Bradley followed in his father Brett's footsteps, which is not uncommon here. (Courtesy of the Helm family.)

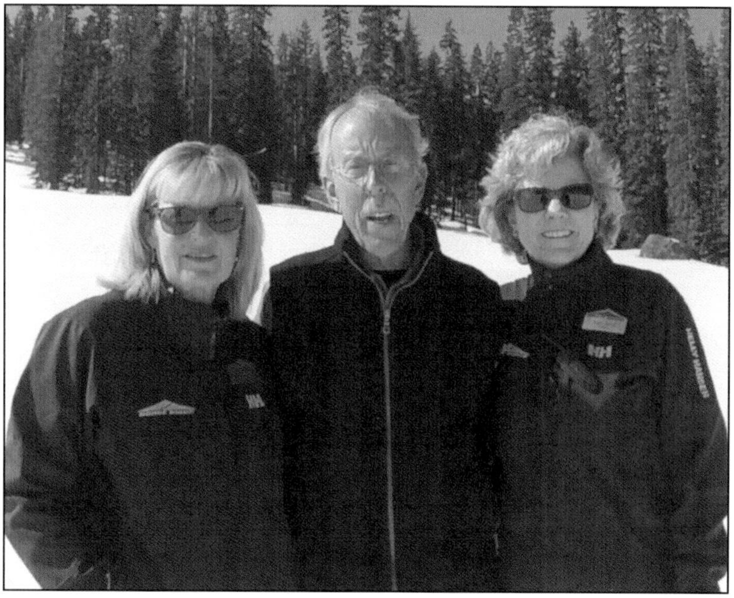

From left to right are Jenni Smith, Frank Helm, and Sally Helm near Chair One. Smith rose through the ranks and became the general manager at Park City, Utah. Smith was prepared for a career shift, and Sally Helm recognized her value, thus offering her the role of general manager. Smith continues to hold this position to date and oversees just about everything at the resort. (Courtesy of the Helm family.)

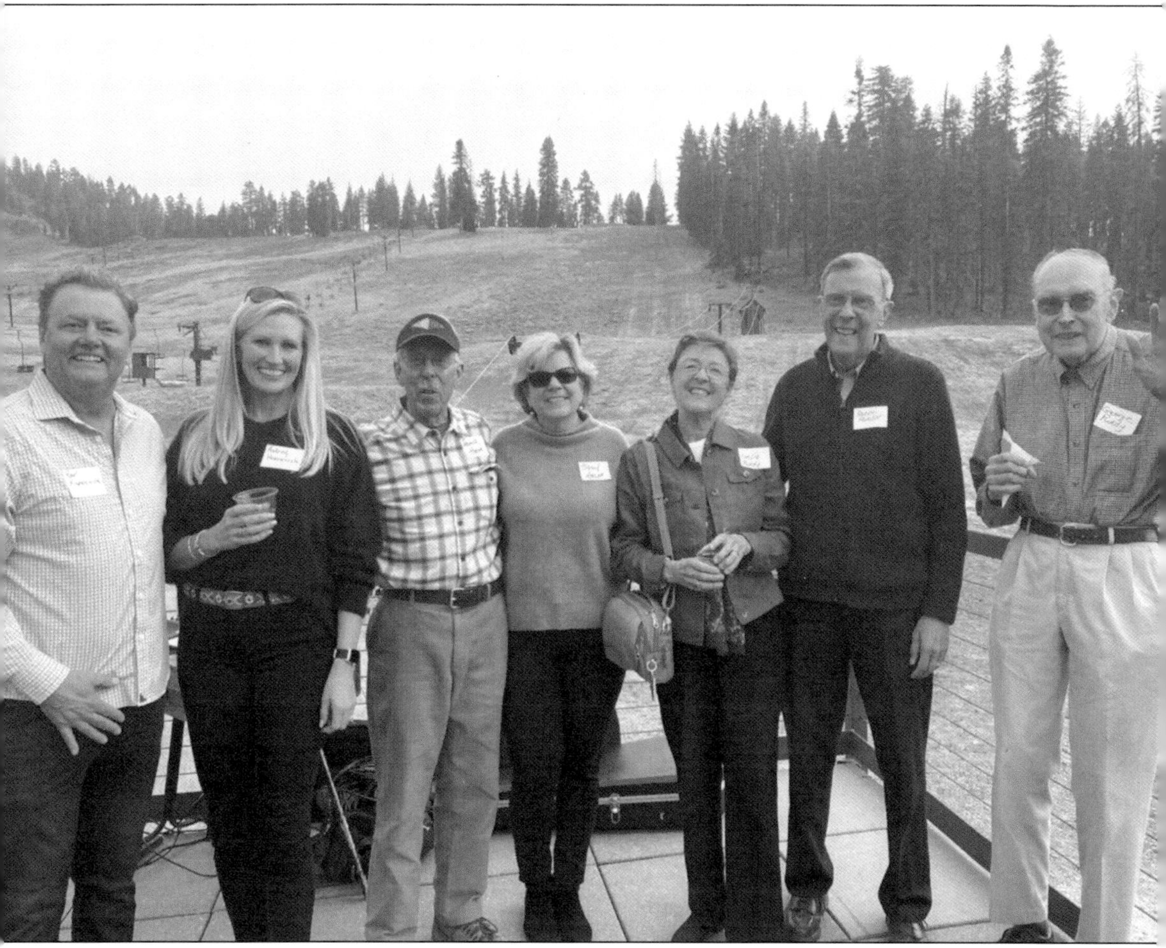

This group is celebrating and welcoming the changing of the guard at Dodge Ridge. From left to right are Karl Kapuscinski, Audrey Kapuscinski (who just took over), Frank and Sally Helm (owners for 46 years), Leslie Purdy, Ralph Purdy, and George Purdy (family members of the first owner Earl Purdy, who owned it for 26 years).

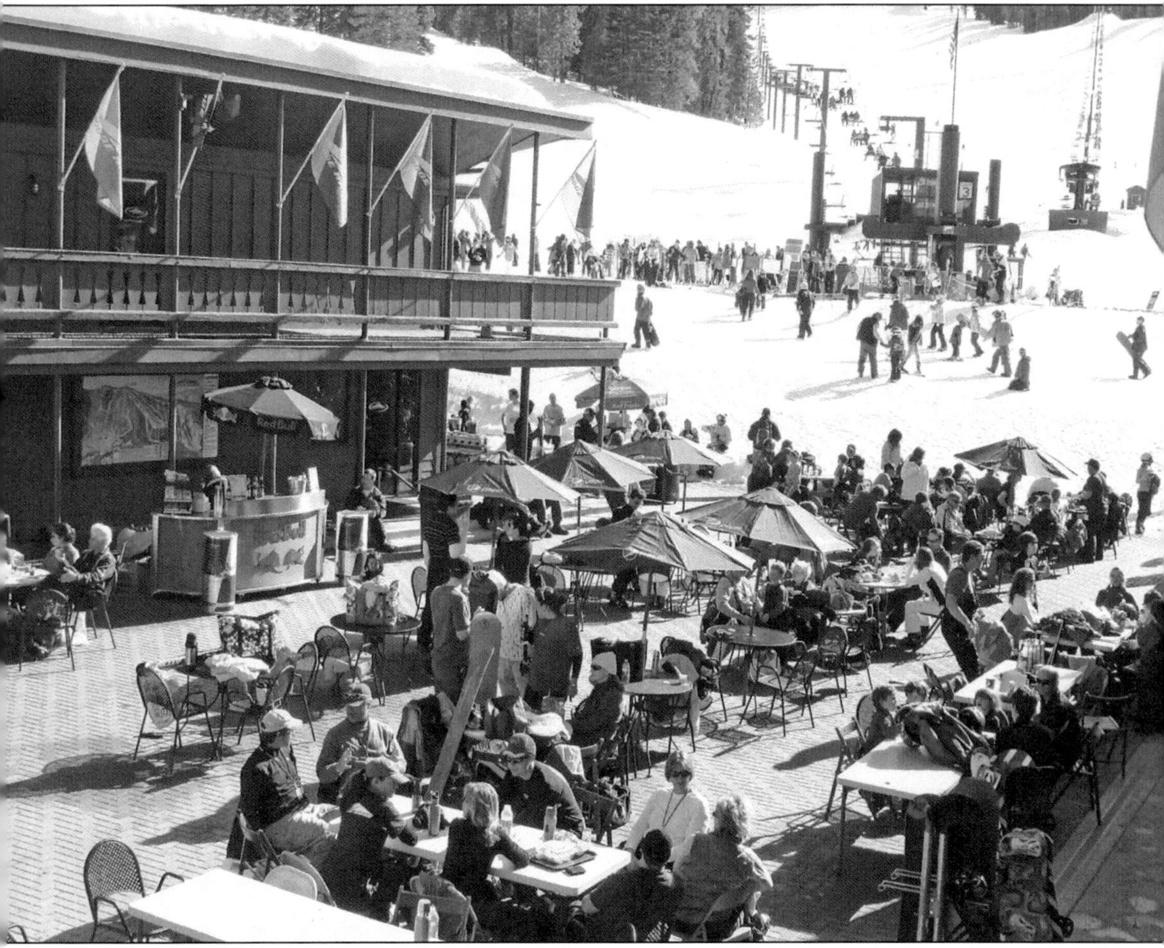

Dodge Ridge has evolved into a more structured environment. Gone is the mud-and-gravel ground that was messy and hurt one's feet. Now, the plaza is properly paved and filled with tables, chairs, and fire pits so guests can relax, eat, and enjoy the outdoor environment with views of the mountain. Events are often held in this area, such as pop-shopping and demonstrations of new equipment.

Quite a bit of effort goes into hosting events. Here, the mountain crew is building a venue for the Courtyard Rail Jam event, replicating a run on the mountain. They gather snow from higher elevations and truck it to the parking lot, where they create a mini mountain for this special event. Participants start in the parking lot and end up in the plaza below.

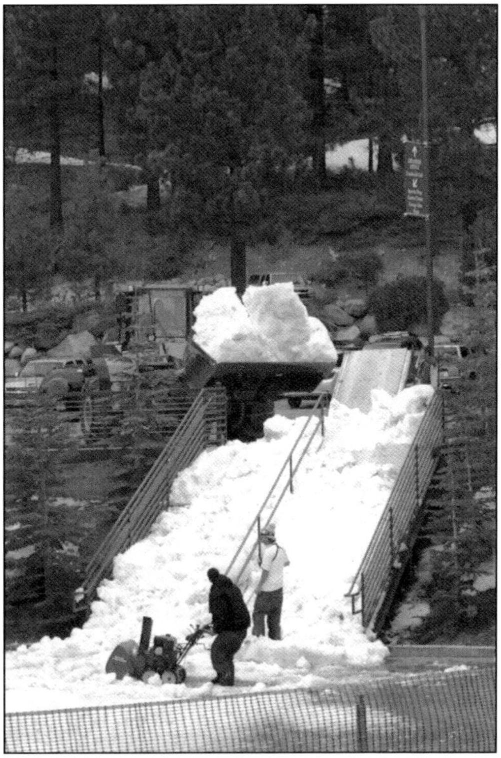

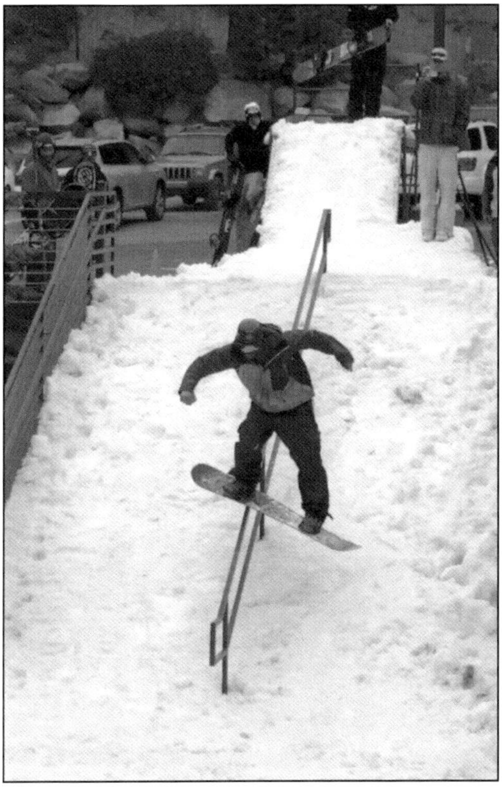

Courtyard Rail Jam participants are judged on their best trick coming off the rail. Shown here is a crew member testing the platform. There are high consequences at the venue due to dangerous cheese-grating steps, so this is not for beginners. It is a fun, high-energy event and a true crowd-pleaser.

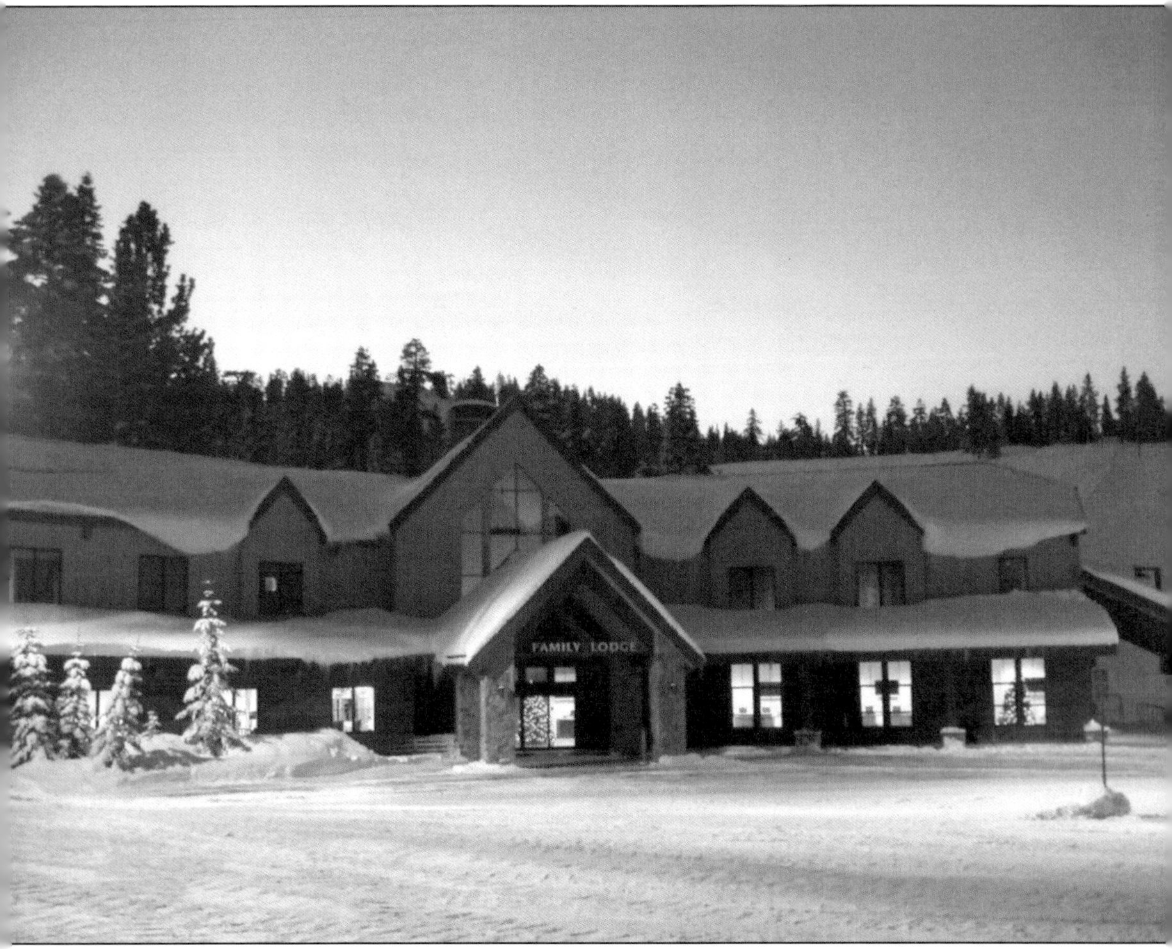

Dodge Ridge is known as a great place to learn how to ski. In the past, ski school, rentals, food options, and check-in were scattered around the grounds. The Family Lodge provides one location for everything a family needs to have a simplified experience in getting children suited up, fed, and on their way to ski lessons without being worn out by the time they get there.

On October 8, 2022, during the winter kickoff and Oktoberfest festivities, Dodge Ridge dedicated the Family Lodge to Frank and Sally Helm. Shown from left to right are Sally Helm and Karl and Audrey Kapuscinski announcing the dedication to the crowd of primarily season passholders.

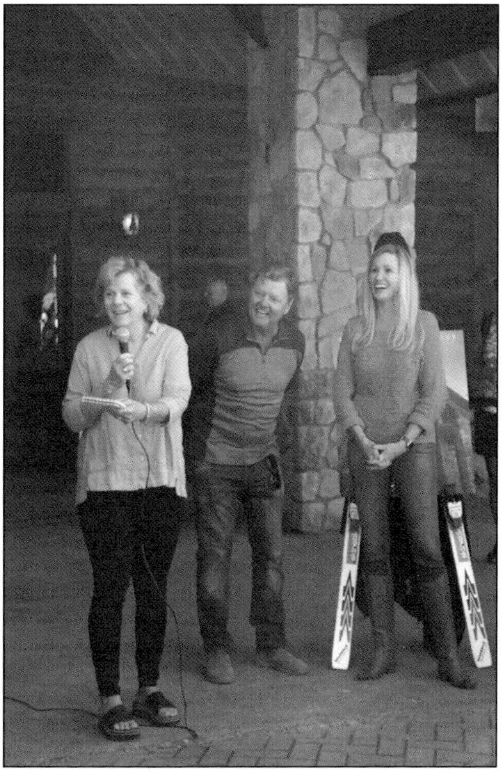

Sally and Frank Helm stand under the banner of the newly dedicated Helm Family Lodge, named in their honor when they recently retired after 46 years of ownership and dedication to the community.

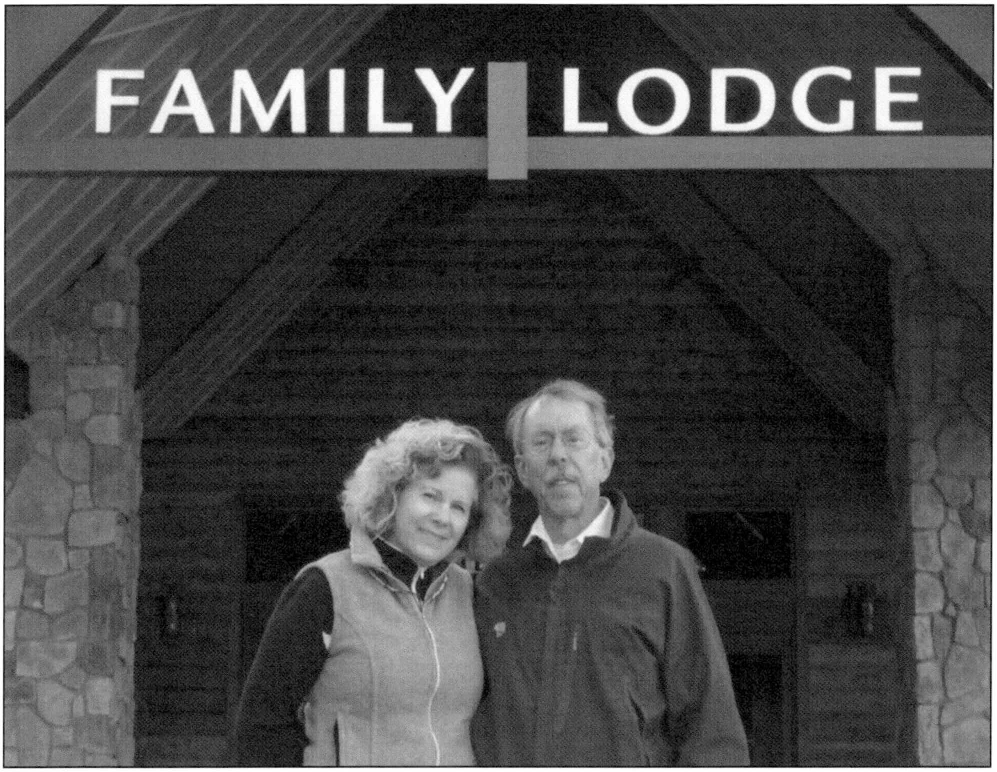

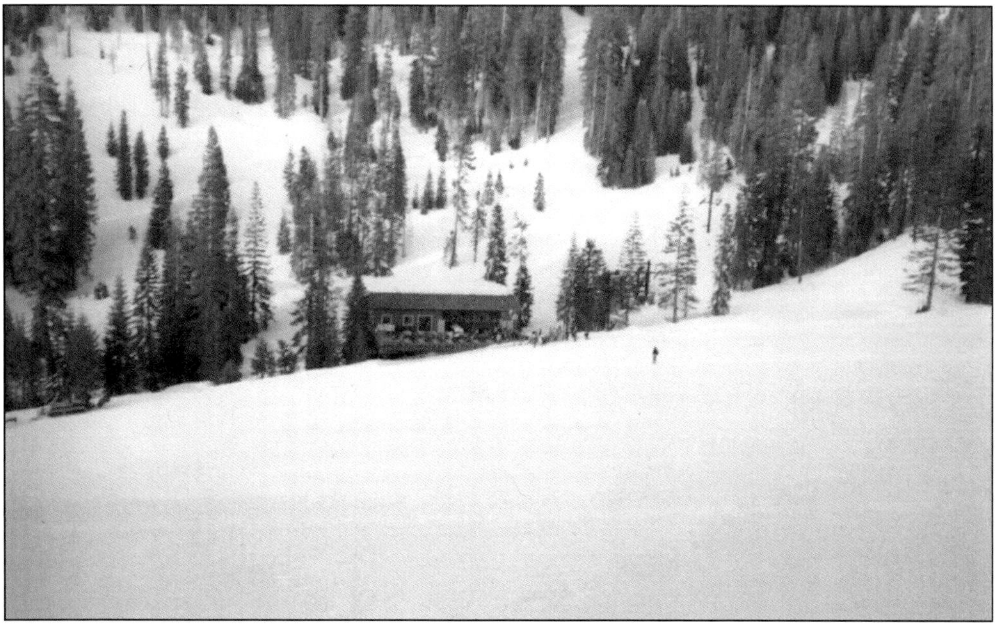

A skier makes their way down the mountain to the Waystation at the base of Chair Seven. Guests used to bring their own barbecues and leave them outside to cook their lunch and hang out until the Forest Service deemed this practice unsafe. As a result, the Waystation got a facelift to accommodate an employee-staffed grill and more seating. This building is only accessible to skiers and not foot traffic.

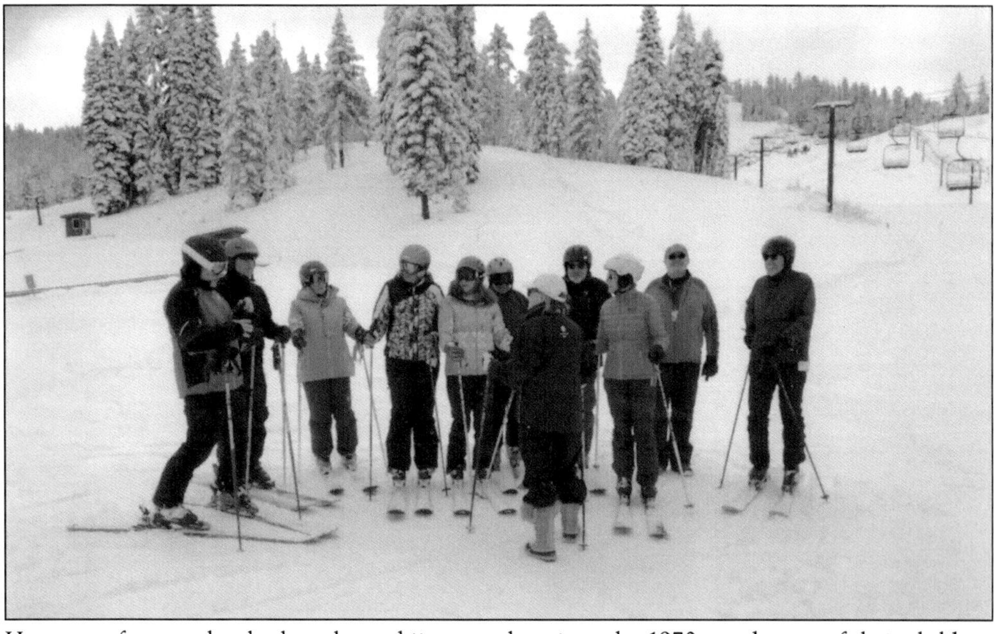

Here are a few people who have been skiing together since the 1970s, and some of their children skied and raced together as well. Some in the group have moved away, so they started an annual reunion celebration. Sharing fond memories are, from left to right, Bob Patton, Steve Lavagnino, Debi Twining, Melissa Lindell, Melanie Curtis, unidentified, Sue Lavagnino, Mike Kline, Bobbie Kline, Preston Hough, and Al Bernat. (Courtesy of the Lavagnino family.)

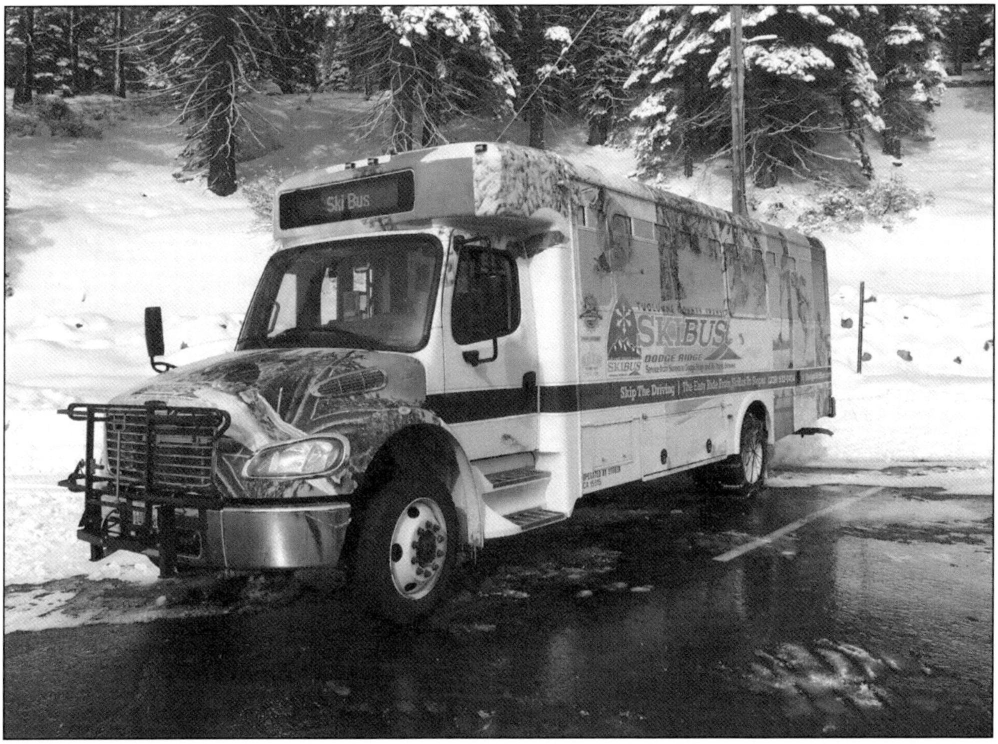

The ski bus is a great way to travel to Dodge Ridge from numerous places in Tuolumne County. If someone is afraid of driving in the snow, the bus can handle that. It is inexpensive and takes the burden of driving up the hill away from guests.

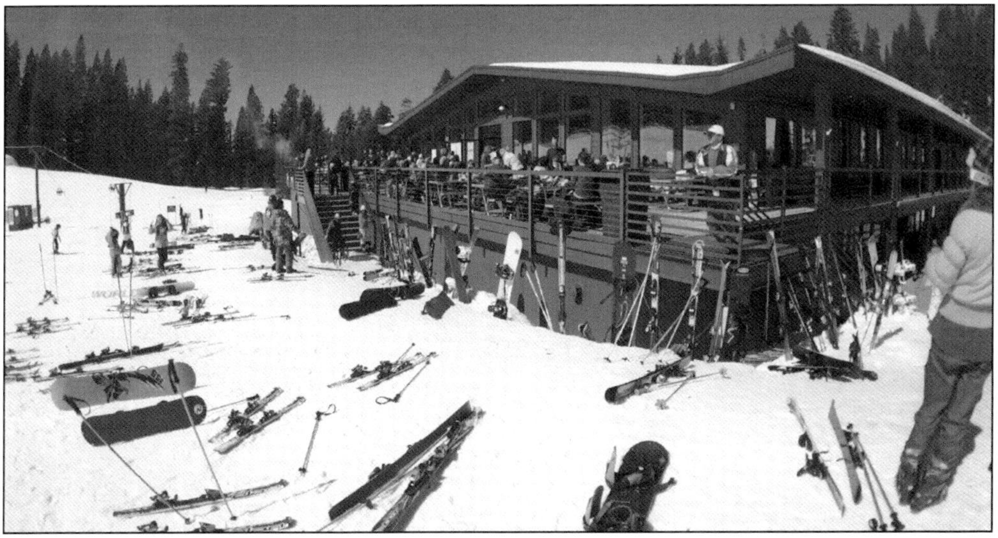

This is the Creekside Motherlode Lodge, which sits at the base of the resort near the beginning of the North Fork of the Tuolumne River. It houses the cafeteria, sports bar, sports store and ski shop, lockers, restrooms, bike rental and repair, and executive offices. Creekside is a fun place to hang out. The wrap-around deck offers seating, tables, and fire pits for guests to use while relaxing, enjoying the views, or listening to music. It is accessible on foot or by skis, snowboards, or mountain bike. It is accessible in the winter and the summer seasons.

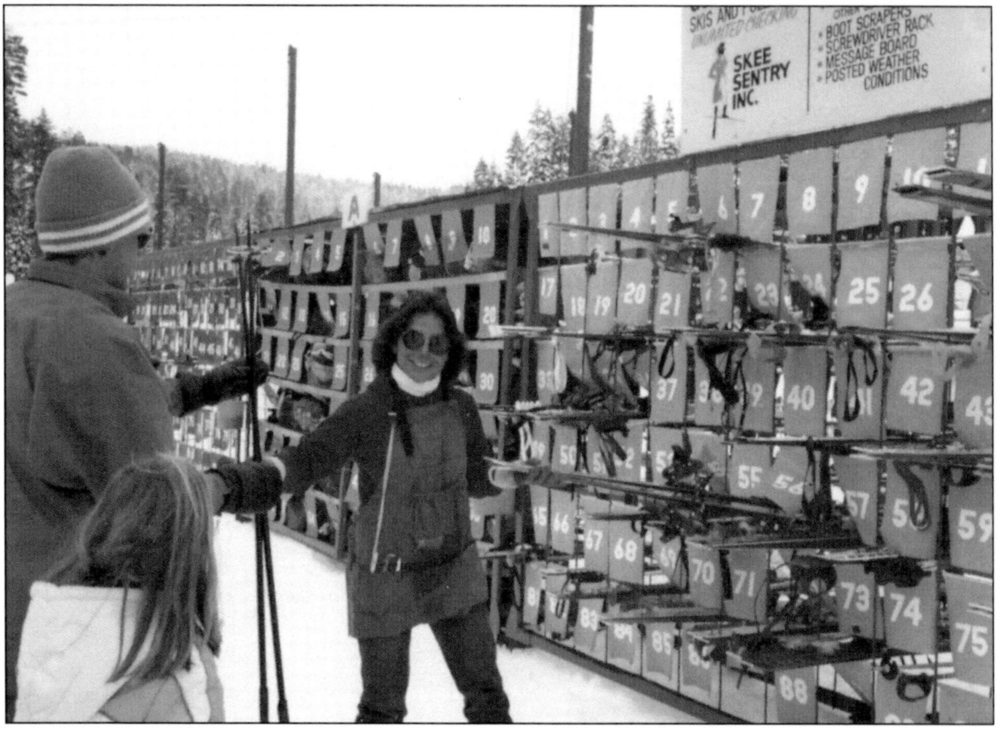

Prior to lockers and ski slots, guests enjoyed concierge service to have their skis safely stored during lunch breaks. Once locker rooms were built, a whole new social scene was created. Some claim that the real fun was finding out what was left over at the end of the ski season—it was mostly booze since there was not a bar until recently.

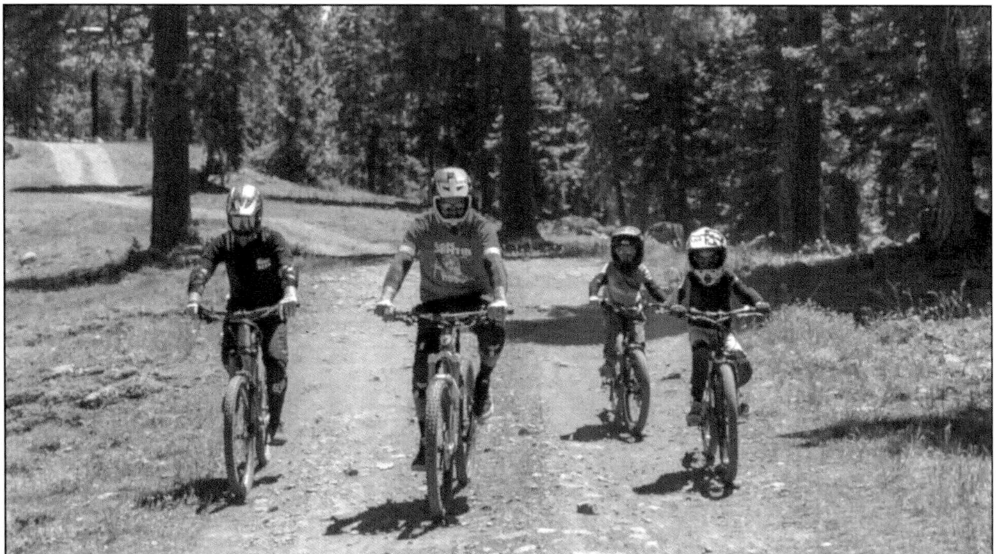

While Sally and Bob Hohne worked with the Forest Service on a new master development plan, they also made sure to secure approval from the Forest Service to implement a sophisticated mountain biking operation. The plan was accepted in 2007. When Karl Kapuscinski took over, he built a top-notch trail for mountain bikers in the spring through fall.

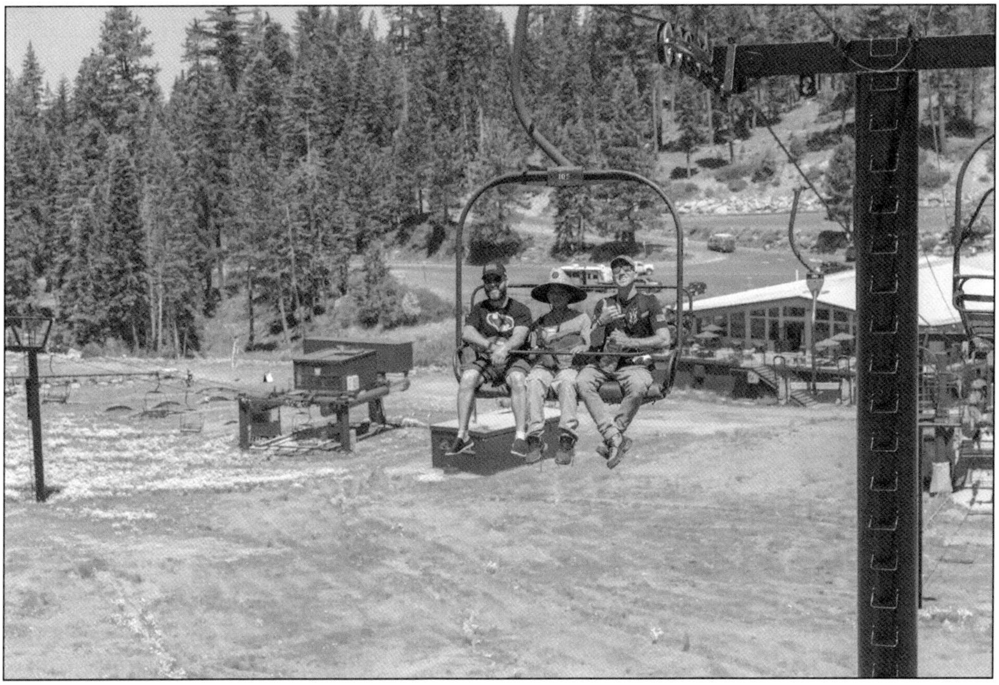

A leisurely ride up Chair Three never disappoints, no matter the season. Here, guests enjoy a warm-weather ride with the option of a picnic at the summit, a game of disc golf, putting a mountain bike on a lift and then riding down the mountain, or hiking or walking about to explore the natural beauty of Dodge Ridge and the surrounding views.

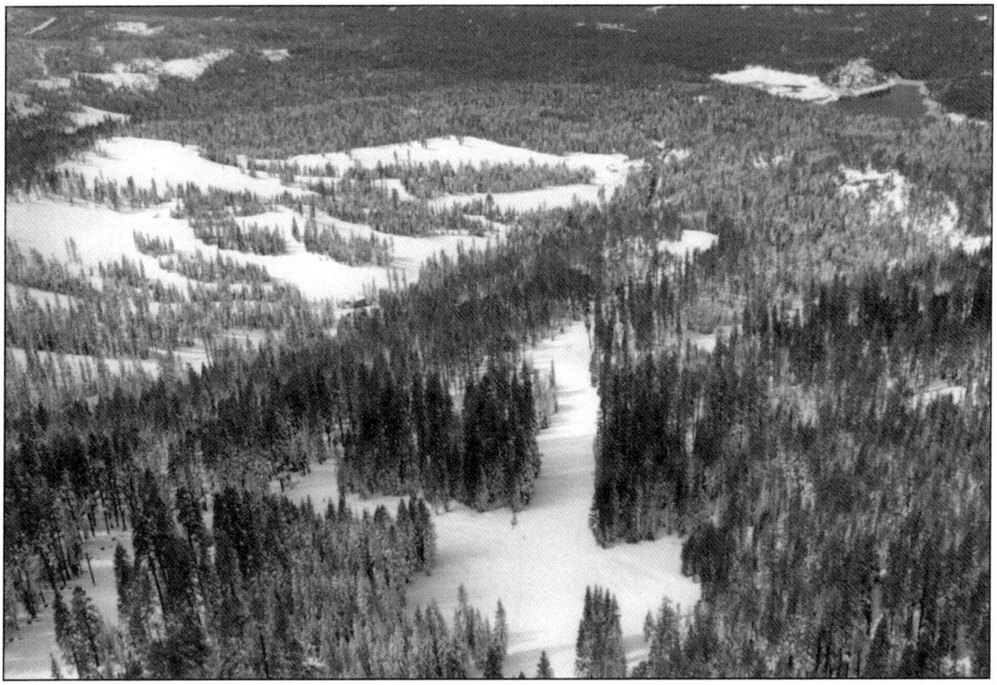

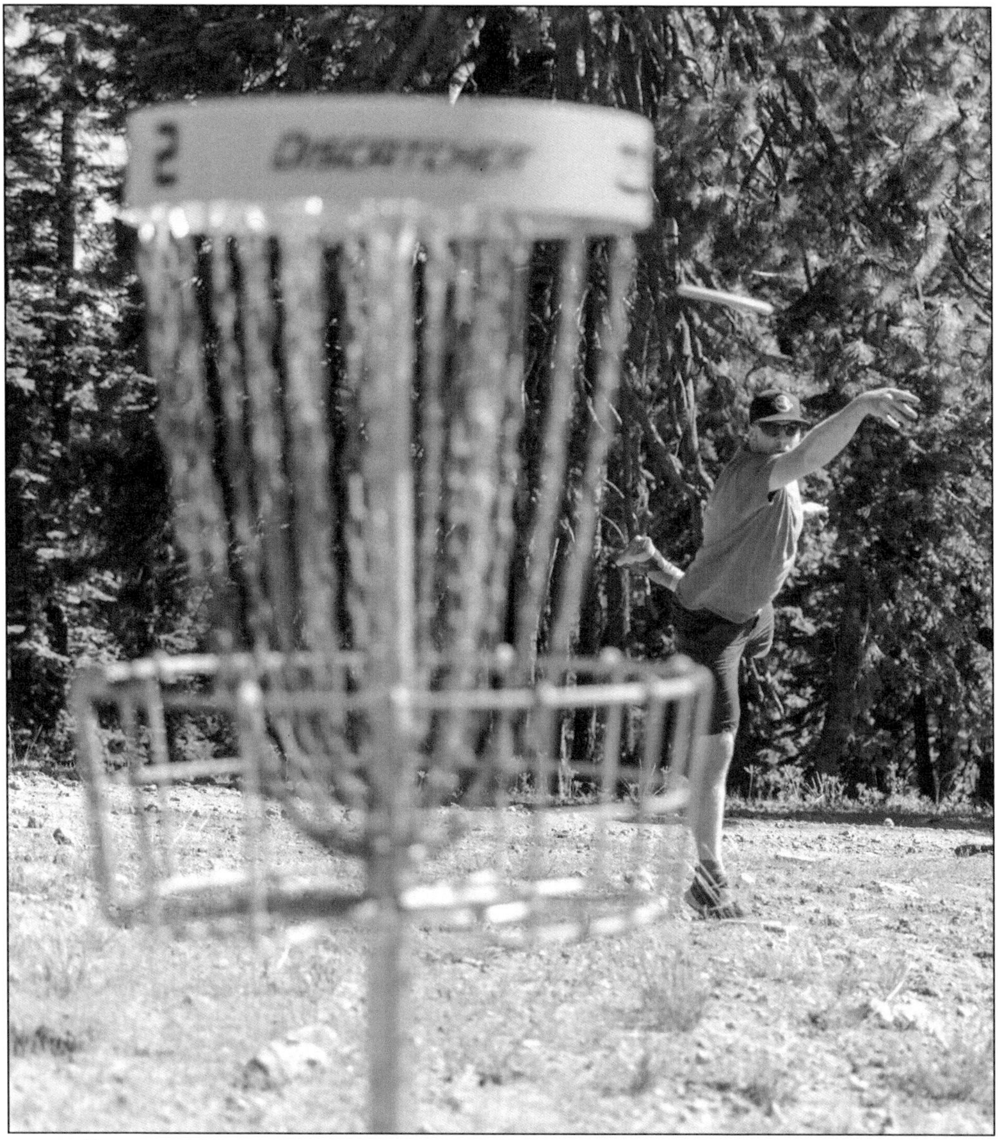

Disc golf is one of the activities for spring and summer. There is a well-laid-out course throughout the resort. It offers a variety of holes with a variety of characteristics that players can enjoy. Plus, there are incredibly gorgeous views throughout the course. Players can ride the lift to the top and back or hike their way up or down.

This shows a well-tracked-out mountain after an epic powder day. The tracks indicate that guests enjoyed themselves. After the resort closes, the mountain team gets together to prepare the slopes for the next day of great skiing, keeping with the mission of this mountain resort.

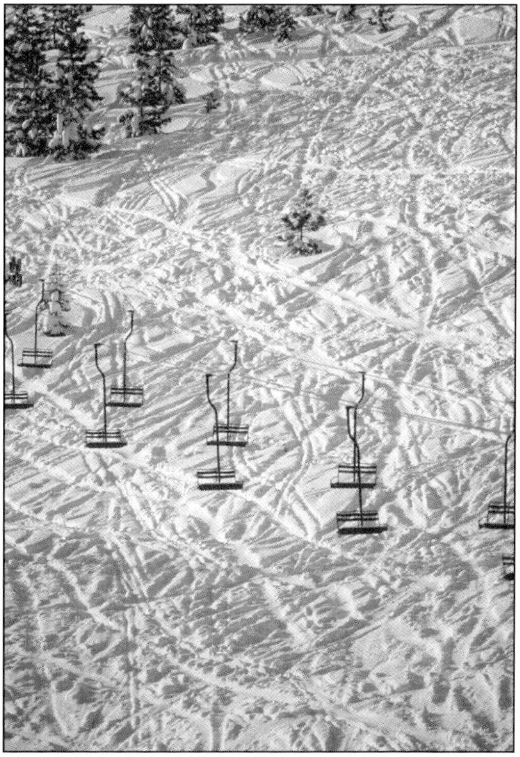

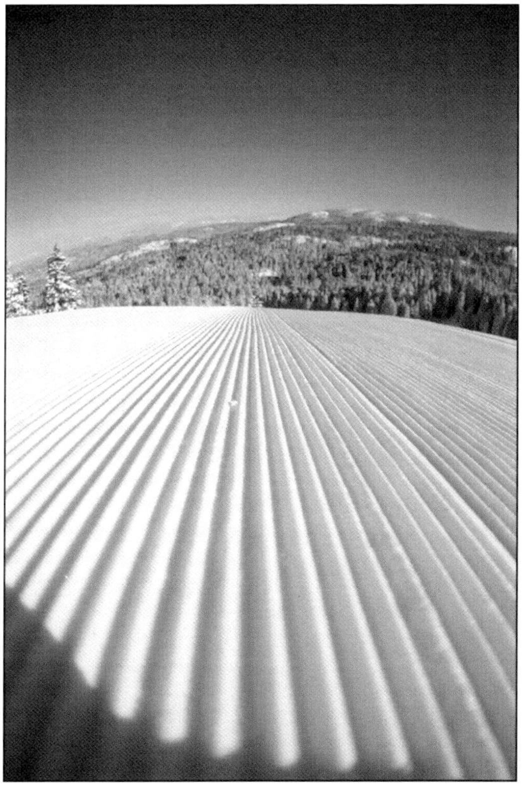

The mountain crew works through the night to create the best possible grooming for guests to enjoy the next day. This is an example of perfectly groomed corduroy just waiting to be ridden. Guests often line up way before the first lift opens at 9:00 a.m. in order to ski fresh tracks. Dodge Ridge is poised to provide corduroy for a long time if Mother Nature cooperates.

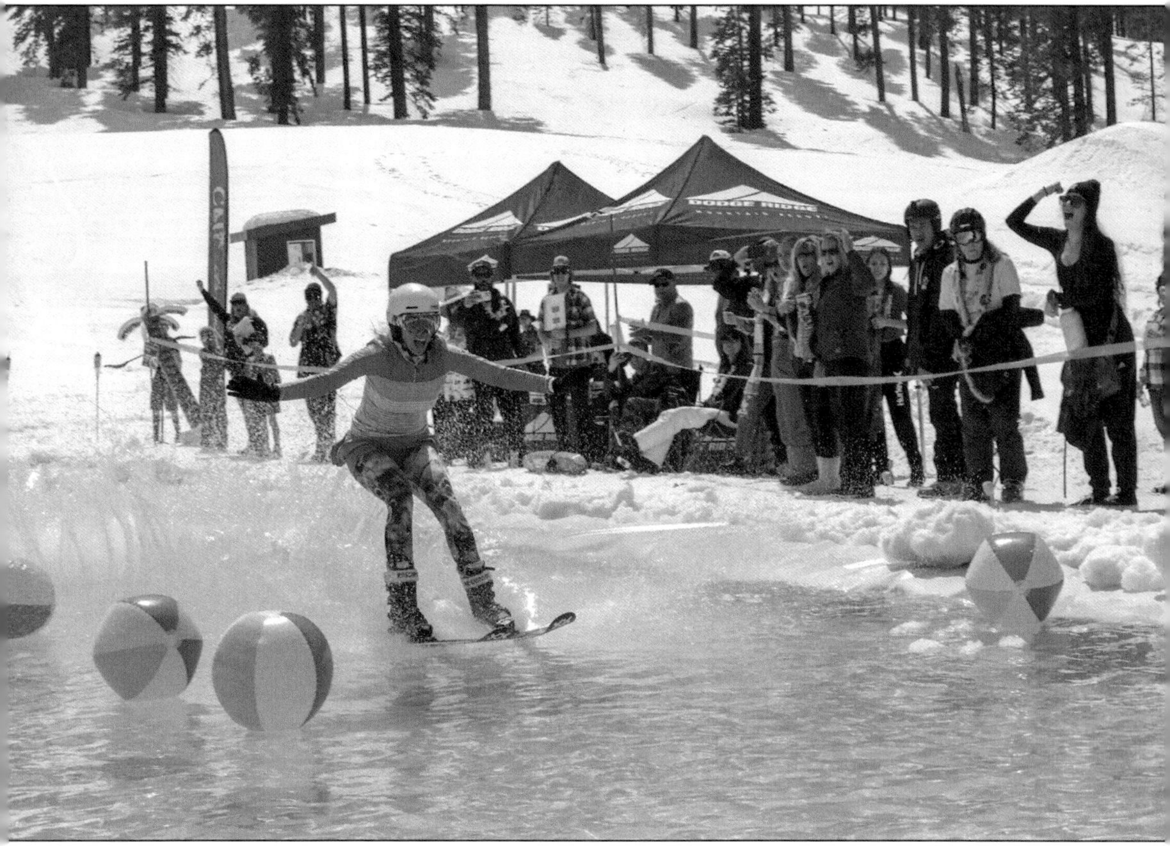

The Pond Skim event is held every spring, provided there is enough snow. Skiers and snowboarders, typically in costume, start at Gentle Ben, gather speed, and enter the pond located at the bottom of Chair One, hoping to make it across the entire pond. Many try, but not all succeed. Audrey Kapuscinski felt the need for speed (hint for aspiring pond skimmers) and had no problem successfully skimming the pond at the end of the 2022–2023 season.

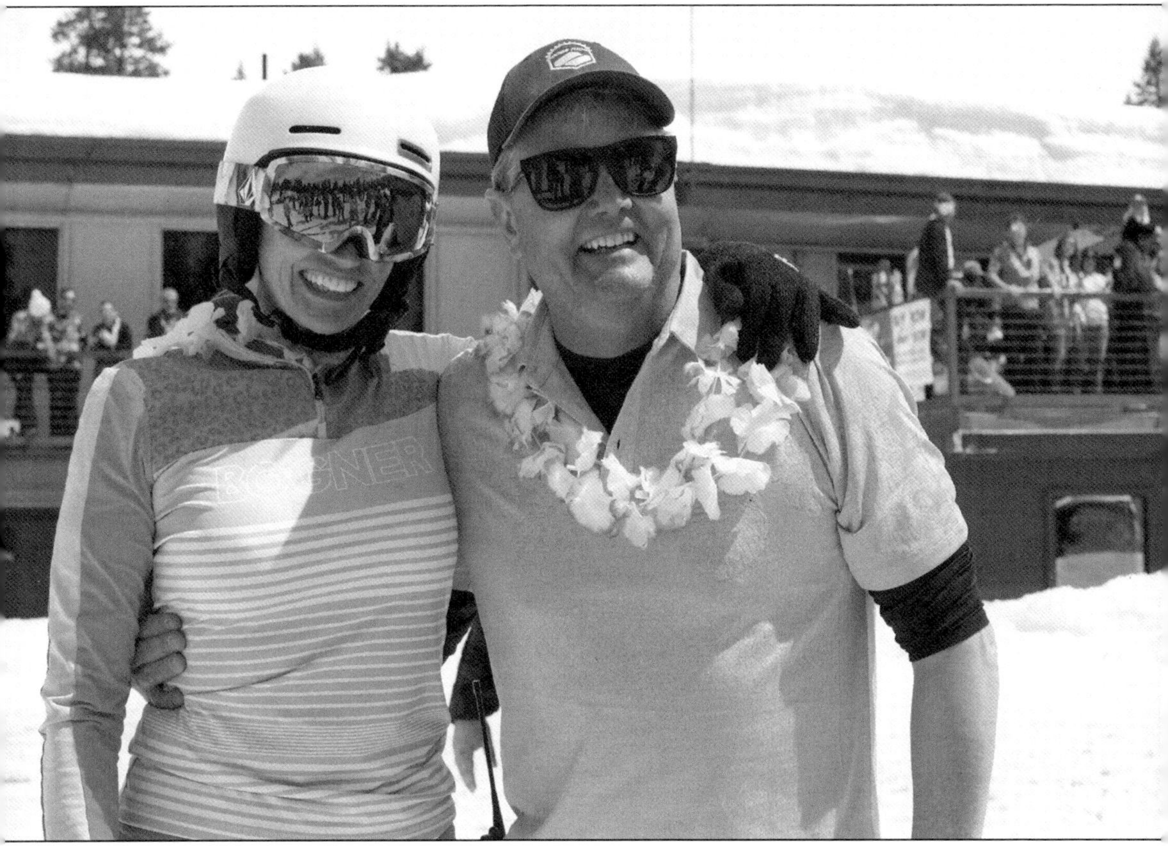

Karl and Audrey Kapuscinski and Invision Capital plan to preserve and enhance the Guest First culture that Dodge Ridge was founded upon. Ski resort life has been a part of Karl's life since childhood; it is a passion and a way of life that he does not take for granted. In a few short years, he has already made an impact on the community and enhancements to the resort with snowmaking efforts and no-snow activities for year-round enjoyment. Food and beverage choices have been elevated, as have entertainment options for music lovers, children, those who ski, and those who do not ski but love the environment. Following the principles of previous leaders who valued every position and those who held those jobs and prioritized guest experience, Dodge Ridge Mountain Resort is set for a promising future under Karl's leadership and knowledge. Family fun, learning to ski, and enjoying the nature provided at Dodge Ridge will continue for years to come. Early into their ownership, Dodge Ridge experienced one of the longest seasons ever, perhaps an auspicious tale for the future.